Pan American Visions

Pan American Visions

Woodrow Wilson
in the
Western Hemisphere
1913–1921

MARK T. GILDERHUS

THE UNIVERSITY OF ARIZONA PRESS/TUCSON

About the Author
Mark T. Gilderhus, well-known authority on diplomatic and military history of the twentieth century, is the author of *Diplomacy and Revolution: U.S.-Mexican Relations Under Wilson and Carranza* (1977). He has taught United States history at Colorado State University since 1968 and has served his department as professor and chair.

THE UNIVERSITY OF ARIZONA PRESS

Copyright © 1986
The Arizona Board of Regents
All Rights Reserved

This book was set in 10/12 V.I.P. Baskerville.
Manufactured in the U.S.A.

Library of Congress Cataloging-in-Publication Data

Gilderhus, Mark T.
    Pan American visions.

    Bibliography: p.
    Includes index.
    1. Pan-Americanism. 2. Latin America—Foreign
relations—United States. 3. United States—Foreign
relations—Latin America. 4. United States—Foreign
relations—1913–1921. I. Title.
F1418.G487 1986   327.7308   86-16024
ISBN 0-8165-0936-0 (alk. paper)

In Memory of My Parents

Contents

Preface   ix

Acknowledgments   xiii

CHAPTER ONE

The First Initiatives, March 1913–August 1914   1

CHAPTER TWO

The Quest for Integration, August 1914–February 1917   37

CHAPTER THREE

The Effects of Waging War, February 1917–November 1918   81

CHAPTER FOUR

The Consequences of Making Peace, November 1918–
    March 1921   129

Notes   159

Bibliographical Note   177

Index   191

ILLUSTRATIONS

Map: South America in the Wilson Era   4

If I Had Only Done That (cartoon)   36

A Few More Supports for the Nest (cartoon)   82

Room for All Under the New Umbrella (cartoon)   128.

Preface

THIS BOOK SEEKS TO EXPLORE more or less systematically a line of policy developed during Woodrow Wilson's presidency. Although many scholars have alluded to it, no published accounts have examined the implications in any detail. The theme centers on Pan Americanism or, in more current jargon, what contemporary social scientists would call "regional integration." This work is presented as a case study, but it seeks also to address a larger issue—namely, the ongoing efforts of the United States to manage the affairs of the western hemisphere and to bestow more orderly and predictable structures upon its relations with the countries of Latin America. In the United States, the advocates of Pan Americanism have always argued their case by holding that the cultivation of more intimate ties would demonstrate self-evident virtues and necessarily would serve mutual interests in peace, prosperity, and security. The proponents presumed the existence of natural harmonies in the western hemisphere and reasoned that the creation of a functioning, regional system would benefit all participants by facilitating, among other things, the settlement of disputes, the expansion of trade, and the diminution of European influences.

As an approach to political and economic organization within the western hemisphere, Pan Americanism always has had more appeal in the United States than elsewhere. The champions affirmed their belief in the existence of a common bond with Latin Americans. The historian Arthur P. Whitaker characterized their view as "the western hemisphere idea," according to which a unique community of nations had developed out of a shared history, geography and ideology.[1] To put it another way, Pan Americanism came into being as a result of republican rebellions in the New World against the decadent monarchies of the Old. In graphic contrast, the inhabitants of Latin America were more impressed by the disparities of wealth, power, and culture. They worried that too close an affiliation with "the colossus of the North" might overwhelm and submerge them. Early in the 1820s, Simón Bolívar, the liberator of South America, advised close cooperation among the newly independent Spanish-American states to ward off domination by the United States. Similar mistrust later obstructed Secretary of State James G. Blaine's wish for the establishment of a customs union and a system of compulsory arbitration at the First International American Conference in Washington, D.C., in 1889. For many Latin American nationalists, any credible approach to regional integration would have to exclude the United States. They preferred a Pan Hispanic or Pan Latin alternative.

One of the difficulties in studying Pan Americanism is trying to comprehend the implications of the term. Though coined in the 1880s and popularized by the New York *Evening Post*, the expression has always projected vague, elusive, and contradictory images. One authority, the historian Thomas L. Karnes, has remarked that "Pan-Americanism is more easily traced than defined."[2] For some observers, it has connoted a more equitable system of association and partnership, a relationship based on courtesy, consideration, and justice, as Woodrow Wilson often claimed. For critics, in contrast, it has meant an exercise in deception and disguise, a subtle method of hegemony and exploitation. The Chilean historian, Hernán Ramírez Necochea, depicted Pan Americanism as "a movement inspired and impelled by American imperialism with the purpose of winning absolute political and economic supremacy in the western hemisphere."[3] In the present day, Marxist scholars and dependency theorists concur in this view, arguing that international relationships in the western hemisphere invariably drain away wealth and resources from the poorer countries, held in thrall to an alien and overweening authority, and enrich the United States.

The issue entails fundamental and profound conceptual dilemmas. Statesmen and scholars do not agree whether a strong, dynamic state can function in any way as an equal in close proximity with weaker and often more disorganized neighbors. Just what the leaders in the United States intended of their policies and what they actually accomplished as consequences are subjects of ongoing debate. A central question asks whether natural harmonies or structural dependencies best characterize the nature of relations in the western hemisphere. Can political cooperation attain common goods, or will it result in dominion? Can an expanding trade and investment spread prosperity from the metropolis to the provinces, or is the prevalence of poverty in Latin America a direct outcome of such processes? The authorities do not agree. Advocates of what Ronald H. Chilcote and Joel C. Edelstein call "the diffusion model" will insist upon the existence of compatibilities, while the adherents of "the dependency model" will convey an impression of disharmony. How best to conceive of inter-American relations has elicited a great deal of controversy which, so far, has allowed for no concensus.[4] In an appeal for methodological diversity, two political scientists recently voiced a disturbing suspicion that each theoretical construct tends to define its own reality and to confirm facts in its own support. The result, an uncomfortable predicament for scholars, implies the possibility that two irreconcilable interpretive perspectives are both demonstrably true.[5]

The matter intrudes upon this study in that the differences produced by Wilson's Pan Americanism largely prefigured the broad outlines of the contemporary debate. Wilson, a classical liberal, believed that the diffusion of United States' influence in Latin America would have uplifting and beneficial effects. The Latin Americans, in contrast, though perhaps less analytically sophisticated than modern-day social scientists, often shied away, choosing their grounds carefully out of concern for establishing unwanted dependencies. The ensuing narrative follows Wilson's efforts to develop and to act upon a Pan American vision. The president aimed at regional integration in the western hemisphere under United States' leadership, and the responses to his initiatives often ran counter to his expectations.

This book holds that Pan Americanism, a subject much neglected by Wilson specialists, occupied importance as a kind of centerpiece in the unfolding of Wilson's policies toward Latin America. It became a sort of blueprint according to which Wilson tried but failed to reform and to regulate the conduct of international relationships in his part of the world. The first chapter considers the formulation of the policy and some early experiments with implementation. The second examines some ambitious undertakings once the onset of the Great War in Europe altered significantly the political and economic milieu. The third explores the impact upon the Americas when the United States entered the First World War, and the final chapter looks at the place of United States–Latin American relations in the process of peacemaking after the armistice. Some concluding observations follow. The intended focus throughout the text centers on the Pan American theme and gives foremost attention to the roles of Argentina, Brazil, and Chile, the principal, prospective partners in Wilson's scheme of things.

Acknowledgments

In bringing about the completion of this project, I wish to acknowledge my indebtedness to Colorado State University for providing research funds and a sabbatical leave, particularly to Frank J. Vattano, the dean of the College of Arts, Humanities, and Social Sciences, and to George M. Dennison, the former associate vice president for academic affairs. My colleagues, George M. Dennison, Liston E. Leyendecker, and John P. Vloyantes, two historians and a political scientist, read portions of the manuscript in various stages. Deborah Ann Clifford provided editorial assistance and typed clean copies with skill, accuracy, and good humor. To an extent, I owe my interest in the subject to David F. Trask of the United States Army Center for Military History and Michael C. Meyer of the Latin American Center at the University of Arizona, although I attribute no responsibility to them or to anyone else for my handling of it. The dedication recalls the memory of my mother, Thea Enderson Gilderhus, who supplied love and encouragement, and my father, M. R. Gilderhus, who served unheroically in Pershing's army, happily for me, in safe places. As for other members of my family, my wife Nancy and my daughters Kirsten and Lesley engaged in unspoken conspiracies to ward off the effects of certain obsessional tendencies. They have had to live with an unnatural concern over Woodrow Wilson for a long time.

CHAPTER ONE

The First Initiatives

March 1913—August 1914

THE PROMISE OF LATIN AMERICA held great allure during the Wilson presidency, and the expectation for years in the future ran high. For two decades, an expanding commerce had buoyed the hopes of trade enthusiasts and other promoters. Meanwhile, an assortment of publicists, reformers, and peace advocates hailed the efficacy of international law and other organizational devices as the proper means to uphold order and security within the region and to exclude foreign intrusions. In 1913, the anticipated fulfillment of such aims heralded the advent of a new era in which intimate ties would bind the peoples of the western hemisphere.

The impending completion of the Panama Canal, a powerful symbol of unity and progress, signified a contraction of geographic distance and a new access to the markets of South America. Fulfilling the ancient dream, the modern techniques of medicine and engineering had created the Straits of Anián, the mythical passage between the oceans long sought by the Spanish *conquistadores*.[1] The incoming Wilson administration took advantage of propitious circumstances by embracing Latin America as a place of special importance and developing a Pan American vision of friendship and cooperation. Conceived as a strategy for peace and prosperity, the plan called for regional integration, an attempt to bring into existence an autonomous, self-sufficient community of nations, independent of Europe and committed to an enlightened conception of mutual self-interest under the benign guidance of the United States. In his approaches to Latin America, President Wilson presumed the existence of natural harmonies and fundamental compatibilities.

[1]

OPPORTUNITIES AND EXPECTATIONS

Leaders in the Wilson administration believed that regional integration could serve both economic and political ends. An expanding and potentially lucrative trade had established Latin America as an important market, yet impediments retarded the rate of advance. The absence of adequate shipping and banking facilities, for example, handicapped North America entrepreneurs and rendered them dependent upon European capabilities, thereby less able to compete. In addition, Latin America's historic mistrust of the United States' power and alleged hegemonial ambitions intensified the problem by encouraging the cultivation of European ties as a counterbalance. To provide redress, President Wilson proposed a tactical shift, seeking to reduce the European presence and also to win over the Latin Americans by showing that closer relations could entail advantages.

The new administration had a high regard for trade promotion. In times of economic distress throughout the course of United States history, trade expansionists had identified the acquisition of foreign markets as a vital goal. Indeed, they saw it as a means of promoting recovery and maintaining good times henceforth. The perceived alternative held frightening implications. Ongoing surplus production would result in forced gluts, high unemployment, low prices, and endless cycles of panic and depression. In support of this analysis, the economic patterns since the 1870s appeared as confirmation and suggested compellingly that the application of new technologies and techniques in industry and agriculture had accentuated the ingrained tendency toward instability. To gain access to the outside world, the proponents favored an open-door policy. That is, they claimed the right of unrestricted access to the markets of the world, unhindered by discriminatory treatment, exorbitantly high tariffs, or other special arrangements such as spheres of influence. First articulated formally in reference to China at the turn of the century, United States' leaders during the ensuing years sought to apply the open-door policy in as much of the world as possible. If open conditions could prevail, trade enthusiasts had confidence in their country's capacity to outproduce and undersell potential competitors and thereby to obtain effective control. They reasoned that the United States previously had neglected unduly the export trade.[2]

The arguments in favor of trade expansion held persuasive power within the Wilson administration. During the campaign of 1912, Wilson endorsed them as conventional wisdom. In an exuberant talk before an audience of farmers in New Jersey, he affirmed in classic terms that "we have not established ourselves in foreign markets very successfully as yet" because "we have been so complacently content with the domestic market." But such indifference could not persist. The great changes wrought by the industrial revolution meant that "America . . . is now so productive of almost everything that the human race uses that she has got too much to sell to herself." To assure prosperity in the years to come, he urged that "we must broaden our borders and make conquest of the markets of the world." To permit a freer trade, he wanted a reduction of tariffs, and to guarantee a carrying fleet, a reconstruction of the merchant marine, allowed to languish and to deteriorate after the Civil War.[3] Wilson also noted implications for Latin America. As he told a group of merchants in New York City while commenting upon the completion of the Panama Canal, "that ditch . . . will switch the route of trade around" as much as when "the Turks captured Constantinople" and forced "the venturesome seamen down the coast of Africa to discover a route around the capes." In recent years, he asserted, the expansion of exports had accelerated by "leaps and bounds." "We have ceased to be a provincial Nation."[4]

The steady expansion of the Latin American trade over two decades raised high hopes. As observed by John Barrett, the executive director of the Pan American Union, "Although the volume of our trade at the present time with Latin America is only a small part of our total foreign trade . . . no section of the world . . . offers greater opportunities for development in the future."[5] The published statistics bore out some of his claim. Annual exports from the United States had increased in value from $1,394,000,000 in 1900 to $1,745,000,000 in 1910, to $2,466,000,000 in 1913. These figures reflected a shift away from agricultural commodities in favor of manufactured goods. Europe remained the favored trading partner, absorbing in 1913 about 60 percent of the products coming out of the United States, but the degree of preponderance had shifted downward from 1900 when it stood at nearly 75 percent. The amount going to Latin America, meanwhile, moved upward to around 20 percent.[6]

The statistical aggregates, not wholly accurate, represented different methods of appraisal in customs house evaluations but nevertheless showed impressive rates of increase for Latin American commerce. The estimated value of Latin American exports to and imports from all countries rose several times over from $910,422,000 in 1893 to $2,864,876,000 in 1913. For sixteen years, the annual rate of expansion had averaged 13 percent, meaning that Latin America accounted for a growing measure of the world's commerce, a turn of events described in the *Bulletin* of the Pan American Union as "a larger trade development than has taken place in any other considerable part

South America in the Wilson Era

of the world."[7] In 1913, the United States controlled almost 30 percent of the Latin American trade, the largest single share, but the nearest rivals, Great Britain and Germany, posed tough competition, especially in the larger, more populous countries. The United States had negative trade balances with Brazil, Chile, Colombia, Cuba, Mexico, Peru, and Venezuela, the result of purchasing more coffee, sugar, and other such raw materials than selling finished goods. Nonetheless, the *Bulletin* predicted optimistically that within a few years the imports and exports of "nearly every one of the Latin American countries would . . . move north and south and not east and west," with the United States coming out as the principal beneficiary.[8]

Still, an assortment of obstacles stood in the way. Cultural and language barriers and other difficulties placed the United States at a disadvantage in remote regions and caused acute worry. Charles Lyon Chandler, an official in the Counsular Service, enumerated some of the reasons. In an essay entitled "The World Race for the Rich South American Trade," published in the *World's Work*, Chandler warned of the consequences of "strenuous" European activity and also of insufficient shipping and banking facilities, meager sources of reliable information, and poor representation in the field. Before the United States could take control, it would have to acquire independent means to finance trade and to issue bonds in host countries. The latter held special utility in the construction of railroads, canals, and highways, the necessary prerequisites to an extensive trade. Similarly, Lincoln Hutchinson, an agent of the Commerce Department, urged the need for skill and perseverance. Although convinced that "a new era" lay ahead in international trade, he believed that only "intelligent knowledge" of actual conditions could take full advantage.[9]

The United States government already had taken steps. In 1912, the Taft administration created the Bureau of Foreign and Domestic Commerce within the Department of Commerce. It had as a charge "the duty of fostering, promoting, and developing the various manufacturing industries of the United States and their markets at home and abroad" and also the obligation of gathering and publishing "all available and useful information concerning such industries and markets."[10] To such ends, a variety of outlets provided dissemination, notably the *Daily Consular and Trade Reports*, consisting of useful résumés of market conditions from all over the world, and also the monographic studies set forth in the *Special Agents Series* and *Miscellaneous Studies*. These specialized and detailed investigations presented an array of facts and figures for interested readers.

Private groups also mobilized for action in efforts to win over many customers among the 74,000,000 inhabitants of Latin America. In

1913, trade associations and commercial groups from eastern cities
planned publicity campaigns and undertook excursions. Late in the
spring, a delegation from Boston traveled some 14,000 miles in
eighty-five days and visited ten countries. The participants reportedly
returned "with a deeper and better knowledge . . . of Latin American
civilization and culture" and "a clearer idea of the vast resources
awaiting development," for which the venture earned commendation
as "a splendid expression of enterprise." Similar aspirations animated
plans among the Galveston Chamber of Commerce, the Nashville
Board of Trade, the Grain Dealers' National Association, the Illinois
Manufacturer's Association, the Mississippi Valley Medical Association, the Louisville Commercial Club, the Birmingham Chamber of
Commerce, and the St. Louis Businessmen's Club. The accelerating
interest expanded the membership roster of the Pan American Society
of the United States from 130 to 500 within three years of its founding
in 1912. Mainly the creation of John Barrett of the Pan American
Union, a tireless advocate, the organization comprised businessmen in
New York City who favored "closer relations" with Latin America.[11]

Business leaders understood the principles of reciprocity. If North
Americans seriously proposed to sell in Latin America, they also had to
buy from Latin Americans. When the Chicago Association of Commerce opened a showroom for wares in Belgrano Street in Buenos
Aires, the group signaled readiness to purchase Argentine products.
John Barrett established the point on grounds of self-interest, noting
that such practices actually would bolster the consuming capacities of
prospective customers. As observed by the Pan American Union *Bulletin*, "In the economic field, a people must have something to sell and
must be able to sell it before they can be buyers." This concern necessarily impinged upon another. Prospective entrepreneurs in the
United States worried that Europeans enjoyed unfair advantages,
"monopolies," and "special concessions." Early in 1913, the Latin
American Chamber of Commerce in New York advised the Wilson
administration to take action against such favors, urging "free" and
"open" economic intercourse with Latin America and also the establishment of competitive steamship and telegraph lines.[12] Wilson later
emphasized these themes in his famous address at Mobile, Alabama,
before the Southern Commercial Congress in October 1913.

The idea of political integration also appealed to leaders in the
Wilson administration. They wanted to achieve some method of con-
sultation and cooperation so that other countries could participate in
efforts to police the western hemisphere, to safeguard it against presumed foreign threats, and to maintain the peace internally. Although
Wilson understood some of the adverse effects of the great disparity in

power and influence between the United States and Latin America, he hoped to overcome them by divising more effective, less costly techniques for managing regional affairs. The traditional method based on unilateral measures entailed liabilities and bred mistrust. For almost a century, Yankeephobic sentiments in Latin America typically cast the United States as a natural enemy, the northern colossus, inimical in all things to the sovereignty and values of the Hispanic world.[13]

The image of the United States as an expansive insatiability obtained credence from the Latin American reading of historical experience. The march of conquest across North America in the nineteenth century and the perceived arrogance of the Monroe Doctrine in its several interpretations aroused antagonism and apprehension. Secretary of State Richard Olney's declaration in 1895 that "today the United States is practically sovereign on this continent, and its fiat is law upon the subjects to which it confines its interposition" had such effects. Later, the demolition of Spain's empire in America, the accentuation of the United States' imperial thrust, and the transformation of the Caribbean region into a sphere of influence intensified the fear and foreboding. Indeed, the creation of protectorates in Cuba, Panama, Nicaragua, Haiti, and the Dominican Republic appeared as confirmation of bad expectations. The rationale, as articulated by Theodore Roosevelt in his Corollary to the Monroe Doctrine, affirmed a unilateral right to exercise "an international police power." According to Roosevelt, the United States, "a civilized nation," would uphold the canons of decent and law-abiding conduct when so compelled by "chronic wrongdoing" among unstable, unruly neighbors.[14] The tendency of small countries to default upon loans especially disturbed him, since it tempted the Europeans to take counteractive measures. Rather than sanction an additional European presence in the New World and put up with menaces to the canal, he devised a doctrine of preventive intervention. When things went wrong, the United States would make them right. But such paternalism had vexing implications.

The hegemonic role of the United States in the western hemisphere raised difficult issues for reformers and other critics during the Progressive era. Although the political elites most interested in foreign policy overwhelmingly favored order and predictability as desired ends and wanted such conditions to prevail in as much of the outside world as possible, they also questioned the wisdom and viability of unilateral actions and hoped to subsume the United States' role within some kind of international system. The perceived excesses of intervention and "dollar diplomacy" under Roosevelt and Taft prompted leading dissenters in the organized peace movement, the churches, the universities, and among the guild of international lawyers to put forth

various solutions.[15] Most favored a new emphasis on multilateral approaches in international relations, underscoring the need for countries with similar interests to share responsibilities and to use the power
of the United States in pursuit of broad definitions of the general
welfare. Many observers regarded international law as the proper
device. Indeed, the creation of the Central American Court of Justice
in 1907, though defunct by 1917, inspired grandiose thoughts of a
juridical system for all of Latin America. In 1913, Joseph Wheless, a
noted international lawyer, published just such a plan for a Pan American Court. Other such proposals called for nations to cooperate in
keeping the peace through guarantees of national sovereignty and
independence. In 1911, James L. Slayden, a Texas Congressman and a
trustee of the Carnegie Endowment for International Peace, introduced a resolution into the House of Representatives, calling for a
system of collective self-defense in the western hemisphere. Though
the proposed treaty went nowhere, it sparked Woodrow Wilson's im-
agination. The president called the idea "striking" and later made it a
feature of his Pan American policy.[16]

Wilson's campaign in 1912 centered on domestic issues and never
developed a full-blown discussion of foreign affairs. Nevertheless, his
rhetoric conveyed intimations of readiness to break with the immediate
past. A skillful and enthusiastic orator, Wilson liked to move people
through the power of his words. In speeches and other pronouncements, he employed mainly generalities and appeals to high principle
but sometimes implied criticism of his predecessors. His message to
Democrats across the country just before the election contained a
pledge of proper behavior in the conduct of diplomacy. "We have
become a powerful member of the great family of nations," he
affirmed. "The nations look to us for standards and policies worthy of
America." Once in possession of the White House, he promised, his
administration would take greater care for "the maxims of justice and
liberality and goodwill" and "the advancement of mankind" than for
"the progress of this or that investment," the latter an obvious slap at
"dollar diplomacy." Wilson's priorities required the use of governmental power in service to "the [human] race . . . the moral life . . . and
[the] spiritual betterment of those . . . for whom we profess to have set
government up."[17] During his presidency, he returned to such themes
many times, affirming a close identity between his purposes and the
best interests of humankind. Such conceptions functioned as sources of
conviction and strength when the world collapsed into chaos and
uncertainty. As president, he became more enmeshed with diplomatic
complexities than any president since James Madison.

THE FIRST STEPS

Shortly before the inauguration, Wilson expressed misgivings to a friend, remarking, "It would be the irony of fate if my administration had to deal with foreign affairs."[18] Often interpreted as a kind of portent, his words suggested a measure of insecurity and apprehension, yet, taken too literally, they surely result in an overstatement. Wilson suffered from few doubts about his capabilities. To be sure, he regarded domestic affairs as his expertise. He also recognized his lack of experience with professional diplomacy and perhaps his scant appreciation for foreign countries, cultures, and languages. Nevertheless, his qualifications for taking charge of the nation's foreign relations ranked no worse than other presidents since John Quincy Adams and surpassed those of many. Serious, competent, and highly educated, Wilson had enjoyed successful careers as a professor, a university president, and a one-term governor of New Jersey, all of which provided training grounds of sorts in the political and diplomatic arts. Whatever deficiencies marred his practice of statecraft may have stemmed less from inexperience than from personal rigidity, temperamental quirks, and a touch of arrogance. He intended to perform as a strong leader.

Once established in office, intricate questions engulfed him, the most pressing emanating from Latin America. In Mexico, civil war threatened another round of violence after General Victoriano Huerta's overthrow of President Francisco Madero. Though Wilson had scant knowledge of the circumstances, he had a personal connection. During the revolution in 1910, his daughter Eleanor had been "lost" for a short time during a vacation trip south of the border.[19] Elsewhere in Central America and around the Caribbean, the legacies of political instability and financial disorganization plagued the countries; and in South America, complicated rivalries and territorial disputes traditionally caused resentment and anxiety. After some six weeks in the presidency, Wilson, in exasperation, complained that he had trouble getting hold of "the threads" in Central and South America and wondered how best to find out "just what is going on down there."[20]

Political observers, meanwhile, speculated on his probable responses. During the campaign, Oswald Garrison Villard, the editor of the New York *Evening Post*, recorded ambivalent impressions of the candidate. "To my regret," he wrote after an interview, "I found that the Governor favors a large navy, and that he has been quite deluded by all that silly jingo talk about Germany making a raid on South America." Villard also disliked Wilson's notion that big powers no

longer should put up with "misbehavior" by little countries. Villard
thought Wilson poorly informed, "in ignorance of many things," especially in international affairs, but, as compensation, he also found him
"open to reason," ready to weigh "every argument candidly and on its
merits."[21] Another observer, Willard Straight, a well-connected banker
with J. P. Morgan and Company and formerly a diplomat, also affirmed disappointment. During the campaign, he expected "a more
straight-forward defense of the principles of the Democratic party"
from Wilson and characterized the man, in an arresting phrase, as "a
combination of a pedagogue and Jesuit." Later he remarked, "From all
accounts Wilson is pretty pig-headed and his record apparently, at
Princeton especially, has been one of broken friendships and petty
squabbles." But, in fairness, Straight noted that the harsh judgment
came mainly from Wilson's "enemies." The new secretary of state also
caused misgivings. After meeting with him, Straight reported that
William Jennings Bryan, now "holding down the chair which had held
Webster, Seward, Hay and Root," had emitted intimations "of the
Nebraska hayfield." But Straight conceded that the Great Commoner
had meant well. Somewhat later, Straight expressed enthusiasm over
the president's fast start, getting his administration "off with a bang,"
especially in Latin America.[22]

The distribution of responsibilities within the new administration
reflected priorities. The Latin American Affairs Division within the
State Department took charge of routine matters. As the civil war in
Mexico grew larger, the president became ever more involved with it
and functioned as his own foreign minister. Secretary of State Bryan,
meanwhile, directed projects around the Caribbean, worked on conciliation treaties, and sought means to alleviate Latin American indebtedness. Secretary of Commerce William C. Redfield and Secretary
of the Treasury William G. McAdoo also played significant roles in
foreign affairs. As dedicated trade expansionists, they hoped over the
long term to increase substantially the United States' share in Latin
America and intended also to provide the means to achieve it. Edward
Mandell House, another powerful figure, operated informally as an
outsider, removed from official channels. The "Colonel," a diminutive
Texan and self-styled power broker, had cultivated Wilson the candidate during the campaign and had won his confidence. Subsequently
functioning as a trusted personal advisor, House lived in New York, a
safe distance but a short train ride from the capital, and performed the
role of *deus ex machina* from behind the scenes. He gave himself high
marks for his skill in directing the action. His diary, a remarkable
document, revealed more than a trace of megalomania. Yet, in spite of
it, he became the president's closest friend, ally, and confidant. Wilson
could unburden his cares and speak frankly, and House had a talent

for saying the right things. He also figured prominently in the development of the Pan American policy. Even before the inauguration, House focused Wilson's attention on Latin America, suggesting the need for an international agreement with Great Britain and Germany on the meaning and scope of the Monroe Doctrine.[23]

Initial responses in Latin America implied favorable first impressions. On inauguration day, 4 March 1913, *La Prensa* of Buenos Aires, a premier newspaper in South America, applauded the prospect of a Wilson presidency. After a review of the recent past, an editorial concluded somewhat simplistically that Roosevelt and Taft had stood for the trusts and big corporations, while Wilson represented the people. The paper also anticipated "the beginning of a new era," characterized in the United States by a retreat from imperialism. Ironically, such expectations caused worry within the new administration out of concern for dangerous misimpressions. What if political dissidents in Central and South America misinterpreted the meaning of the election and perceived in Wilson "an encouragement" to acts of violence and revolution? The impending civil conflict in Mexico underscored the importance of the point. No one in the administration wanted several such difficulties. To dissipate misconceptions, the members of the cabinet unanimously resolved to support the president in a commitment to constitutional order in the western hemisphere.[24]

In a statement on 11 March 1913, the first on foreign affairs, the president affirmed his principles and expectations and also set forth a central assumption. Natural harmonies could unite the peoples of the western hemisphere if they manifested good behavior and showed the necessary regard for mutual rights and obligations. As "one of the chief objects of my administration," Wilson promised, he would "cultivate the friendship and deserve the confidence of our sister republics" and also "promote in every proper and honorable way the interests which are common to the peoples of the two continents." He stated "earnestly" his desire for "the most cordial understanding and cooperation between the peoples and leaders of America" and then explained how he proposed to obtain them.

Wilson attached crucial importance to legal procedures. Harmonious relations, he asserted, could take place "only when supported at every turn by the orderly processes of just government based upon law, not upon arbitrary or irregular force." In addition, the principle of self-determination required that "just government rests always upon the consent of the governed" and that "no freedom could exist unless founded upon law and upon the public conscience and approval." Although he intended to make "respect" and "helpfulness" the cornerstone of his policies, he put forth an important caveat, really the crux of his message. "We can have no sympathy with those who seek to

seize the power of government to advance their own personal interests
or ambition . . . . As friends, therefore, we shall prefer those who act in
the interest of peace and honor, who protect private rights, and respect
the restraint of constitutional provision." Only "mutual respect" could
provide "the indispensable foundation of friendship between states."
His conclusion affirmed the pursuit of common goals. The United
States "has nothing to seek in Central or South America except the
lasting interests of the people of the two continents, the security of
governments intended for the people and for no special group or
interest, and the development of personal and trade relationships
between the two continents." The achievement of such harmonies, he
was sure, would redound "to the profit and advantage" of both
partners and interfere "with the rights and liberties of neither."[25]

Wilson's eloquence depicted good faith and goodwill as essential
elements in his unfolding Pan American vision, yet, in the ensuing
years, contradiction and incongruity plagued his efforts, and criticism
ran strong. In response to the 11 March statement, for example,
Estanislao S. Zeballos, a former Argentine foreign minister, raised
some disturbing questions. Writing in *La Prensa*, Zeballos feared that
the United States intended to take sides in civil struggles and then to
determine the outcome. Any such endeavor, he argued, would violate
international law and overturn the tradition of recognizing the existence of de facto governments. Zeballos would not sanction any form
of intervention and urged the Argentines to repudiate it.[26] The per-
plexity became acute when Wilson confronted the full magnitude in
Mexico.

MEXICO AND OTHER MATTERS

The revolution in Mexico bloodied the country for over ten years.
The violence, beginning in 1910, resulted in the ouster of the aging
dictator, Porfirio Díaz, and, shortly thereafter, in the election to the
presidency of Francisco I. Madero. But he could not sustain himself. A
series of revolts culminated in a military takeover on 19 February 1913
and in Madero's death by assassination three days later. General Victoriano Huerta, the army chief of staff and a principal instigator, then
arranged to obtain the provisional presidency but reaped the whirl-
wind. His efforts to impose peace and order provoked a rebellion
against him among northern dissidents. Under the leadership of Venustiano Carranza, the governor of Coahuila, the insurgents pledged
themselves to the cause of constitutional legitimacy and mounted a
march on Mexico City. The Constitutionalist revolt against Huerta
required eighteen months to succeed in its purpose and repeatedly
confounded Woodrow Wilson.[27]

The president, in response, stood by his words of 11 March 1913. Voicing objections to the seizure of power as a violation of constitutional propriety, Wilson withheld diplomatic recognition and resolved to remove Victoriano Huerta from power, even though the European powers, notably Great Britain, accepted the provisional government on de facto grounds. As a solution to the Mexican problem, Wilson advised mediation. In the summer of 1913, his plan called for a cease-fire and early elections. If Huerta would agree to stay out of the contest, the United States would guarantee recognition of whatever government came into existence. To deliver the terms, the president sent an emissary into Mexico. John Lind, a former Democratic governor of Minnesota, undertook the mission, but it turned into a debacle. Wilson, to his sorrow, had underestimated Huerta's determination and resourcefulness. Moreover the episode gave credence to Estanislao Zeballos's apprehension that the United States now aimed at determining the results of civil struggles.[28]

Meanwhile, other concerns in foreign policy required attention. Within the foreign service, the distribution of patronage had important effects and intruded upon Latin America. After the victory in 1912, aspiring officeholders besieged Democratic party leaders, the outsiders for over a decade, and the new administration responded by eliminating Republicans from public office, seeking the spoils as rewards for "deserving Democrats." To an extent, Wilson and Bryan mistrusted the diplomatic corps, a presumed bastion of Republicanism and privilege. Although the State Department controlled only 450 jobs, comparatively small pickings, Wilson and Bryan regarded top diplomatic posts as political and proceeded within a year to replace seven of the eleven ambassadors, twenty-two of the thirty-five ministers, and about half of the lesser employees. Critics complained, meanwhile, that such practices undercut professionalism and competency and had undesirable results. The new appointees characteristically had no diplomatic experience and little foreign language facility.[29]

The onslaught threatened an established group of Latin American hands. Henry P. Fletcher, the minister in Chile, John W. Garrett, the minister in Argentina, and Edwin V. Morgan, the ambassador in Brazil, had entered diplomatic service under Republican presidents and regarded themselves as professionals. Fletcher, a well-connected insider, learned of the danger soon after the election when his friend, Willard Straight, told him to "sit tight in Chile" and "see how the wind blows." Nevertheless, Fletcher expressed his anxiety in a letter to William G. McAdoo, saying he was "very much interested" to learn the new administration's attitude. Since "only about a dozen of us . . . have come up from the ranks," he hoped that Bryan could "satisfy party claims" and "still maintain the service." But the insecurity persisted. In October

1913, Fletcher complained that Garrett, Morgan, "and myself are about all that's left of the old guard and we feel none too safe."[30]

Secretary of State Bryan, meanwhile, undertook ambitious projects in support of peace and prosperity. One set of plans called for the negotiation of conciliation or "cooling off" treaties. Designed as deterrents against the precipitous outbreak of war, they required nations engaged in disputes to submit to an investigation by a nonpartisan commission before resorting to hostilities. In the meantime, the mobilization of world opinion presumably would further reduce the likelihood. Bryan likened the process to conciliation in labor disputes. Secretary of the Navy Josephus Daniels underscored the earnestness of the endeavor by reporting that "The Administration is sincerely desirous of promoting the peace of the world" and recording that Woodrow Wilson liked the idea. It reminded him of a method employed to ward off fights which he had heard of in a military school. If quarrels developed, the boys had to state their grievances before the headmaster and then act according to the Marquis of Queensbury rules. As a result, Wilson said, no spats took place at all.[31]

Bryan wanted to negotiate conciliation treaties with every country in the world and almost succeeded. In Latin America, only Mexico, unrecognized, and Colombia, still aggrieved over the loss of Panama, failed to take part. Otherwise, thirty-six of the forty nations represented in the United States accepted the plan in principle and thirty endorsed it in formal terms. Nevertheless, Bryan's zeal caused critics to scoff. Senator Henry F. Ashurst, a Democrat from Arizona, remarked that "no one, except Bryan, believed that his treaties will preserve the peace."[32]

Bryan also sought ways to relieve conditions of impoverishment in Latin America. While endorsing the conventional wisdom that an expanding trade would enlarge the wealth, he also believed in liberation from European financial control. The magnitude of indebtedness and the high interest rates outraged him. For example, he found out that the cost to Nicaragua for European loans usually ranged from 18 to 24 percent and sometimes reached 36 or 48 percent. As a preferred alternative, he suggested that the United States make government loans available at 4½ percent, in which case the small republics could pay back their European debts and also "our country" could acquire "such an increased influence . . . that we could prevent revolutions, promote education, and advance stable and just government." Although Wilson disapproved of government loans, he favored addressing the problem by providing cheaper credit through United States banks. Subsequent attempts at implementation made Bryan, the erstwhile anti-imperialist, confusingly appear as an advocate of "dollar diplomacy." While reflecting upon the irony, one biographer, Paolo Coletta, described Bryan as a practitioner of "paternal despotism." As Coletta argued, "By practically banning all but American investments, exercising financial control, prohibiting revolutions, approving treaties which included protectorate features, and even using force, he made the Caribbean more than ever an American lake." As a consequence of United States' actions, the countries of Nicaragua, Haiti, and the Dominican Republic moved ever closer toward the Cuban and Panamanian models. A tinge of racism also colored his thinking. After hearing a briefing on Haiti in 1912 before becoming the secretary of state, Bryan exclaimed quizzically, "Dear me, think of it! Niggers speaking French."[33]

The persistence of such issues produced a high level of interest in the meaning and application of the Monroe Doctrine. For critics in the United States, this hallowed creed symbolized better than anything the hegemonial and unilateral pretensions of the United States, especially the definition advanced in the Roosevelt Corollary. Some radicals wanted to overturn traditional practices altogether. Otto Gresham, the son of former Secretary of State Walter Q. Gresham, thought outright repudiation better than constant interference in "the internal conditions" of foreign countries. Moderates more characteristically wanted a new definition of the Monroe Doctrine, cast in multilateral terms, and an enlistment of partners whenever disturbances required some action. For example, E. G. Stafford of the Cananea Cattle Company advised such a course in a letter to Woodrow Wilson, explaining that "in this way, should intervention in the affairs of some Latin American republic become necessary a group of nations would bear the expense." For him, the joint expedition against the Boxers in China struck the proper precedent.[34]

The debate elicited a great deal of public notice. When the delegates assembled at the nineteenth Lake Mohonk Conference on International Arbitration in May 1913, a prestigious event, they heard a series of presentations on Latin America, including one entitled "Some Recent Forms of the Monroe Doctrine and Their Relation to International Arbirtration" by William R. Shepherd, professor of history at Columbia University. Later in November 1913, a symposium on Latin American affairs at Clark Univeristy in Worcester, Massachusetts, devoted six sessions to various facets of the Monroe Doctrine, featuring such authorities as F. E. Chadwick, rear admiral in the United States Navy, Charles H. Sherrill, former minister to Argentina, Albert Bushnell Hart, professor of government at Harvard University, James Morton Callahan, professor of history and political science at West Virginia University, and Hiram Bingham, professor of Latin American history at Yale University. From various perspectives, they explained why Latin Americans had come to regard the Monroe Doctrine as a mixed blessing.[35]

Hiram Bingham, renowned as the discoverer of the Inca ruins at Machu Picchu in Peru and one of the founders of Latin American studies in the United States, became a foremost critic. Following a trip to South America, Bingham published an article in *The Atlantic Monthly* in 1913, later a book, entitled "The Monroe Doctrine: An Obsolete Shibboleth." In these publications, he argued that the Monroe Doctrine had lost its original meaning and now manifested an unacceptable degree of paternalism and condescension. Indeed, it appeared "to our South American neighbors to be neither disinterested nor unselfish, but rather an indisputable evidence of overweening conceit." But, he assured, a multilateral definition could remedy the problem. The Latin Americans should join in an understanding so that, whenever trouble developed in the future, the United States and its associates could call "a family gathering and see what if anything needs to be done." Bingham took his case directly to the president. As a distant acquaintance ever since Princeton, Bingham sent a reprint of his article with encouragment to read it. Later, he wrote to the president that "the time is ripe for you to take advantage of the present opportunity to formulate and explicitly enunciate a new foreign policy" because "the Monroe Doctrine is tottering . . . . Something definite must take its place."[36]

REDEFINING THE MONROE DOCTRINE

The Mexican imbroglio galvanized just such a determination. The unsettled state of the neighboring republic produced incessant talk of strong measures and elicited interest in enlisting other countries in joint measures. Early in May 1913, Wilson pondered the possibility of intervention and inquired of Colonel House whether the consequences would have effects "as bad as the Cabinet thought." House, in reply, estimated the 50,000 troops could begin the job but that guerrilla war might follow. Rather than take the risk, he preferred the alternative of holding an election to remove Huerta and to restore the peace. Meanwhile, Argentina and Chile indicated readiness to follow the United States' lead in withholding recognition, an especially heartening sign since Wilson wanted to think that the stable states of South America might play a role in bringing order to the unstable ones around the Caribbean.[37]

Such an approach held intriguing possibilities. Late in July 1913, John Barrett of the Pan American Union reiterated a favorite theme. Convinced that a resort to force would destroy "Pan American com-

merce and comity," he advised mediation as the best option in what had
become "a matter of vital importance." He insisted, "Our prestige, our
influence and our commerce with all twenty countries lying South of us
are involved in this issue." In his view, "An intervention, without first
exhausting every other means of securing peace, may mean war with
Mexico and permanent alienation of Latin American sympathy, the
evil effects of which will last a century." A better course, Barrett urged,
would invoke "the Pan American Doctrine" instead of the Monroe
Doctrine. He pointed out to Wilson, "if you can give a Pan American
tone to mediation, you will strengthen Mexican confidence in your
good intentions and gain the lasting sympathy of the rest of Latin
America." Later expressions of support from Argentina, Brazil, and
Chile lent further credence, bolstering Wilson's hope that "God
[would] grant that no war shall come to this country during my administration."[38]

John Lind, the presidential emissary in Mexico, meanwhile languished in Veracruz, suffering from stomach problems and frustration
over his incapacity to arrange a settlement. According to Lind, the
Mexicans "have no standards." In their politics, "They seem more like
children than men." He attributed their actions to "appetite" and
"vanity." He also articulated a thesis with disturbing implications.
Mexico, he claimed, had become the object of an international competition pitting the United States against Great Britain. Standing behind
Huerta and thwarting Wilson's aims, he saw the power and influence of
the British empire. Such suspicions soon permeated the Wilson administration. The president and the secretary of state shared them, and
so did the American ambassador in London, Walter Hines Page. To
make matters worse, Huerta dashed the American plan to remove him
on 10 October 1913 by dissolving the Chamber of Deputies and promising to stand as a candidate. Sir Lionel Carden, the British minister to
Mexico, presented his credentials on the next day and threw official
Washington into disarray. Carden, reportedly no friend of the United
States, had connections with S. Weetman Pearson, Lord Cowdray, a
large English investor in Mexican railroads and petroleum. Previously
Britain's refusal to withhold recognition from Huerta gave the Wilson
administration cause for concern. Now Carden's arrival appeared as a
studied affront, if, indeed, not nefarious design. Huerta, now perceived
as an agent of foreign imperialism, presumably had an obligation to
respond with economic favors for Great Britain.[39]

The question of Latin American economic dependence upon
Europe dominated Wilson's celebrated address before the Southern
Commercial Congress on 27 October at Mobile, Alabama. The presi-
dent argued that the Europeans, in quest of concessions and special

privileges, constituted a threat to the very right of self-determination. He claimed, moreover, that much of Latin America already had fallen victim but that the United States stood ready to aid in the cause of liberation. He would "never condone iniquity because it is most convenient to do so." Quite the contrary, he would insist upon "the principle that morality and not expediency is the thing that must guide us." Wilson's defiance set him in opposition to an alleged alien menace, but he promised "emancipation" and called upon the United States to make common cause with the people of Latin America in the development of "true constitutional liberty" throughout the world. To show his good faith, he vowed, the United States "never again" would seek "one additional foot of territory by conquest."[40]

The Mobile Address, sometimes misinterpreted as a pledge against intervention, actually anticipated broader forms of involvement in the affairs of Latin America. In what verged on a declaration of economic war, the Wilson administration proposed to engage the Latin Americans in an effort to roll back the European presence. Colonel House understood the intention. He hailed Wilson's words as "a new interpretation of the Monroe Doctrine," enlarging upon the original purpose "to keep Europe from securing political control of any state in the Western Hemisphere" by recognizing that it was "just as reprehensible to permit foreign states to secure financial control of those weak unfortunate republics." House applauded the president's revelation of "this alliance between the Mexican Government and the oil interests" and his readiness to build "a fire back of the British Ministers through the English public." House's fictional creation, Philip Dru, the administrator, had employed similar stratagems. In a diplomatic circular, Secretary Bryan reasoned in a parallel fashion, explaining that "we are attempting to give to the small republics of Latin America the advantage of our experience." Lind, meanwhile, cautioned darkly that if Huerta should remain in power, Mexico would become "a European annex, industrially, financially, politically."[41]

Wilson desired a strong stand. At the end of October, according to Colonel House, "The President [had] in mind to declare war against Mexico even though actual armed entrance into Mexico is not made." Instead, he would apply pressure by blockading the ports, closing the border, and cutting off the revenues. Wilson himself wrote that "Many fateful possibilities are involved . . . I lie awake at night praying that they may be averted. No man can tell what will happen while we deal with a desperate brute like that traitor, Huerta. God save us from the worst!"[42] Ambassador Page in London reinforced the determination, echoing the president's demand for "a moral basis of government" in Mexico and "for all the volcanic states in Latin-America." He thought

Mexico was only part of the problem. "We have never had a South- and Central-American policy worth calling so, because we have never based our action in a given conspicuous case on a fundamental moral basis—except in Cuba." He claimed further that the British had difficulty comprehending a truly principled approach. "They have a mania for order, sheer order, order for the sake of order and—of trade." Bryan summarized the prevailing attitude late in November, affirming that "the purpose" in Mexico "is solely and singly to secure peace and order . . . by seeing to it that the processes of self-government . . . are not interrupted or set aside." He said frankly that the United States in Mexico as elsewhere around the world must function as "the consistent champion of the open door."[43]

Such rhetoric impressed British leaders alternately as the product of confusion or hypocrisy. In the middle of November, Lord Edward Grey, the foreign secretary, complained of Bryan's supposedly false notion that British oil companies had determined British policy. As Grey wrote to Carden, the minister in Mexico, "I presume Huerta knows that we cannot support him in any way against the United States, but if not you should make it clear to him." Grey denied further that British interests had acquired any oil concessions. Meanwhile, Grey's personal secretary, Sir William Tyrell, then on a mission in the United States, reported after an interview with the American president that Wilson had a wish to teach unstable countries "a lesson" by driving Victoriano Huerta from power. Tyrell remarked upon the oddity. "The President did not seem to realize that this policy will lead to a 'de facto' American protectorate over the Central American Republics; but there are others who do, and who intend to achieve that object." As John Lind told the president early in January 1914, "however justifiable and ideal your policy may be on ethical grounds its economic and political importance to the United States is greater."[44]

When the tension dissipated, the men in charge of the Wilson administration congratulated themselves for having won a victory over the British. Exultantly, Walter Hines Page observed, "They've done all we asked and more; and . . . they've come to understand what we are driving at." Still, he expressed pique over the suspicion that "we wish to exploit [Latin America] ourselves." Page commended Wilson for delivering countless people in the western hemisphere from the grip of a "dictatorship." The British, he claimed, had "no idea of our notion of freeing men." In a sardonic commentary upon this episode, an English historian remarked with some measure of overstatement that the Wilson administration "deluded itself into believing that the British government was pursuing a policy actively hostile to its own and, having done so, deluded itself out again." The more recent work by Friedrich

Katz concluded differently, showing that legitimate grounds existed
for Wilson's worry. [45]

ARGENTINA, BRAZIL, AND CHILE

While unresolved difficulties with Mexico kept anxiety high, the
administration developed new initiatives, seeking to enfold the stable
states of Latin America in a Pan American embrace, in spite of legacies
of mistrust. As Minister to Chile Henry P. Fletcher observed, "Pan
Americanism has a hard row to hoe" because "many people in South
America . . . misunderstand and misconstrue the acts of the United
States." The policy of seeking new forms of economic and political
cooperation centered on Argentina, Brazil, and Chile. As the most
powerful and influential nations in South America, and potentially
among the best customers, the A.B.C. countries held promise as working partners. In recent years, at least since the Baron of Rio-Branco had
taken over the foreign office in 1902, Brazil had cultivated an "unwritten alliance" with the United States, while Argentina and Chile, a good
deal more aloof, identified with the European powers and welcomed
British capital. As traditional rivals, the A.B.C. countries competed
with one another in many areas—for example, in naval arms construction and over real estate. Specialists in the United States Department of
State wanted to improve relations among them but not too much.
Dismaying rumors floated around occasionally that the three countries
might overcome their difficulties and then put together a Pan-Latin
alignment directed against the United States. [46]

Commercial incentives aroused much attention. A report by the
Department of Commerce noted in October 1913, "In anticipation of
the opening of the Panama Canal, American manufacturers and exporters are showing keen interest in the possibilities of extending their
trade in South America." The demand for information required that
the Bureau of Foreign and Domestic Commerce produce a variety of
publications on specialized subjects, ranging from the demand for
cotton goods in Latin America to the coal trade and the cost of transportation on the west coast. Curiosity also led to eccentric calculations.
A geographer, Walter S. Tower, reported imaginatively that "in pro-
portion to its size and its population South America is commercially
more important than Asia, for Asia has a total foreign trade less than
twice as great as that of South America, while its area is two and a half
times and its population more than sixteen times as large." Nevertheless, many impediments hindered development. Professor Hiram
Bingham told the American Manufacturers' Export Club that distance
and physical barriers in themselves slowed the advance. The Andes

Mountains posed an immense difficulty. Bingham wondered too whether large numbers of poor people with little inclination or capacity to buy products could ever become good customers. Nevertheless, exports from the United States rose from $41,000,000 in 1903 to $150,000,000 in 1913, and the A.B.C. countries accounted for much of the increase.[47]

Economic conditions gave reasons for continued optimism. In Argentina's case, foreign trade in 1913 amounted to $877,711,376, consisting of $408,711,966 in imports and $468,999,410 in exports. The totals marked an overall increase of two and one-half times since 1903. Great Britain, the predominating influence, controlled over 31 percent of the market, followed by Germany with almost 17 percent and the United States with nearly 15 percent. In their purchases abroad, the Argentines bought large quantities of food products, textiles, iron and steel, agricultural implements, locomotive equipment, and electrical apparatus. In return, they sold wheat, maize, linseed, hides, wool, and beef. The United States, the weakest among the main competitors, had an unfavorable balance of trade with Argentina, but indications pointed to better times. As the renovation of the docks in Buenos Aires neared completion, American observers pondered the opportunities for the future, the feasibility of constructing first-class hotels to ease the plight of travelers in the major cities, the reasons why the sale of locomotives lagged way behind the British, and the prospect of selling large amounts of agricultural machinery to Argentine ranchers. Indeed, the P.A.U. *Bulletin* remarked in August 1914 that the United States, Great Britain, and Germany had become engaged in a "great competition" in Argentina.[48]

As Argentina's export-oriented economy boomed, the major trade centers moved enormous quantities of agricultural and pastoral products into the world market. In most years after 1890, the sale of cereals ran to 10 million tons. After the introduction of refrigeration in ships and packing plants in 1900, Argentina sold about 350,000 tons of meat each year. By 1915, the total cultivated area in Argentina encompassed 24 million hectares. Argentina ranked among the most prosperous and productive countries in the world and owed a great deal to Great Britain. As historian David Rock explained, "The export boom was largely a result of the expansion of the British food market and the maturing of British industry in the last quarter of the nineteenth century." While the British imported from Argentina large amounts of foodstuffs, especially meat, they sold large numbers of industrial products. As Rock observed, "The Argentine economy was thus broadly modeled on the classic precepts of Free Trade and international specialisation."[49]

Agricultural production in Argentina rested on a system of large landed estates, the owners of which constituted the dominant political class. According to Rock, "the core" comprised about 400 families out of a population of about 7.8 million, and functioned as "a local collaborating elite with British interests." The wealth centered in the pampas region, running in a wide arch a couple of hundred miles around the major port city and capital, Buenos Aires. The oligarchy depended heavily upon foreign capital. In 1910, the estimated British investment amounted to 300 million pounds sterling, concentrated especially in government loans, railroads, and public utilities.[50]

During the first decade of the twentieth century, a high level of political tension set members of the oligarchy at odds with an emerging urban middle class and large numbers of immigrant workers, mainly Italian and Spanish. Although socialist and anarchist parties agitated against the established order, after 1900 the Unión Cívica Radical, or Radical party, posed the greatest threat as a destabilizing influence. Headed by a contingent of dissident members of the elite, the Radicals sought to enhance their position by mobilizing mass support among the lesser classes. One of the leaders, Hipólito Yrigoyen, later played an important role as president after 1916. In winning the office, Yrigoyen overturned tradition and capitalized upon the Sáenz Peña law of 1912, an electoral reform measure. Largely the work of President Roque Sáenz Peña, it sought to dissipate the prospect of revolution by instituting the secret ballot and male suffrage, thus permitting mass participation in presidential elections for the first time. The oligarchs misguidedly believed that passage would enable them to keep power, since they could not believe that a majority of voters freely would choose a Radical candidate. Contrary to the expectation, the Argentines elected Yrigoyen and turned out the old elite.[51]

In the conduct of foreign policy, the Argentines possessed strong identifications. Seeing themselves as white and European, they traditionally stood some distance from the remainder of Latin America. In addition, they looked toward Europe for a counterbalance against the United States and espoused a strong nationalism. Habitually suspicious of appeals for "solidarity" within the western hemisphere, the Argentines upheld the inviolability of national sovereignty and sought on repeated occasions to write it into international law. The doctrines of the Argentine jurists Carlos Calvo in the 1860s and Luis M. Drago in the 1900s put forth early versions of the principle of nonintervention, inveighing specifically against the use of force in the collection of foreign debts in the Americas. Though consonant with early renditions of the Monroe Doctrine, the Argentine position necessarily ran counter to the Roosevelt Corollary. Intervention by the United States had no more acceptability than by the Europeans. The Argentines also disliked customs unions, compulsory arbitration, and other schemes prejudicial to their European connections and generally resisted United States' bids for leadership within the western hemisphere.[52]

Brazil, a racially mixed country, had, in contrast, cultivated the United States since the turn of the century. Established in 1889 with the overthrow of the empire as the biggest republic in the world, Brazil encompassed half the land mass in South America, an area of 3.25 million square miles. The population, consisting of European, African, and Indian stock, numbered 23 million in 1910, the largest among the countries of the southern continent. Coffee, first, and rubber, second, ranked as the principal exports. Brazil's total commerce in 1912 amounted to $671,038,582, with imports at $308,243,730 and exports at $362,794,846. The United States performed as the major partner in each area, both as a supplier and consumer of goods. The reliance on the export trade accounted for the political dominance of the southern states, São Paulo, Minas Gerais, and Rio de Janeiro. After the ouster of Emperor Dom Pedro II, the first five civilian presidents came from these regions and served the interests of the great planters, the Brazilian oligarchs who supplied 75 percent of the world's coffee. The principal port, Santos, shipped most of the coffee to markets in the United States, Great Britain, and Europe. The amount doubled from 5,742,362 sacks, each weighing 130 pounds, in 1900 to 11,308,784 in 1914.[53]

The vast demand for the Brazilian beverage in the United States had great effects upon the country's foreign policy. In 1912, purchases in the United States made up 36 percent of Brazil's exports. Sensibly reluctant to jeopardize such sales and also eager to enlist friends in the ongoing rivalry with Argentina, the Brazilians established as a central tenet of their international behavior the need to cultivate the United States. As the historian E. Bradford Burns has explained, from 1902 until 1912 an "unwritten alliance" prevailed during the tenure of the Baron Rio-Branco, the foreign minister. He recognized an interdependence of aims and ambitions and brought about a working partnership that survived his death. Among the countries of South America, only Brazil acquired the diplomatic status necessary for a United States embassy. Elsewhere in the other countries, diplomatic posts bore the title of legation. Although some difficulties developed in 1913 over a valorization scheme—that is, an effort by Brazilian planters to raise prices by buying up coffee and holding it off the world market—the tension eased during the summer when the United States invited the Brazilian foreign minister, Dr. Lauro Müller, to undertake a visit of courtesy and friendship. In the course of a month, he

traversed the country from New York on the Atlantic to San Francisco
on the Pacific in a journey widely hailed as the analogue of Secretary of
State Elihu Root's call upon Rio de Janeiro in 1906.[54]

Chile favored a different stance. Traditionally suspicious of the
United States, Chileans often talked about the need for a Pan Latin
union and also advocated devices in international law as means of
restraining and containing the Yankee colossus. Some 3.5 million
people inhabited Chile. They produced raw materials for export and
maintained close connections with Great Britain, the main supplier of
capital, markets, and finished goods. By 1890, British investors controlled nearly one-half of the nitrate industry, the most important
economic sector. Britain ranked as preeminent in other areas as well.
By 1912, the value of British sales in Chile amounted to $38,616,866,
some $5,000,000 more than Germany, and $22,000,000 more than the
United States. Chile bought overseas mainly textiles, mineral products,
machinery, and hardware. The country paid for the imports with
exports of borite of lime, copper, iron ore, iodine, and nitrate of soda,
the largest amounts of which went to Great Britain, worth $55,102,
650 in 1912, to Germany, $28,060,697 and the United States,
$24,515,565.[55]

With the opening of the Panama Canal in August 1914, North
Americans anticipated a good chance of challenging British dominance. As the P.A.U. *Bulletin* remarked, "No longer can it be charged
that Chile must suffer from being 'on the wrong side of the world'."
Indeed, this long, narrow, geographically freakish country stretched
along the seaboard "is naturally adapted for commercial activities."
Other observers shared the view. An agent of the United States Office
of Naval Intelligence reported that "The future outlook for trade
expansion . . . is bright." Already the Bethlehem Steel Company had
acquired iron ore deposits near Coquimbo; the American Smelting and
Refining Company had under construction at Chuquicamata a plant
described as "the largest in the world," and the Du Pont Powder
Company had developed an interest in Chilean nitrates.[56]

Nevertheless, legacies of ill will and alienation posed a problem.
Indeed, Chilean mistrust of the United States had intensified in recent
times. During the War of the Pacific, a conflict pitting Chile against
Bolivia and Peru from 1879 until 1883, the maneuvers of Secretary of
State James G. Blaine impressed Chileans as designed to deny them the
fruits of the victory, principally the acquisition of the nitrate-rich
provinces of Tacna and Arica. Relations deteriorated further during
the next several years. Chilean elites harbored suspicions of Blaine's
motives at the First International American Conference at Washington
in 1889; they disliked United States policy during the civil war in 1891

because of presumed favoritism for President José Manuel Balmaceda, the loser in the struggle against the parliamentary faction; and they took umbrage over the *Baltimore* affair, a lamentable incident at the port city of Valparaíso in October 1891 in which drunken sailors from the United States naval vessel provoked a war scare by brawling with Chileans at the "True Blue" Saloon. Henceforth, Chilean leaders performed as outspoken critics of the Monroe Doctrine and the Pan American movement, regarding both as cosmetics and subterfuges to obscure the imperial extension of United States' influence into South America.[57]

After the civil war and the removal of President Balmaceda, the Chileans practiced a turbulent kind of factional politics among rival elites. Between 1892 and 1920, the era of parliamentary ascendancy, some 120 cabinet changes took place, many of them resulting in a new minister of interior, the key position. In the spring of 1913, Henry P. Fletcher, the United States minister in Santiago, reported his impressions, observing that "All thoughtful men in Chile deeply deplore these constant ministerial changes and recognize . . . that the parliamentary system . . . makes for governmental inefficiency." But, he added, "there seems at present no way to escape." The Chileans "fought the Balmaceda war to establish this principle." The president, lacking real power, "is practically a figurehead," and the army and the navy, distant and aloof, leave the government to operate through acts of compromise among the factions, "delicately balanced on patronage." Although "politically all is chaos and disorganization," according to Fletcher, the Chilean elites had a remarkable facility for pulling together on international questions. He thought the Tacna and Arica dispute the most likely "to disturb the peace of the American continent." Although Chile had taken possession of the region after the War of the Pacific, the Treaty of Ancón in 1883 stipulated that at some point a plebiscite ought to determine ownership. By 1913, no such proceeding had taken place, and Chile had no wish to make the issue an object of international concern. The country particularly bridled at the suggestion of compulsory arbitration, still another reason why Chile shied away from the United States' Pan American initiatives.[58]

Political relationships engaged the A.B.C. countries in intense rivalry and competition. Such conditions had deep historical roots and entailed cultural, racial, and geographical components. Territorial controversies figured prominently. Portuguese-speaking Brazil, the giant, shared boundaries with all of the Spanish-speaking countries of South America, except for Ecuador and Chile, and husbanded its domain with jealousy. On another plane, Argentina and Chile competed for leadership as white countries in the Indian regions and also contested with each other in claims over land and water. As a consequence, Brazil and Chile often lined up together against Argentina.[59]

Still another manifestation entailed a naval arms race just before the First World War. Since neither Argentina nor Brazil nor Chile had the capacity to build modern warships, they had to go shopping in other countries. Their expressions of interest resulted in a bidding war among British, European, and North American firms, all wishing to sell vessels of the H.M.S. *Dreadnought* class. These mighty battleships, introduced by the British in 1906, had heavy armor and ten big guns with twelve-inch bores in five turrets. Brazil, the first South American country to seek an expanded, modern navy, appropriated monies in 1904 and awarded a contract for the construction of two battleships in British shipyards. In response, the Argentines, fearing for their capacity to maintain jurisdiction in the crucial waters of the Rio de la Plata, then developed plans of their own and attracted a multitude of armaments salesmen to Buenos Aires. The North Americans in this instance pulled off a coup, thanks in large measure to the good work of Minister Charles H. Sherrill, when in January 1910 the Argentine government placed orders for two 27,800-ton battleships with the Fore River Shipbuilding Company of Quincy, Massachusetts. The *Rivadavia* and the *Moreno*, outfitted with twelve big guns and driven by engines with 40,000 horsepower, would cost an estimated $22,000,000. North Americans also opened negotiations with Chile but had bad luck. Long established as a seafaring nation with an interest in naval power, Chile identified with Great Britain and placed orders for two 30,000-ton vessels of the dreadnought class in 1911 and 1912. They bore the names *Almirante Latorre* and *Lord Cochrane*, important figures in Chilean naval history.

The naval arms race collapsed precipitously at the end of 1912, resulting in something akin to high farce. The Brazilian government developed second thoughts in November 1912, when the crews of the two recently delivered dreadnoughts mutinied against their officers and then trained the big guns on Rio de Janeiro, threatening to open fire, pending better pay and working conditions. Although the authorities eventually reasserted control, the episode eroded confidence in the navy and public willingness to pay for the big ships. Brazil subsequently sold the *Rio de Janeiro* to Turkey. The immensity of the financial burden also dissuaded Argentina and Chile from proceeding. Indeed, when the Argentines attempted to back out on their deal with the United States, the Wilson administration insisted upon holding them to their contract and may have agreed in 1914 to elevate the legation in Washington to embassy rank as part of a trade-off. The Chileans, meanwhile, also eager to cut their losses, reduced their commitment to the purchase of a single dreadnought.[60] The naval arms race in the New World thus ended less catastrophically and a bit more comically than the one in the Old.

INITIATING A COURTSHIP

The United States launched a drive into South America early in 1914, seeking to develop specific initiatives for the purposes of weakening European ties and reorienting relations along a north-south axis. The leaders in the Wilson administration especially wanted improved systems for banking and transportation, necessary capabilities for expanding the trade, and their attention centered particularly upon Argentina, Brazil, and Chile. Charles Lyon Chandler, a consular official, expressed one line of thinking, based on a common prejudice and environmental and racial grounds. While insisting upon the need to maintain a distinction between temperate and tropical South America, he claimed that "The white race not merely degenerates in the tropics through climate, but fully as rapidly by intermarriage with inferior stock of whatever color." Since the temperate regions would always dominate "commercially and economically over the tropical part," he advised powerful efforts to obtain the trade of Argentina, Chile, and Uruguay. Although most of his superiors in the Wilson administration probably agreed, they saw no reason to write off Brazil out of simple bigotry.

The timing appeared propitious for pursuing working understandings with the three countries. From Buenos Aires, the United States chargé d'affaires, George Lorillard, optimistically reported, "Not for many years have the relations of Argentina with its neighbors been so satisfactory." Secure in their "hegemony" over South America, the Argentines wanted "to place no obstacles in the way of the present material prosperity." From Rio de Janeiro, the secretary of the embassy, J. Butler Wright, testified to a growing, mutual interest in trade but complained that North American exporters suffered from disadvantages, notably inadequate representation by foreign firms and a dependency upon European banks. From Santiago, Don Eduardo Carrasco, chief of the commercial section of the foreign ministry, affirmed his country's wish to attract United States investments and trade. To show good faith, the Chilean government helped the Chilean American Permanent Exposition Company to arrange a display of North American products in Santiago, making free space available in the building erected for the Chilean centennial in 1910. The United States consul in Valparaíso, Alfred A. Winslow, meanwhile cautioned

that, although investments in nitrates and copper had increased steadily, the lack of banking facilities hindered United States citizens.[61]

The issue became a major concern. As Consul Winslow lamented
early in 1914, the city of Valparaíso had twelve banks—five Chilean,
three German, two English, one Italian, but not one North American.
The same condition prevailed elsewhere. Under the terms of the
National Banking Act of 1864, national banks could not establish
branches in foreign countries; for the next half-century, bankers resisted any change. They anticipated low returns and lacked the capital
to finance such ventures. But circumstances changed, and promoters
of trade defined the shortcoming as fundamental. A comprehensive
study published by the Commerce Department in 1914 demonstrated
in detail the degree of disadvantage. Holding that banking and credit
are "indispensable elements" in our trade with South America, the
report underscored the undesirability and unworkability of depending
upon foreign banks, those institutions organized not for the United
States but "for the development and defense of the commerce of our
competitors." Although many different kinds of banks existed in South
America, most fell into two categories. Domestic or "native" banks
catered mainly to local interests. Foreign banks, in contrast, mainly
British and German, served international commerce and had as "their
chief concern . . . the advancement of trade of their own nationality."[62]

The report explained at length the four principal functions of
foreign banks. The first, exchange, facilitated the conversion of one
currency into another and long since had established London as the
center of the world's money markets. Before 1914, a "bill on London"
reigned as the most common currency in world commerce. The process entailed several handicaps for non-English. United States importers, for example, had to pay commissions to British bankers and also,
through the conversion, lost opportunities for sales in Latin America
when dollars became pounds. The second function, collections, also
incurred expense. The cost of bills paid through London could run as
high as an additional 1 percent. The third, loans and discounts, constituted at once "a source of large profit and great risk" to foreign banks
in South America. Characteristically, they imposed high rates in normal times and exorbitant ones in duress. The fourth, the extension of
credit, impinged significantly upon the entire process of exchanging
the raw materials of America for the finished goods of Britain, Europe,
and the United States, since without some means, no trade would take
place at all.

After identifying many of the liabilities of the existing sytem, the
report concluded that "American banks were imperatively needed in
South America as a dependable resource in the campaign for greater

trade." Leaders in the Wilson administration, convinced of the same point, already had provided the method of deliverance. Under the terms of section twenty-five, the Federal Reserve Act of 23 December 1913 authorized national banks to establish branches in foreign countries. The P.A.U. *Bulletin*, often a cheerleader, immediately exhorted members of the financial community to act upon the provision as soon as possible. Frank A. Vanderlip and the National City Bank of New York, the first to do so, led the way during the next five years by establishing banks in many cities, including Buenos Aires, Rio de Janeiro, Santiago, Montevideo, Havana, Caracas, São Paulo, Santos, Bahia, and Valparaíso.[63]

The lack of adequate transportation on land and sea also presented problems. Trade expansionists wanted to improve railroad systems within Latin American countries and steamship lines to and from them. Construction projects usually attracted favorable notice in the United States. For example, in Chile late in 1913, the last rails connected Punto Montt in the south with Iquique in the north. Plans also called for improvements of the port at Valparaíso, a double-track railroad to Santiago, and a line into the interior toward the southeast. All these activities stemmed from anticipation over the opening of the Panama Canal. Utopians, meanwhile, dreamed of an intercontinental railway, linking the countries of North, Central, and South America with tracks of the same gauge.[64]

Steamship lines also had importance. Before the First World War, American shippers and traders in South America depended primarily upon European carriers. For example, in Brazil, over 4,500 foreign trading vessels entered port cities annually, but not more than ten in recent years had come from the United States. Great Britain, in contrast, accounted for about half of the total, followed by Germany, France, and Italy. The Wilson administration intended to alleviate the circumstance and supported the reconstruction of the merchant marine.[65] Beginning in 1913, the United States and Brazil Steamship Line, an affiliate of the United States Steel Corporation, established regular service between New York, Rio de Janeiro, and Santos. Three modern steamers, the *California*, the *American*, and the *Hawaiian*, would alternate departures on the fifteenth of each month, make the Brazilian capital in twenty days, and carry freight at rates 10 percent lower than the competition. The effect accentuated the absence of regular connections with Argentina and Chile.[66]

To highlight the growing prominence of Argentina and Chile in South America, Pan American enthusiasts in the United States wanted to exchange ambassadors, thereby placing those countries on par with Brazil, where an embassy had existed since 1905. The indefatigable

John Barrett argued in favor of the proposal, pointing toward the importance of "the moral effect" while lobbying before senators and congressmen. The P.A.U. *Bulletin* reasoned simply that the recent increase of commerce between the two countries in itself would justify the act. During the deliberations in Congress in the spring of 1914, other reasons emphasized a general United States' interest in prompting closer ties, the lack of much additional expense, and the overall incentive for business expansion. In addition, a kind of clincher, Argentina and Chile wanted to exchange ambassadors. When the State Department recommended in favor, President Woodrow Wilson signed a bill on 16 May, elevating the legations in Argentina and Chile to the rank of embassies. He saw the move as an important advancement of his Pan American policies. Chile reciprocated quickly, establishing an embassy in the United States on 24 July. In Argentina, political divisions within the Chamber of Deputies, and possibly unhappiness over the battleship deal, delayed a decision until the fall, but in the end a favorable outcome took place and the Argentina legation became an embassy.[67]

INTERVENTION AND MEDIATION

The Mexico issue remained the foremost concern of Woodrow Wilson during the early months of 1914. Although the prospect of British defiance had diminished, Wilson still had to cope with Huerta. He remarked in a letter to a confidante, "The thorn in my side is Mexico." Although he confessed to "a sneaking admiration for at least the indomitable, dogged determination of Huerta," which he attributed "in large part to ignorance," Wilson intended to place in Huerta's way an "insuperable stumbling block." But Wilson found "the problem . . . most puzzling" because he had to keep "the men in Europe quiet" and "at the same time . . . steer our own public opinion in the right path." In frustration, he anticipated "growing cross-eyed with watching people in so many separated quarters at the same time."[68]

Meanwhile, leaders in the administration monitored attitudes in Argentina, Brazil, and Chile, wondering especially what might transpire if intervention should take place. An alleged rapprochement among the A.B.C. countries held some unnerving implications. Indeed, early in 1913, a rumor made the rounds that the three nations had agreed to follow a common course, presumably in opposition, if the United States should put military forces in Mexico. George Lorillard, the chargé d'affaires, reported that he could neither confirm nor disprove the rumor, but he was convinced that an armed action, "no matter what the provocation," would produce "a deplorable impres-

sion in Argentina" and might result in "a violent anti-American out-
burst," very prejudicial to "our influence here" and "the friendly good
feeling . . . toward our Government and people."[69]

Reasons for uncertainty persisted. Early in 1914, illness forced the
Argentine president, Roque Sáenz Peña, to retire. When Victorino de
la Plaza took over as acting president, the reputation of this former
foreign minister as "aggressive" and "unbending" caused concern that
he might move toward a more antagonistic stance. But relations remained cordial. Indeed, Argentina subsequently took the lead in efforts to resolve the Mexican issue through multilateral action and
mediation. The proposal, first advanced in March 1914, stirred the
interest of the editors of *La Prensa*, who commended the notion and
remarked upon the economic ramifications. More intimate ties might
invite larger sales of meat, corn, and wheat in the United States, which,
in turn, might promote larger levels of North American investment in
Argentina and have "a great influence upon finance and diplomacy."
Somewhat later, *La Prensa* complained of Argentina's tradition of
diplomatic isolation in the New World and urged countermeasures. A
dramatic opportunity to accomplish such ends appeared late in April
1914.[70]

The incident at Tampico on 9 April 1914 transformed the Mexican
imbroglio into a crisis. The arrest of United States sailors in an unau-
thorized zone by Mexican federal troops precipitated a demand for a
formal apology from Admiral Henry T. Mayo. When President Wilson
backed him in it and escalated the pressure, the difficulty became acute,
compounded further by the imminent arrival of the *Ypiranga*, a German vessel carrying arms to Huerta. In response, Wilson asked the
Congress for authority to use military force. On 21 April 1914, a naval
contingent with Marines took the city of Veracruz, the principal port on
the east coast, in a move designed to weaken Huerta by cutting off the
flow of customs revenues. Though Wilson persuaded himself that he
could accomplish his goal and topple the regime cheaply, the Mexicans
surprised him by defending the city. Over two hundred died. Moreover, a threat of outright war ensued. Also contrary to Wilson's expectations, the seizure of Veracruz failed to rally much support among
Huerta's enemies. Only Francisco Villa expressed approval. Venustiano Carranza and Emiliano Zapata, in contrast, denounced the act as
an invasion and threatened a great patriotic struggle against the Yankee presence.[71]

The intervention, a kind of culminating event, issued logically
from Wilson's evolving policies in Latin America yet revealed incom-
patibilities and contradictions. Paradoxically, Wilson intended this
blow against predatory militarism and foreign imperialism to serve the

cause of self-determination in Mexico. By smiting the dictator Huerta
and, by extension, his confederates the British, he would aid in restoring the constitutionality of government, thereby acting out the dictates
of the Mobile Address. But he exaggerated the effects of natural
harmonies. Mexican nationalists, disparaging the mutuality of common interest in this case, refused to let him function as their surrogate,
out of concern for eroding their own prerogatives and independence.
Rather than run such risks, they preferred to entertain the possibility
of a fight.[72]

Happily for Woodrow Wilson, the unwanted war with Mexico
never took place, an outcome made possible by an offer of mediation
from the A.B.C. countries. On 25 April 1914, Rómulo S. Naón of
Argentina, Domicio da Gama of Brazil, and Eduardo Suárez Mújica of
Chile proffered the good offices of their countries as means to assure
"the peaceful and friendly settlement of the conflict between the
United States and Mexico." Argentina performed conspicuously in
striking the arrangement. Initially, the Argentine Foreign Office had
taken a correct but studiously critical position in response to the intervention, but then, on 25 April, Naón, the minister in Washington,
suggested a joint offer of mediation with Brazil and Chile. Naón already had won over da Gama and Suárez Mújica.[73]

United States' acceptance of the offer got Wilson off the hook and
opened the way for a conference of mediation late in May at Niagara
Falls, Canada. Although the ensuing negotiations succeeded in the
primary purpose of averting an international conflict, they failed otherwise to contribute much toward a settlement in Mexico. Indeed, the
main determinants resided far beyond the control of the conferees.
Although the United States' delegates wanted to remove Huerta from
office and to create a new government through elections, the representatives of Huerta and Carranza obstructed any such move by
insisting that the purview of mediation could not extend to Mexico's
internal affairs. When at last an innocuous protocol required the contending factions to establish a provisional government through direct
negotiations, the advance of the victorious Constitutionalist armies had
rendered the outcome irrelevant. On 15 July 1914, General Victoriano
Huerta fled the country, leaving Mexico City to General Alvaro Obregón's triumphant army.[74]

The mediation, nevertheless, earned acclaim as a precedent and
as a useful guide for the future. In Buenos Aires, Chargé d'Affaires
Lorillard averred that "our Government has never taken a more successful and profitable step toward closer relations with Latin America."
La Prensa bestowed its sanction, applauding Wilson for demonstrating
the sincerity of his commitment to Pan Americanism and the Argentine

government for its role in championing a multilateral solution. The paper speculated that such shows of unanimity would deter European adventures in the western hemisphere. In Santiago, Chile, the newspaper *El Mercurio* hailed the event as immensely important for Latin America because it marked a significant departure from the traditional unilateral measures in United States foreign policy. *El Mercurio* even anticipated the possible emergence of "a concert of American powers," combining the Latin with the Anglo-Saxon in a show of "mutual confidence" in the readiness to maintain "the peace and prosperity of the New World."[75]

Similar expressions became current in the United States. For John Barrett, unrelenting in his enthusiasm, the mediation had inaugurated "a new era in Pan American relationships" and would "have a favorable influence upon the attitude of sister American Republics." He regarded the episode as a form of personal vindication, since he had unsuccessfully advocated such an approach during the Madero uprising in 1910. Other observers affirmed their support. Late in May at the twentieth Annual Conference on International Arbitration at Lake Mohonk, New York, the delegates in attendance, the largest number on record, passed resolutions supporting and encouraging mediations of the sort carried out at Niagara Falls. After taking part in a symposium on Mexico with three hundred other "serious-minded men," President Charles W. Eliot of Harvard University wrote to President Wilson, suggesting the adoption of three rules of conduct. First, "No American republic shall acquire territory from another republic by means of force." Second, "No American republic shall protect or support by force of arms its citizens who venture of their own accord into the territory of another republic." Third, "When an American republic gets into trouble with a neighbor, an appropriate combination of other republics shall be called in to settle the difficulty."[76] The third suggestion struck an especially responsive note.

Within the Wilson administration, the efficacy of multilateral initiatives retained great appeal. Six days before the intervention at Veracruz, Colonel House, according to his diary account, advised the president "to stand firm and to blaze the way for a new and better code of morals than the world had yet seen." As House explained, "If a man's house was on fire he should be glad to have his neighbors come in and help put it out, provided they did not take his property, and it should be the same with nations." By such reasoning, Mexico "should not object to our helping adjust her unruly household" if Mexican leaders "understand that our motives were unselfish." But of course they had suspicions. House had no more empathy for the dictates of Mexican nationalism than Wilson. After the capture of Veracruz,

House welcomed the mediation as a way to ease the crisis and wanted, in the event of full-scale intervention, "to invite the A.B.C. Powers to join."[77]

Wilson still affirmed the justice of his cause. Though perhaps chastened by the experience at Veracruz, he told the journalist Samuel G. Blythe of his commitments in an interview published in *The Saturday Evening Post* late in April. His "ideal" required "an orderly and righteous government in Mexico"; his "passion" demanded sympathy for "the submerged eighty-five percent of the people . . . who are struggling toward liberty." He repudiated selfish motives and denied further that the Monroe Doctrine provided "merely an excuse for the gaining of territory for ourselves." Quite the contrary, he argued, "our friendship for Mexico is disinterested." Accordingly, he held that any acceptable plan for reconstructing the country would have to take into account the well-being of "the people" and not "the old time regime . . . the aristocrats . . . the vested interests . . . the men who are responsible for this very condition of disorder." His insistence upon participating in the creation of a "new order" based upon "human liberty and human rights" promised to perpetuate involvements in Mexican affairs.[78] Wilson subsequently reiterated his views in letters to Walter Hines Page, the ambassador in London. Noting his preference for the Constitutionalists, Wilson said they "are much less savage and more capable of government than Huerta . . . . The mediation is by no means to be laughed at." He depicted Carranza as "honest" but "very narrow and rather dull," a person "extremely difficult to deal with" but eager "to try to do the right thing." Wilson claimed that "A landless people will always furnish the inflammable material for a revolution."[79]

The disjunction of positions flabbergasted the British. Sir Cecil Spring-Rice, the British ambassador in Washington, disconcertedly wondered whether the president really understood the ramifications. Wilson now claimed as a "foremost duty . . . the internal reform" of Mexico, "this unhappy neighbor." Spring-Rice noted that no government since the Holy Alliance had so asserted its mission to expunge "the moral shortcomings of foreign nations." He expected Latin American countries at some juncture to react with alarm. At the present time, the A.B.C. mediators occupied the untenable position "of prescribing internal legislation for an American state at the instance of the President of the United States."[80]

The alleged incongruity escaped much notice in Washington. Indeed, the administration persisted in seeking ways to roll back the European presence while wooing Latin America. Robert Lansing, the counselor of the State Department, aimed toward such goals when he submitted his memorandum on the "Present Nature and Extent of the Monroe Doctrine and Its Need for Restatement" in the middle of June 1914. In substantial agreement with Woodrow Wilson, Lansing presumed the existence of natural harmonies with Latin America. In the course of a historical overview, he described the Monroe Doctrine as a unilateral instrument of national policy—more particularly, a means of obtaining security by ensuring against the European acquisition of political power in the western hemisphere through the occupation, conquest, or cession of territory. But circumstances had changed. After ninety years and because of "modern economic conditions," the traditional policy no longer applied in reality. Echoing Wilson's claims in the Mobile Address, Lansing argued that foreign financial control now posed the main threat to national independence. A European power in control of the public debts of an American state and also with large investments in transportation, agriculture, and mining could achieve domination just as "completely as if it had acquired sovereign rights." Lansing implied a need for a new statement of the Monroe Doctrine by which the United States would forbid "European acquisition of political control through the agency of financial control over an American republic." It would also underscore the growing sense of "fraternal responsibility . . . in all our international relations."[81]

The Lansing memorandum set forth a strategic design widely shared by leaders in the Wilson administration. By severing the European bonds of trade and debt and embracing the Latin Americans as friends, they hoped to forge a self-sustaining, regional community of nations. Yet misconceptions, contradictions, and other difficulties placed many obstacles in the way of tactical solutions. Colonel House tried to address the issue during a visit to Europe early in July 1914, just before the outbreak of the Great War. Seeking to reduce Latin America's dependency upon European banking houses, he asked British, French, and German leaders whether they would join in an international agreement with other lenders to guarantee the safety of loans and also to bring about lower borrowing rates. In his diary, House denounced the subversion of weak, debt-ridden states by outsiders who demanded "concesssions" and "usurious interest." But the timing was all wrong, and he met with little receptivity as the Europeans prepared for armed combat.[82] The onset of the First World War changed many things, including the international environment in which Woodrow Wilson pursued his Pan American vision.

Europe: "If I Had Only Done That," by Cartoonist Westerman [?].
Reprinted from the *Ohio State Journal*, 1916.

CHAPTER TWO

The Quest for Integration

August 1914–February 1917

THE ONSET OF THE GREAT WAR IN EUROPE had reverberations all over the world. In the western hemisphere, the initial effects devastated the economies of Latin America by destroying traditional affiliations and forcing reorientations in the flow of capital and goods away from Europe and toward the United States. For over six months, Latin America languished in a state of virtual paralysis until the spring of 1915, when intimations of recovery appeared. The conflict compelled the establishment of new relationships. In the New World, the United States took over customary European roles by becoming the prime purchaser of raw materials and the principal supplier of finished goods. To illustrate the point, the magnitude of trade with Latin America between 1 July 1914 and 30 June 1917 increased by more than 100 percent, transforming the United States into the predominant partner.[1] A parallel drive to advance the cause of political integration never produced a similar measure of change. In spite of repeated efforts by the Wilson administration to attain the goal through new definitions of the Monroe Doctrine and the negotiation of a Pan American treaty, these endeavors fell short of their aims, suggesting thereby some of the limitations of Wilson's conception of natural harmonies. The war both presented opportunities and precipitated rebuffs.

ECONOMIC CONSEQUENCES: CONFERENCES ON FOREIGN TRADE

The advent of war produced economic hardships in Latin America and highlighted the traditional dependency on Great Britain and the western European countries. Historically, the Europeans had provided the means and mechanisms of economic intercourse—not only the markets, the manufactures, and the investment capital but also the facilities of finance, communication, and transportation.[2] Wartime conditions reduced access to the European networks and cut off the Latin Americans, exposing them to the full effects of their own vulnerabilities. The movement and sale of raw materials became ever more difficult because of German raids on commerce and the British blockade, both of which rendered the customary markets inaccessible. Meanwhile, the conversion of European economies to a war footing limited the availability of capital and goods for Latin Americans. The crippling outcome accentuated already depressed economic conditions as shown by the experiences of Argentina, Brazil, and Chile.

Argentina had enjoyed a markedly expanding commerce in 1912 and 1913, but even so, according to United States consular reports, a high level of uncertainty kept the inhabitants in "a state of economic suspense." The trouble resulted in part from falling levels of foreign investment and a poor harvest. In Buenos Aires, United States Consul General Richard M. Bartleman described the year 1913 as "one of serious economic depression" and "panic," the result, according to Argentine businessmen, of imposing tight money policies after a period of easy credit and excessive speculation. The ensuing boom-bust cycle meant that business houses, overstocked and often in debt, could not maintain current operations, and business failures became "general" and "continuous." Nevertheless, Bartleman noted with satisfaction an increase in imports from the United States. Similarly, George C. Lorillard, the chargé d'affaires, issued gloomy appraisals. He detected "no change by way of improvement in the economic situation" and anticipated little positive help from the government. Victorino de la Plaza had succeeded to the presidency after Sáenz Peña's death early in August 1914. Although "practical," "cool headed," and "a keen intellect in spite of his advanced age," he favored official inactivity, insisting that only the passage of time and the practice of austerity could provide for much betterment. Meanwhile, United States diplomats worried that the Argentines might cut their losses by selling their dreadnoughts to one of the nations at war.[3]

Everything became more difficult when the war got underway. Although one consular report in the middle of September predicted no intensification of "the critical financial and industrial condition" in Argentina on grounds that things could not get much worse, the argument proved baseless. By early October, *La Prensa* reported that the Argentine people had never been more worried about their economic future. "We have crops to sell, but cannot because of paralysis brought on by the war. We need manufactured goods, but cannot get them." The article complained further that the tariff policies of the

United States placed Argentine exports at a disadvantage because the two countries produced so many of the same things. As a remedy, the paper urged the adoption of long-term policies to develop an independent merchant marine and industrial capability, the acquisition of which would heighten the need for European capital after the war. *La Prensa* argued against Woodrow Wilson's charges in the Mobile speech about the evil effects of exploitative foreign capital, claiming to the contrary that such fear amounted to "a simple illusion" which, if accepted, would jeopardize Argentina's national hopes for the future.[4]

Consular reports chronicled events in abundant detail. By the middle of October, the initial expectation for a short war dissipated and despair over the depression deepened. Although no runs on banks took place, the market value of stocks and bonds had fallen by 25 percent and showed no signs of rallying. Moreover, overseas markets for meats and cereals collapsed. Very few freight vessels left port, and service on passenger and mail steamers became sporadic, the consequence of German attacks against British ships and skyrocketing insurance costs. The pain at home took the form of rising prices and increasing unemployment. By the middle of November 1914, the embargo on coal sales in Great Britain had reduced railroad traffic in Argentina by 40 percent. Nearly all of the meat plants curtailed operations and discharged employees, retaining only enough to meet local demand. Thirty thousand men lost their jobs in Buenos Aires, and food prices increased by 100 percent. Such figures so impressed Chargé d'Affaires Lorillard that he characterized the circumstance as having reached a "most serious stage."[5]

In response to dire straits, Argentine leaders sought relief in the United States, hoping to work out closer economic ties. Rómulo S. Naón, the minister in Washington, created a branch of the legation in New York City to help meet the unique financial situation and also urged the early extension of the National City Bank of New York into Argentina to meet the emergency. United States consular reports, meanwhile, heralded an "unprecedented" Argentine interest in North American goods. Consul L. J. Keena noted that "the present crisis presents an unparalleled opening for the American manufacturer in Argentina." Another dispatch advised an obvious solution to the difficulty. Steamers from the United States should carry machines, implements, iron, and petroleum to Argentina and return loaded with meats, woolens, and hides. Still another showed that the growth of the Argentine electrical industry invited the sale of all manner of technical goods.[6]

Brazil also suffered from hard times. In May 1914, the *Jornal do Commércio*, a leading newspaper in Rio de Janeiro, characterized the economic difficulty as "a crisis." It stemmed from a sharp fall in world prices for coffee and rubber, a large measure of foreign indebtedness, some $997,000,000 for the federal government and another $388,000,000 for the states, and also a high rate of inflation. For several months before the onset of the war, the Brazilian government had attempted to achieve redress through financial austerity and the negotiation of new loans from foreign bankers. The Ministry of Finance reportedly sought deliverance from the House of Rothschild in London, the Banque de Paris, the Banco Commercial de Milan, and Kuhn, Loeb and Company of New York, by transacting a multimillion dollar deal, secured against anticipated customs receipts in the future. In a highly critical vein, United States Ambassador Edwin V. Morgan attributed the trouble to extravagance and excessive spending habits which he regarded as ingrained. According to him, "Money has been loaned to Brazil too freely. . . . Goods have been imported on too large a scale and the balance of trade is badly against the country." Even worse, he averred, "the provisions of the budget have not been respected." Sardonically noting that "the Brazilian . . . is not thrifty," Morgan warned, nevertheless, unless the country secured a new loan, "the present credit crisis will grow disastrous."[7]

Brazil held a presidential election amid the difficulties on 1 March 1914. Although the campaign produced scattered outbreaks of violence and declarations of martial law in the states of Rio de Janeiro and Ceará, the outcome entailed no surprises. Members of the established elite brought into power Wenceslau Braz Pereira Gomes, a resident of the state of Minas Gerais and a member of the *Partido Republicano Conservador*. As president-elect, Braz placed a high priority upon the need to secure financial resources and intimated his readiness to go personally to Europe to talk with the bankers, only to have the outbreak of the war dash his plan. Ambassador Morgan reported in August that the conflict had "gravely accentuated" the financial crisis in Brazil, since the redirection of revenues into European military expenditures meant that the proposed loan might become impossible. Morgan worried that Brazil, in the extreme, might have to default, thereby losing its good reputation for never having done so. Elsewhere, Brazilians experienced inflation, unemployment, and bad effects. In Pernambuco, the cost of foodstuffs trebled, and hundreds of dockworkers fell idle as foreign trade closed down. Although conditions worsened each day, Consul Merrill Griffith reported optimistically that most Brazilians, in spite of the hardship, sympathized with the Allies. In Santos, the major coffee port, meanwhile, the threat of German commerce destroyers and the lack of currency exchange kept coffee-laden vessels in port with nowhere to go. Similarly in all of the major cities, coal shortages threatened to shut down mills, factories, and railroads and possibly to provoke mass protests among people without jobs.[8]

In spite of the maladjustments and dislocations, Morgan anticipated the possibility of happier outcomes. Because the war had
wrenched Brazilian trade out of the usual patterns, he detected "an
unusual opportunity" for extending the market share of the United
States. Opportunities existed especially for coal and fuel oil. Similarly,
Consul Maddin Summers in Santos advised that the United States
could proffer significant relief and assistance by exchanging foodstuffs
and consumer goods for coffee, but he too emphasized a serious
obstacle. Before much of anything could take place on a large scale, the
United States would have to develop the means of extending credit. He
hoped for the establishment of a branch of a North American bank in
Santos as soon as possible. On a related point, a good chance to improve
communications appeared in September 1914 when the Brazilian government allowed to lapse the British monopoly on telegraphic communications with Argentina and thereby animated interest in the
United States. Overall, economic prospects had improved by the end of
the year when the Finance Ministry concluded the negotiation of a loan
calculated at £15,000,000 sterling with Rothschild and Sons of London. Expressing his relief and approval, Morgan now believed that
Brazil's creditors in the long run had a chance of receiving adequate
compensation for their "inconvenience."[9]

The damage inflicted upon Chile also worsened the effects of an
economic slowdown. In the middle of July, Consul Alfred A. Winslow
in Valparaíso reported that lagging business conditions discouraged
much hope for significant improvements before the end of the year.
Chileans, nevertheless, enthusiastically anticipated the consequences
of opening the Panama Canal, looking forward to new opportunities
for trade and travel. Winslow noted too a growing influx of United
States capital into Chile, particularly in the extractive industries—iron,
copper, and nitrates. He urged even fuller participation in the future
so that North American capitalists could benefit from the better conditions sure to follow the passing of the present "depression."[10]

The war precipitated a near calamity. In the middle of August,
Henry Fletcher, the United States minister, described the severity of
the consequences. The closing down of European markets destroyed
the sale of nitrates and deprived the government of its principal source
of revenue, the export tax, causing still further embarrassment over an
already unbalanced budget. Fletcher expected that such duress might
compel the sale of warships then under construction in England and
also the negotiation of emergency loans to meet outstanding obligations. He remarked that Chileans, though "intelligent and patriotic,"
had "wasted their public money" on unwise expenditures. Matters got
steadily worse. By the middle of October, large numbers of unem-
ployed men had flooded into Valparaíso and Santiago, presenting a

problem for government authorities who wanted to develop public works projects to alleviate the distress but lacked the means. Fletcher, meanwhile, affirmed the need for an American branch bank as a stimulant to trade and also the necessity of improved means of transportation. At the end of the year, Consul Winslow's résumé stated that the government's action had mitigated the bad effects by propping up endangered businesses with loans but that conditions overall remained "far from normal."[11]

Two other issues required attention in United States' dealings with Chile. The Tacna-Arica dispute, the central preoccupation in Chilean-Peruvian relations, defied all prospect of solution and engaged the interest of the United States out of concern for keeping the peace. As a means of resolution, the possibility of mediation sometimes came under discussion, but United States officials hesitated to make a formal offer unless both parties consented in advance. The degree of sensitivity in Chile ran high. For example, the newspaper *El Mercurio* attracted much attention by publishing a series of patriotic articles on the War of the Pacific in May and June.[12] The other question concerned the proposed fifth Pan American International Conference, tentatively scheduled to take place in Santiago in September 1914. Chilean leaders had offered to host the assembly in the spring of 1913 but then developed misgivings, and the meeting never took place until 1923. The persistence of troubles with Mexico, the onset of the war in Europe, and the inability of Secretary of State Bryan to arrange his schedule for attendance became public excuses, but the more substantive reason may have been Chile's worry over Tacna and Arica. The Wilson administration's advocacy of arbitration schemes could cause embarrassment if the fate of the two provinces came under scrutiny. This matter, and the Wilson administration's own hesitancy, resulted in the postponement for nine years.[13]

The United States and the countries of Latin America all assumed positions of neutrality in the First World War and maintained them until the early months of 1917, when the United States first broke relations with Germany and then entered the conflict. During the interim, occasional breaches of neutrality took place—for example, when warships entered neutral waters—but overall, leaders in the western hemisphere tried to isolate the region from the violence. The United States, in turn, inaugurated a campaign to capitalize upon propitious circumstances and to consolidate ties with Latin America. The opening of the Panama Canal in August 1914 became a focus of international attention and a symbol of the larger undertaking. In an instant, the canal reduced the distance from Colón on the Atlantic side to Balboa on the Pacific from 10,500 nautical miles, the journey around South America, to 45, the passage through the canal. As a consequence,

New York became 7,873 nautical miles closer to San Francisco. If Magellan had sailed his voyage late in 1914, he would have traveled 5,262 nautical miles instead of 13,135.[14]

An assortment of promotional activities directed observance toward Latin America. The National Foreign Trade Convention had such effects. It met at the Raleigh Hotel in Washington, D.C., on 27–28 May 1914 under the auspices of the American Manufacturers' Export Association, the American Asiatic Association, and the Pan American Society. The representatives, mainly spokesmen for commercial organizations and business houses, expressed special interest in tariff reform and reciprocity, noting particularly the beneficent consequences of such measures in promoting an expansion of trade with Cuba and Brazil. The convention recommended that the United States president and secretary of state pursue the negotiation of new treaty arrangements with the other countries of Latin America, a course made feasible by the Underwood tariff of 1913. Later in the summer, the Commerce Department developed a plan to establish "a permanent and travelling force in South America," consisting of men who knew the languages, customs, and business methods of Latin America and who also had practical experience. To supplement the activities of commercial attachés at the diplomatic posts in Rio de Janeiro, Buenos Aires, Santiago, and Lima, six additional agents would traverse the continent, including specialists in hardware, textiles, and lumber. To defray the cost, the Bureau of Foreign and Domestic Commerce proposed to set aside $50,000 for the fiscal year and also planned to organize a "Latin American section" in the Washington office.[15]

With the outbreak of the fighting in Europe, enthusiasm over the possibilities became greater. As observed by the *Bulletin* of the P.A.U., the circumstances called to mind the old saying that it is an "ill wind that blows no good." The Great War, though lamentable as a human disaster, had expanded "a general appreciation" of the importance of Latin America and introduced "great opportunities." Seeking to pursue them effectively, government officials held an informal conference on 7 August 1914 to organize an Inter-Departmental Committee on Pan American trade. The men in attendance, Jordan H. Stabler of the State Department's Latin American Affairs Division, Robert F. Rose of the Foreign Trade Adviser's Office, and E. A. Brand and Dr. Frank R. Rutter, both of the Bureau of Foreign and Domestic Commerce, agreed that such a coordinating group could greatly benefit American exporters, particularly by systematically collecting accurate information about market conditions from consular officers overseas.[16]

The recommendation appeared especially sound because the trade statistics at the end of the fiscal year on 30 June 1914 showed a marked fall-off. Although United States commerce with other American countries in that year amounted in aggregate to $1,303,000,000, the figure represented a decrease of 33 percent from the record high in 1913. Trade balances favored the United States in the northern regions, where imports had a value of $427,000,000 and exports, $529,000,000, with Canada absorbing the greatest share, $345,000, 000, Cuba, $69,000,000, and Mexico and Central America, each with $39,000,000. In these countries, the United States had greater sales than any competitor. On the other hand, unfavorable balances existed in the south. Imports into the United States from South America reached $223,000,000, of which nearly one-half came from Brazil, about one-fifth from Argentina, and the rest primarily from Chile, Colombia, Venezuela, and Peru. Exports to South America in comparison totaled only $125,000,000, of which one-fourth went to Brazil and about one-third to Argentina. As the Commerce Department noted succinctly, "In sharp contrast with the high position of the United States in North American markets is its low rank among the nations selling goods in South America." The purchases of Argentina, Brazil, and Chile in the United States consisted only of 15 percent of their totals.[17]

The Latin American Trade Conference in Washington on 10 September considered some means of redress. Assembled at the request of Secretaries Bryan and Redfield, the meeting brought together government officials and business representatives, including delegates from the United States Chamber of Commerce, the Southern Commercial Congress, and the National Foreign Trade Council. As a promotional gimmick, they discussed the feasibility of sending to South American ports a fleet of six merchant ships, replete with salesmen and samples, but ruled it premature. Redfield could see no point because, before a substantial trade could take place, the national banks had to provide credit facilities and dollar exchange. The leaders in attendance then called for the creation of such capabilities so that Latin Americans could buy extensively in the United States and draw drafts upon New York City. They also established a committee to oversee the development of the Latin American trade. Headed by a chairman, James A. Farrell of the National Foreign Trade Council, the group consisted of seventeen trade enthusiasts, including the omnipresent John Barrett of the Pan American Union, William Bayne of the New York Coffee Exchange, J. P. Grace of the W. R. Grace Company, Fairfax Harrison of the Southern Railroad Company, C. J. Owens of the Southern Commercial Congress, and Willard Straight of J. P. Morgan. Straight later told his friend Henry Fletcher that "there is a very great emergency in New York City to find the credits to handle our South American business."[18]

Elsewhere across the United States, commercial ties with Latin America provoked "unprecedented interest," according to the *Bulletin* of the P.A.U., as chambers of commerce, boards of trade, and business associations of all sorts mounted investigations, inquiries, and campaigns. In a letter to Ambassador Edwin V. Morgan, Willard Straight testified to the magnitude, noting the existence of "considerable excitement up here regarding South American trade." Because of sheer proximity, observers thought that the states of the Mexican gulf and the south Atlantic would have the competitive edge. Further to advance the cause, Secretary of the Treasury William Gibbs McAdoo proposed late in October 1914 that the State Department sponsor a conference attended by finance ministers so that all of the American republics could explore methods of improving financial connections. United States bankers might also wish to take part. As McAdoo told Redfield, "Finance is . . . at the bottom of all trade. It is essential that improved financial facilities and relations be created between the Central and South American Governments and this country." He also urged the development of steamship lines.[19]

Woodrow Wilson also favored such measures. In his annual address before the Congress on 8 December 1914, he explained his critique and analysis. The war in Europe "has interrupted the means of trade not only but also the processes of production." As a result, the economies of European countries could no longer supply their own people with manufactured goods, to say nothing of their former trading partners, "our own neighbors," the countries of Central and South America. Wilson characteristically identified a "duty" and an "opportunity." As he remarked, "Here are markets which we must supply, and we must find the means of action." He called upon the United States, "this great people for whom we speak and act," to react vigorously and "be ready, as never before, to serve itself and to serve mankind; ready with its resources, its forces of production, and its means of distribution." Once again Wilson found evidence of natural harmonies.[20]

POLITICAL CONSEQUENCES: THE PAN AMERICAN PACT

The war also accentuated a concern for achieving higher levels of political integration in the western hemisphere. Almost as soon as the fighting began, interest developed in the possibility of stopping it through joint action, conceivably by means of mediation. A related issue centered attention on the collective defense of neutral rights. But rival and cross purposes often got in the way, confusing the initiatives, and persuaded leaders in the Wilson administration to bide their time. While waiting for the appropriate moment to act in Europe, they would put together an organization of peace-loving states in the western hemisphere to serve as a model for emulation. The proposed Pan American pact had just such a purpose.

At the beginning of the conflict, some measure of institutional disarray still beset the diplomatic corps. Bryan's purge of Republicans kept Henry Fletcher on edge well into the fall. Even though Fletcher, a Republican, had impressed Bryan as "a very good man" who had the support of McAdoo and others in the administration, the secretary of state still wanted to use "our prominent Democrats, not only as a reward for what they have been, but because distinction puts them in a position to do something in the future." He fussed over the fact that "We have been quite short of prefixes, while Republicans have been able to introduce Secretary so-and-so, Ambassador so-and-so, and Minister so-and-so. . . . We have usually had to confine ourselves to 'Mister' or 'Honorable'."[21] Fletcher, meanwhile, relied upon his connections at home to save him. His friend, Willard Straight, had cautioned earlier that Bryan sought "nice fat salaries for nice sleek Democrats" and might give the post in Santiago to some "long-haired apostle of free silver." Straight later employed influence in high places in Fletcher's behalf and beat back "the wolves" by obtaining support from Colonel House, who, as a kind of patron, used his persuasive talents in the White House and later facilitated a promotion to the rank of ambassador.[22] Fletcher became the first United States diplomat in Chile to possess that status.

The mission in Argentina also caused a problem. After taking leave, John W. Garrett, the minister, decided against returning because of his wife's inability to tolerate the climate. Eager to find a replacement, Bryan regarded Argentina as "an important post" and also "an expensive place to live." Because the ambassador "must combine fitness for the place and an ability to spend considerably more than his salary," two candidates, unnamed, already had turned down the job. The administration later located another possibility in the person of Frederick Jesup Stimson. A wealthy, cosmopolitan, and well-traveled man of affairs, and also a Democrat, Stimson taught constitutional law at Harvard University, and his personal ties ran through the upper classes in both the United States and Great Britain. His correspondents included Richard Olney, the former secretary of state, Theodore Roosevelt, the former cowboy and chief executive, and Lord James Bryce, the former British ambassador and author of *The American Commonwealth*. However, the administration had trouble tracking him down to make an offer. Stimson, a widower, and his second wife, Mabel, had taken a trip to Europe in the summer of 1914, a singular exercise in ill timing, and for a while found themselves stranded behind

German lines. Upon concluding the harrowing venture by making their way to London in the middle of September, they learned of the nomination and Stimson initially reacted with misgivings. As he recorded his impression, "a South American post had hitherto been regarded as the *pis aller* of a diplomatic career, and I had no disposition to abandon for it my work in teaching the United States Constitution to our future leaders at Harvard." But Ambassador Walter Hines Page argued in favor of taking the post, emphasizing that the administration's promotion of Pan Americanism amounted to much more than merely the defense of commerce and also that Argentina had become the leading country in South America. Lord James Bryce further assuaged Stimson's vanity in a telegram by providing assurance that "you can do a great deal of good there by instructing the Argentines in your ideas of self government" and, further, "you will come back an authority on Latin American conditions and tell the Americans how much harm thoughtless talk about the Monroe Doctrine does." Stimson, to be sure, would have to learn some Spanish, but as Bryce noted, "that language is . . . exceptionally easy."[23]

Stimson took the oath of office early in October 1914 and then traveled to Washington to obtain instructions. By his own account published later, he disliked Bryan's "perfunctory" and "ungracious" manner. It made him think that Bryan disapproved of his appointment. President Wilson, in contrast, engaged Stimson in "a good long talk," the first "since that Harvard commencement." Stimson had spent a week in the State Department reading over the correspondence with Argentina during the past twenty years, and when he affirmed his opinion on the importance of getting cable lines down the Atlantic side to Buenos Aires, Wilson claimed ignorance of the matter, explaining that "They never told me of that." Stimson later focused on the episode as a portent, his "first experience" with the "secretive" Department of State, the faults of which became obsessional with him. In his memoirs, he characterized his superiors as unimaginative, tradition bound, prejudiced, and ill mannered, lacking in proper respect for confidentiality. He also stated his distress because neither Wilson nor Bryan gave him any instructions before his departure for Argentina.[24]

The European war, meanwhile, compelled ever greater concern. For leaders in the western hemisphere, an important question centered on the extent to which they could do anything to mitigate the effects and to halt the fighting. The possibility of mediation aroused some interest, especially when Woodrow Wilson reacted to the outbreak by tendering his good offices. Even though the gesture accomplished nothing, Bryan told the president on 17 August that several foreign ministries had taken heed, inquiring whether any good would accrue if

the Pan American Union endorsed Wilson's offer by commending it to
the belligerents as a means toward peace.[25] But parochial concerns and
other differences made cooperation difficult, as shown by collapse of
plans for the fifth Pan American International Conference in Santiago
that September.

Fletcher reported that a variety of things caused Chilean reluctance. The war made the meeting seem inopportune; Bryan could not
attend; and the Chileans hesitated to participate in a situation in which
Tacna and Arica might attract international attention. In addition, the
"special severity" of the financial crisis in Chile further reduced enthusiasm. According to Fletcher, "most leading men" favored postponement. As it turned out, the same held true for leaders in the
Wilson administration who disliked the timing and anticipated embarrassment. For example, the Brazilians reportedly intended to recommend an expansion of the Pan American Union by including "other
political divisions" in the western hemisphere not presently represented. This idea produced strong opposition in the State Department's Division of Latin American Affairs, which advised against it
"on trade bases alone." As the position paper stated, "the inclusion of
Canada would mean the inclusion of English workshops, the inclusion
of French Guiana, those of France, and through the inclusion of Dutch
Guiana the colonial products of Holland would surely compete with
American goods." Wilson also grew suspicious of some of the more
ambitious appeals for the nations to act in tandem, calculating that
"more mischief than relief" would probably ensue.[26]

A limited response by the governing board of the Pan American
Union on 7 October gave sanction to a resolution addressed to the
warring nations and affirmed "an earnest expression" of hope for
peace, but the issue of whether to go any further remained unsettled.
On the same day, Bryan told Wilson that Latin American diplomats
again had raised the possibility of a mediation offer, prompted presumably by inquiries from Europe, but the secretary reported that he
had put off all discussions of united action because he did not know
whether "an opening" conducive to such a course existed. By his own
calculation, "We will find less embarrassment if we act alone than if we
act with a number of others," but at the same time, "it would be hard to
refuse the other nations desiring the honor of joining with us." He had
"no doubt" that they would follow the United States' lead and wanted
Wilson to consider whether to act unilaterally or cooperatively with the
A.B.C. countries, with all of the Latin American republics, or conceivably even with the European neutrals. Wilson's response on the following day downplayed the chances of a Pan American initiative having much effect. He remarked, "My own expectation is that the matter

will not lie with us. I do not think we will be called upon to choose which nations shall participate in the mediation or that we shall be at liberty to invite others to participate." To the contrary, he calculated, "when the time comes we shall receive an intimation that our intermediation would be accepted," and he reasoned, moreover, "it is very desirable that a single nation should act in this capacity rather than several." Any other approach would provoke "difficulties" and "complications" and render the outcome "much more doubtful."[27]

Late in 1914, the Wilson administration devised an inventive course designed, among other things, to impress upon the Europeans the sheer sensibility of providing alternatives to armed conflict. The undertaking, largely the work of Colonel House, resulted in the formulation of a Pan American treaty, a project that called for the adoption of a system of collective security and compulsory arbitration. Envisioning nothing less than a formal, political structure to give meaning to regional community in the western hemisphere, the idea would have established machinery for policing the region and also moved some distance toward a multilateral definition of the Monroe Doctrine. But the effort failed, in spite of a large investment of time and energy for over two years, largely because of Chilean objections and the inability of the Wilson administration to find ways to overcome them. In this instance, the president exaggerated the degree to which natural harmonies and mutualities of interest could govern international relationships in the western hemisphere. Nevertheless, the abortive pact, in many ways prototypical, held importance for revealing an evolving pattern in Wilson's conception of statecraft. A direct line ran from it to the League of Nations.

The discussions got underway late in the year. House initiated them on 25 November by advising the president "to pay less attention to his domestic policy" and "greater attention to the welding together of the two western continents." House applauded Wilson for his achievements in domestic affairs, notably his role in bringing about passage of the Federal Reserve Act, "his greatest constructive work," but now the times required "a constructive international policy." Wilson already had made headway "by getting the A.B.C. countries to act as arbitrators at Niagara." According to House, "the time had arrived to show the world that friendship, justice, and kindliness were more potent than the mailed fist." The European war showed the futility of any other course. Alluding by implication to Wilson's address at Mobile, House emphasized the irony in traditional policies toward Latin America. "In wielding the 'big stick' and dominating the two Continents, we lost the friendship and commerce of South and Central America and the European countries had profited by it." House saw a special danger in Germany and worried particularly that the United States would have to account for its attitudes if the Germans should win the Great War. He speculated further that Kaiser Wilhelm II had designs on South America, notably Brazil, presumably hoping that the United States would limit jurisdiction under the Monroe Doctrine to areas north of the equator, thereby permitting Germany "to exploit" the regions to the south. Wilson, in response, observed that war might have engaged Germany and the United States if it had not come in Europe.[28]

House addressed the subject again on 30 November. According to his diary, he told the president that "the wise thing for you to do is to make your foreign policy the feature of your Administration during the next two years," and he recommended further a Pan American focus to "weld North and South America together in a closer union." The circumstances favored such a plan. On 1 December, Eduardo Suárez Mújica presented his credentials as the Chilean ambassador, followed by the Argentine, Rómulo S. Naón, two days later. On 8 December, another sign of common purpose, a resolution by the governing board of the Pan American Union, this one enacted at Argentina's suggestion, affirmed the need for a special commission of nine members to investigate breaches of neutral rights and to recommend solutions. Although unsure whether "much immediate good" would come from it, Bryan told Wilson, "The discussion will draw the American countries nearer together and show the unity of interest that really exists but has not always been recognized."[29]

A week later on 16 December, House visited Washington and urged a major initiative upon the president. Again by his own account, House told Wilson flatly that "he might or might not have an opportunity to play a great and beneficent part in the European tragedy." But, "there was one thing he could do at once, and that was to inaugurate a policy that would weld the western hemisphere together." House had in mind a plan, once agreed upon, which would function as "a model for the European nations when peace is at last brought about." His idea, a preliminary version of the Pan American pact, thoroughly excited Wilson who wrote down the terms while House dictated them. First, to reduce the threat of war in the western hemisphere, House proposed a system of collective security: "mutual guaranties of political independence under republican form of government and mutual guaranties of territorial integrity." Next, to regulate the arms trade, House suggested the development of international supervisions: "Mutual agreement that the Government of each of the contracting parties acquire complete control within its jurisdiction of the manufacture and sale of munitions of war."

Wilson had encountered similar notions before and previously had reacted with caution. Early in 1914, for example, when S. Pérez Triana, a Colombian diplomat, suggested a treaty outlawing "the conquest of territory" as a method of giving certainty to Wilson's pledge at Mobile, the president feared the results of a mistake if the United States went ahead without clear indication that the other countries favored such a course. On this occasion, he responded with less reticence. Indeed, he went to his typewriter, reproduced a copy, and instructed House to feel out the ambassadors from Argentina, Brazil, and Chile with whom he thought it best to start the discussions. He also advised informality in order to avert precipitous acts and to avoid any bruising of "Mr Bryan's sensibilities."[30]

On the following morning, House arranged to brief Bryan on the essentials of the plan "for the linking of the Western Hemisphere" and then set up separate meetings with Naón, da Gama, and Suárez for 19 December. When they took place, Naón "warmly approved," especially the first article, claiming in House's paraphrase that "it struck a new note and would create an epoch in governmental affairs." When told that Wilson personally had typed the draft, Naón asked if he could keep it for its historical importance, and House let him have it. In subsequent dealings with the others, House found da Gama very receptive to the plan and "easy of conquest." But Suárez was more difficult, in House's view "because he is not so clever" and also because "Chile has a boundary dispute with Peru,"the Tacna-Arica controversy, and therefore hesitated to raise the question of territorial integrity.[31] But House underestimated the degree of opposition, as it turned out, a serious misjudgment.

After ten days, officials in the Wilson administration learned of Argentina's readiness to pursue discussions on the understanding, as House noted, "that such a proposition tends to transform the one-sided character of the Monroe Doctrine into a common policy of all the American countries." House ebulliently advised Wilson, "This is a matter of such far reaching consequences that I feel we should pay more attention to it just now than even the European affair for the reason that if brought to a successful conclusion the one must have a decided influence upon the other." House saw the proposed Pan American pact as a way to move the Europeans in favor of peace, but his enthusiasm led him to inflate the chances of his success. When Naón cautioned that Chile might object because of Tacna and Arica, House brushed aside his concerns, insisting instead upon discussing "the best means of buttoning-up the South American proposition." When Naón asked whether the United States intended twenty-one different treaties or a single convention for all of the countries, House favored the latter course, thinking that the exact terms would take form in negotiations with the A.B.C. states before transmittal to the others. When he received word of Brazil's favorable response early in January 1915, he wanted to drive through to a conclusion as soon as possible so that the Senate could ratify the document before adjournment in sixty days. But he never got his way. The Chileans delayed a formal response, explaining that another ministerial change had made a quick reaction impossible.[32]

PURSUING THE MULTILATERAL ALTERNATIVE

In 1915, the Wilson administration developed an even more explicit vision in Pan American policy but experienced frustration in pursuit of the Pan American pact. A vague Chilean reaction, conveyed by Suárez on 19 January, appeared to offer some grounds for hope by expressing agreement with the proposal "in principle" and applauding the idea as "a generous and panamerican one." But it affirmed no express commitments and, indeed, hinted, to the contrary, that in certain instances Chile would have difficulty finding "the proper expressions to render an idea agreeable to several parties." Heartened nevertheless, House somewhat impetuously told Wilson, "Everything now seems to be in shape for you to go ahead." He expected that "the country will receive this policy with enthusiasm and it will make your Administration notable, even had you done but little else."[33]

House, meanwhile, perceived ever more clearly a relationship between deteriorating circumstances in Mexico and the prospects of joint action with the A.B.C. group. Toward the end of the month, he suggested that collective measures perhaps could best solve "the Mexican problem" by imposing a settlement. The president, intrigued, characterized the notion as "an excellent idea" but held back for various reasons, including timing. The configuration of events and the expected outcomes in Mexico remained unclear, and the A.B.C. ambassadors seemed disinclined to run risks. The onset of a new round of civil war had dashed Wilson's hopes for a quick return to peace, order, and legitimacy. Following the triumph over Huerta in the summer of 1914, the Constitutionalists fell to feuding among themselves over questions of power, prestige, and ideology. When Villa and Zapata lined up in opposition to Carranza and Obregón, another wave of violence convulsed the country.[34]

On 26 January 1915, House left the United States for a mission in Europe. While seeking to promote the cause of mediation among the warring nations, he left the Pan American pact in Bryan's hands, hoping for an early conclusion, but the negotiations made no progress.

An edited version of the draft treaty drawn up on 29 January elicited discussion for two years but failed in the end to overcome Chilean resistance. This version consisted of four parts. The first reiterated the guarantee of territorial integrity and political independence "under republican forms of government." The second, a new addition, stipulated that "all disputes now pending and unconcluded" over territories and boundaries would become eligible for settlement by an arbitration board three months after ratification of the treaty. If direct negotiations failed during the interim, the compulsory feature would take effect. The third, a part of the original draft, would commit the member nations to institute controls on the manufacture and sale of munitions, and the fourth, also new, incorporated Bryan's favored "cooling off" formula. No resort to the use of force should take place before the quarreling nations had submitted to an investigation by an international commission.[35]

Bryan showed the proposed draft to the three ambassadors at his home on the evening of 1 February 1915, but his persuasive techniques still failed to win over the Chileans. Their misgivings remained strong. Several years later, Henry Fletcher recorded his understanding of the course of events and the reasons for it. At the outset, he had suffered embarrassment because the project, initiated secretly in Washington, had taken him by surprise. Indeed, he learned of it while sitting in the patio of the Club de la Unión in Santiago, when Enrique Villegas, the foreign minister, called him aside and asked about the "plan Wilson." Nonplussed, Fletcher had to confess ignorance, and Villegas then sketched the details as obtained in a long telegram from Suárez. While sympathetic with "the high motives" of President Wilson, Villegas doubted that the Chilean government could accept the proposal. The Chileans objected for several reasons. They regarded the commitment to a republican form of government as a limitation upon the attributes of national sovereignty; they anticipated adverse effects upon the Tacna-Arica dispute with Peru, and they feared that any such pact would encourage United States intervention in the domestic affairs of other countries. Fletcher noted glumly after the encounter that he had merely expressed "keen interest" and a desire "to be kept in touch with the progress of the negotiations."[36]

For Wilson, the stakes became ever higher as the spring progressed. Perhaps seeing parallels between Mexico's lamentable condition and the future prospects of his own country, he charged in a letter to a favorite correspondent that "the influences that have long dominated legislation and administration here are making their last and most desperate stand to regain control." The fight with the opposition forces in the United States had become "a very grim business, in which

they will give no quarter and in which . . . they will receive none."
Somewhat alarmingly, he declared, "If they cannot be mastered, we
shall have to have a new struggle for liberty in this country, and God
knows what will come of it. Only reform can prevent revolution." Such
apocalyptic convictions undoubtedly spurred a sense of urgency in
settling the Mexican issue, for which Wilson received a great deal of
advice, much of it pointing toward the utility of multilateral approaches.[37]

Charles W. Eliot, the president of Harvard University, favored
such a course. In February 1915, he proposed that Argentina, Brazil,
Chile, the United States, and possibly Spain "should combine to set
Mexico in order" and perhaps also "Hayti" and "San Domingo." He
anticipated additional good effects. Such an "American League" would
strike "a suggestive precedent for a European League to keep the peace
of Europe." As an advocate of "the Christian Brotherhood point of
view," he had difficulty in standing aside and letting Mexico "stew in
her own juice." A few days later, he added that his wish to do well by his
neighbors in no way ruled out the use of force "when all other measures
failed" in coping with "the passions and primitive savageries of the
nations."[38]

Similar sentiments also surfaced in the State Department. Early in
March 1915, Robert Lansing, the counselor, looked "to the possibility
of the necessity of employing force in Mexico" but hoped to find an
alternative to any unilateral moves by the United States. Some method
of "joint action" with the A.B.C. group would reduce the cost and
divert ill will. It would also "ally [*sic*] alarm in Mexico," "remove Latin
American suspicions," and undercut any demands in the United States
for the annexation of territory. From Paris, meanwhile, Colonel House
advanced the same recommendation, describing cooperation with the
A.B.C. countries as "the wisest solution." Wilson, too, inclined in favor.
On 18 March, he told Bryan that, although intervention amounted
only to "a remote possibility," if it should come about, Lansing's suggestion made a great deal of sense. Wilson thought it "in thorough
accord with what we are hoping for in the Americas."[39]

The Pan American treaty, meanwhile, languished. After the first
week in March, Bryan reported that Brazil and Argentina retained
enthusiasm for the idea but that Chile so far had withheld any additional formal response. He wondered whether to wait awhile longer or
to go ahead without Chile. Somewhat tentatively, he advised the latter
course on grounds that Chile could always sign later, and Wilson, in
reply, wrote, "This is very good news indeed." He wanted Bryan to
obtain the assent of Argentina and Brazil. Mexico still functioned as a
powerful incentive for maintaining the courtship, and the possibility of

joint action still existed. Indeed, on 11 March, the Argentine ambassador issued a personal suggestion "that all of the American republics join in an appeal to all of the factions in Mexico to adjust their differences and agree upon some means of establishing and maintaining a stable and orderly government in Mexico." Although Wilson, in this instance, had reservations, regarding any such move as premature, possibly even an "irritation" likely to repel the Mexicans, he kept his options open.[40]

Negotiations over the treaty remained at issue throughout the spring and entailed some twisting maneuvers. Fletcher took leave from Santiago in March 1915 but could not escape them. On the way home, he stopped by Rio de Janeiro for conversations with Ambassador Edwin Morgan over how best to win over the Chileans, and he encountered the same question when he disembarked in the United States. The Brazilians, in the interim, suggested one way of easing Chile's sensibilities over Tacna and Arica, simply by exempting matters of national pride from the treaty's provisions, and they won a responsive hearing. The Chileans incorporated the essentials of the idea into a formal response early in April and urged a complete revision of the proposed terms. Specifically, they wanted to limit arbitration to disputes arising in the future and also to eliminate the commitment in defense of republican forms. But Bryan didn't like the changes. He feared emasculation of the original version, claiming that it held no real menace.[41]

A peripheral but related issue attracted a good deal of attention in diplomatic circles in the spring of 1915. While the United States pursued the Pan American pact, the countries of Argentina, Brazil, and Chile engaged in independent conversations among themselves over a proposed treaty of defense and alliance. Mainly the brain child of the Brazilians and the Chileans, the plan called for allegiance to the principles of nonaggression and arbitration. When difficulties arose, the participants would seek peaceful solutions; moreover, they would regard an attack against any one of them as an attack against all of them. When the United States learned of the project early in 1915, State Department officials declared it "unobjectionable," perhaps even useful, but, in private, they harbored concern that it might compete with the Pan American pact. Even worse, what if it turned into a Pan Latin alignment directed against the United States? Ambassador Morgan in Brazil somewhat pessimistically forecast "increasing intimacy" among the A.B.C. countries, possibly efforts to strike a counterpoise against the United States, and President Wilson wanted to make certain that "nothing in the proposed arrangement . . . will stand in the way of or embarrass our own American plans." The signing of the document by the foreign ministers, Alejandro Lira of Argentina, Lauro Müller of Brazil, and José Luis Murature of Chile, took place at a formal ceremony on 25 May 1915 in Buenos Aires but signified very little. Not one of the signatories ever bothered to ratify the treaty.[42]

THE PAN AMERICAN FINANCIAL CONFERENCE

On the preceding day, 24 May 1915, the delegates attending the first Pan American Financial Conference half a world away in Washington, D.C., convened in opening session. In a speech of greeting and welcome, Woodrow Wilson seized the opportunity to elucidate favorite themes. The occasion, he proclaimed, grew out of a shared purpose, an attempt "the draw the American republics together by bonds of common interest and of mutual understanding." The achievement of this end, a "union of interest," could never take place if "any one of the parties" possessed as its aim the "exploitation" of the others. Wilson denied any such intent. Quite the contrary. In a succinct affirmation of a basic premise, he asserted that "The basis of successful commercial intercourse is common interest, not self interest. It is an actual interchange of services and of values; it is based upon reciprocal relations and not selfish relations." His concluding point emphasized that "We are not . . . trying to make use of each other, but . . . to be of use to one another."[43]

The Wilson administration had ambitious goals. It conceived of the Pan American Financial Conference, primarily the work of Secretary of the Treasury William Gibbs McAdoo, as a way of addressing economic issues and responding to some of the changes produced by the war. The leaders in the administration especially hoped to promote the cause of regional integration. Although the legacies of economic dislocation still lingered in Latin America, intimations of recovery prompted a new sense of optimism about the future, and North American publicists trumpeted the theme of opportunity beckoning. In February 1915, for example, John Barrett published an essay in *World Outlook* in which he conferred plaudits upon the twenty-one nations in the Pan American Union for maintaining their solidarity. As a case in point, he eulogized the attempt at mediating the Mexican question at Niagara Falls and depicted it as a model of harmonious conduct for the entire world, a vivid contrast with the mayhem so prevalent in Europe. As a consequence of the war, he also anticipated a great expansion of United States trade with Latin America, a view developed in his book, *Pan America and Pan Americanism, the Great American Opportunity, War Time and After.*[44]

Several particular issues required consideration at the Financial Conference and aroused special interest. They centered on relationships between finance and commerce. In the middle of January 1915, Professor Leo S. Rowe, a Latin American specialist at the University of Pennsylvania who later became executive director of the Pan American Union, drew attention to various deficiencies after his return from an extended tour through Latin America. For one thing, the United States needed to learn more about the prevailing wants and needs of Latin Americans and the extent of market demands. To find out the answers, he advised extensive programs of investigation and research. For another, he reasoned that concerted efforts to boost United States investment in Latin America would strengthen the trade, and he recommended in favor of them. But most important, he regarded the improvement of credit facilities as "the first requisite" for commercial entry into the field. United States exporters operated under a special handicap because they had no effective means of making long-term credit available to Latin American buyers. In contrast, as an article in the *Bulletin* of the P.A.U. explained, European competitors traditionally had made credit available for periods of three to six months because their banks bought and sold commercial acceptances and could transfer the credit due from merchants in Buenos Aires, Rio de Janeiro, and Santiago to institutions in London and Berlin. The British and German practice of treating the bill as bankable paper created many advantages for their citizens. In contrast, entrepreneurs in the United States suffered liabilities. If they wished to extend credit over a long term, they had to carry the burden themselves by allowing for deferred payments, thereby adding their own costs and possibly straining resources. Rowe's message held simply that the institution of branch banks would alleviate the difficulty.[45]

Another troublesome matter, an object of much misunderstanding, concerned Latin American tariffs. An analysis in the *Bulletin* of the P.A.U. claimed that businessmen in the United States habitually thought of customs duties as protective devices for growing industries. In Latin America, in contrast, manufacturing enterprises hardly required such safeguards because so few of them existed. Instead, tariffs served the function of generating revenues for governments and required different kinds of responses. For foreign sellers, the exact rate of the tariff and the ratio in comparison with the value of goods should matter less than the magnitude of demand for the product and the willingness and ability of consumers to pay the price with the duty added. In other words, the existence of a tariff duty presented no necessary handicap for exporters because of the absence of domestic competition. Still another source of confusion, the Latin American use of specific tariff schedules differed markedly from the usual practice in the United States where *ad valorem* calculations fixed the rate as a percentage of the value of the imported goods. In Latin America, specific tariffs required payments determined by a definite weight, number, or volume. Though irrationalities sometimes resulted—for example, when cheaper grades of an item had to pay the same duty as the more expensive—the Latin American system could result in administrative efficiencies and would not necessarily discriminate against the North Americans in favor of the British or the Germans. When United States citizens put forth such complaints, as they often did, they showed that they had failed to discern the rationale for rate distinctions and to comply with it. As an illustration, the article pointed out, a problem existed in the importation of metal goods into Latin America. The presence of small brass ornaments on a product could have the effect of raising the schedule from the lower one on iron or steel to a higher rate. By leaving the decorations off, the seller might gain the advantage of taking the goods into the country at a lower cost. The Europeans, presumably, knew of the technique, while the North Americans had yet to learn it.[46]

To mitigate the effects of the war upon them, the South Americans especially had large incentives for enhancing the trade with the United States. In an address before a business audience in New York City early in 1915, Ambassador Rómulo S. Naón appealed for closer ties, emphasizing the obvious point that the Argentines needed finished goods and had the capacity to exchange for them high-quality and abundant agricultural and animal products. Although Naón worried that shortages of merchant ships would handicap any large-scale efforts to redirect the trade, an event on 18 February gave credence to his hopes when the Dutch steamer *Tenbergen* arrived in Boston with a sumptuous cargo of wools and hides, estimated in value at $2,500,000. In the following month, the apparent resumption of the Argentine export trade persuaded Consul General Leo J. Keena that economic health had returned to the country and that overseas sales among the Allied nations and the northern neutrals had indeed increased because of the war.[47]

Recovery lagged behind in Brazil, and financial difficulties plagued the government. Brazilian leaders faced up to the crisis by initiating austerity measures in efforts to cut costs and to reduce the imbalances in the national budget. One emergency device, for example, proposed the elimination of commercial attachés in Mexico and the United States. The country also sought large, international loans but had difficulty in obtaining them because of an inability to guarantee repayment against future coffee sales. In March 1915, Consul General Alfred L. M. Gottschalk described the conditions produced by the war as still acute. Brazil remained cut off from European markets and unable to tap foreign sources of credit. Although Gottschalk hoped that the United States could provide some relief by supplying more foodstuffs and manufactured goods, he could conceive of no way that his country could absorb much more of Brazil's main exports. Nevertheless, the establishment of a branch of the National City Bank of New York in the city of Santos on 5 April 1915 raised hopes for the future of United States' sales in Brazil.[48]

Chile also sought benefits by expanding the export trade. In March 1915, Eduardo Carrasco Buscañán of the Foreign Ministry announced plans for a mission in Central America and the United States for such a purpose, since the well-being of the country required it. Chile depended upon foreign trade and also upon foreign merchant ships to haul it. More rapid forms of transportation, in addition to the opening of the canal, underscored the availability of readier access to new markets. In March 1915, the steamship *Pennsylvania* from the American-Hawaiian line made the fastest voyage ever from San Francisco to Iquique in eleven days and ten hours. In the same month, another record fell when mail cargos out of New York and New Orleans on 11 March traversed the canal aboard the *Oriana* of the Pacific Steam Navigation Company in time for a daylight arrival at Iquique on 26 March.[49] In the spring of 1915, consular reports indicated "a marked increase" in world demand for nitrates and "a considerable revival" in commercial activities, very good news because Chile's financial condition and the government's revenues rested upon them. According to one set of figures, nitrates accounted for some 75 percent of the country's total exports and the export tax for about 35 percent of the government's income. Although the collapse in 1914 had resulted in widespread distress, the Chileans now anticipated a strong recovery, especially it they could develop markets in the United States. Reasoning similarly in the spirit of reciprocity, Consul General Leo J. Keena advised United States investors that the present marked a good time to move capital into Chile. Excellent opportunities had arisen especially in public utilities and the coal and copper industries, those sectors traditionally favored by the British and the Germans. As a case in point, an electric power plant installed in May at Tocopilla in the north would drive a copper mill at Chuquicamata. The owners, the Chile Copper Company, headed by President Daniel Guggenheim of New York and Vice-President Albert Burrage of Boston, proposed to open mines in a region thought to possess the largest deposits of copper in the world.[50]

To give focus to mutual aims and common interests and also to avoid distractions, the planners of the first Pan American Financial Conference wanted to rivet attention on germane subjects and achievable goals. During the preliminary stages, Otto Willson, an official in the Commerce Department, established the theme by warning against

"the danger that the meeting will waste itself in a flow of words."
Specifically, he advised in favor of confining the discussions as much as
possible to particular financial and commercial questions. He ranked
them in two categories. The most important included the promotion of
investments, the whole matter of dollar exchange, and the establishment of branch banks. In introducing these concerns, he reasoned that
United States investors really preferred to keep their money safely at
home. If Latin Americans truly proposed to obtain capital from them,
they would have to provide proper inducements with guarantees of
security and high rates of return. A recently transacted loan to Argentina of some $15,000,000 showed that such methods could succeed. He
calculated further that the problems with dollar exchange would simply disappear with the creation of branch banking facilities. As Wilson
explained, the unfavorable balance of trade against the United States
in South America should make "reasonable" exchange easily accessible.
"The only reason this is not the case is . . . because of the lack of
machinery for handling the exchange and the custom of financing
trade through London, Paris, and other European points." The second
category of goals aimed at trade expansion, the achievement of which
depended largely upon attainments in the first. Nevertheless, Wilson's
agenda placed heavy emphasis upon obtaining more and better information about market conditions in Latin America, more skillful techniques of salesmanship and merchandising, and greater uniformity in
the rules, regulations, and customs governing commercial activity.[51]

When President Wilson extended invitations to the countries of
Central and South America, asking that they take part in a financial
conference, eighteen governments, not including Mexico and Haiti,
responded by sending delegations, consisting of the finance minister
and two or three banking specialists. When they assembled on the
morning of 24 May at the Pan American Union, they settled down to
sessions with Secretary of the Treasury McAdoo and about two-
hundred representatives of the political and business elites in the
United States, including cabinet members, diplomats, senators, and
bankers. In the initial speeches, the assembly heard inspirational rhetoric about the lofty purposes and recent advances of Pan Americanism.
Secretary of State Bryan effusively described the special relationship
among the republics of the western hemisphere "as resembling a
great Banyan tree." As depicted by this unfortunate and condescend-
ing metaphor, "The United States is the parent stem; the branches
extending to the South have taken root in the soil and are now permanent supports, yes, important parts of that great tree." Later on, John
Barrett delivered a self-congratulatory panegyric on the progress of
the Pan American Union under his stewardship:

Eight years ago . . . the organization . . . was housed in a little old house on Lafayette Square. To-day its building, this palace of commerce and comity, and its grounds, represent an investment of $1,100,000. . . . Eight years ago a staff of only twenty-five persons took care of all the work that this organization carried on. To-day there is a staff of seventy-five. . . . In this building is the Columbus Memorial Library, which eight years ago had less than 10,000 volumes. Now it has over 35,000 volumes, and the most practical collection of Americana to be found in the Western Hemisphere. . . . Eight years ago this office distributed less than 80,000 pieces of printed matter in a year. This year the distribution will pass the mark of 800,000!

Nevertheless, even when measured against such attainments, Barrett ascribed great significance to the first Pan American Financial Conference. He characterized it as "the inevitable climax of a great present-day Pan American movement. . . . The whole Western Hemisphere is in sympathy with it, and the entire world is watching." After enduring such close scrutiny until the end of the formal sessions on 29 May, the delegates perhaps found some measure of relief in the relative anonymity of a two-week railroad tour through Philadelphia, Pittsburgh, St. Louis, Chicago, Detroit, Buffalo, and Boston.[52]

The conference, though short on tangible achievements, provided face-to-face opportunities for the exchange of views and the expression of goodwill. In a summary appraisal of the outcome to President Wilson, Secretary McAdoo explained his understanding of the United States' stake. "Manifestly enlightened interest in the welfare of our friendly neighbors should induce us to extend to them every facility that our resources permit." He thought it "nothing short of providential" that the Federal Reserve Act had enabled "our bankers . . . for the first time . . . to engage in world-wide operations." The Pan American Conference established a collaborative base from which, the administration hoped, additional and substantive consequences would follow. The delegates recommended in favor of holding another such meeting in the following year. Moreover, they brought into existence the International High Commission. This body, including the finance minister and eight specialists from each participating country, had as its charge the responsibility of devising practical means for achieving the larger goals held in common. More specifically, the members had hopes of finding ways to reduce wide disparities in commercial practices, to render more uniform standards of value among currencies expressed in gold, and to achieve less diversity in the issue of bills of exchange, the classification of merchandise, the regulations for commercial travelers, and the employment of trademarks, patents, copyrights, and postal rates. They also wanted assurances of arbitration in the event of commercial disputes. The representatives to the International High Commission from the United States included Secretary of Treasury McAdoo, John Bassett Moore, a former State Department counselor and presently a professor of international law at Colombia University, John H. Fahey, president of the United States Chamber of Commerce, and Dr. Leo S. Rowe of the University of Pennsylvania. The first meeting with the other delegations was scheduled for Buenos Aires in November 1915.[53]

Overall, the achievements earned praise and commendation in the United States. The *Bulletin* of the P.A.U. predictably described the conference as "undoubtedly one of the most important international meetings . . . ever . . . in the western hemisphere" and looked forward to happy consequences, among them, "a better understanding of the economic conditions of the countries . . . of their interdependence the one on the other and of their relations with Europe," all of which signified "the quickening and birth of new commercial and industrial enterprises." Latin Americans, in contrast, expressed more ambivalent views. *El Mercurio* of Santiago described the event as the beginning of "a new epoch in commercial relations" but harbored doubts that the United States ever could replace Great Britain and western Europe as consumers of Chilean commodities. *La Prensa* of Buenos Aires similarly had reservations about United States motives. Characterizing them as "primarily" commercial, it warned of the dangers of too close an attachment but conceded, nevertheless, that Pan Americanism had "a moral force, useful and advantageous," if defined broadly with proper understanding of "the economic solidarity of the world." *La Prensa* wanted no economic isolation from Europe "upon which depended all the states of this region." Much more outspoken and in frank condemnation, a polemic entitled *La Invasión Yankee* by "Dr. Equis" insisted that North American commercial penetration amounted to a subtle kind of imperialism based on the German model. Claiming that Mexico already had become the first victim, "in spite of Wilson's tranquilizing expressions," the author warned of "the dominating policies of the United States," soon "in full motion initiated on the basis of commercial interchange with the southern countries." Dr. Equis proposed a united front among Argentina, Brazil, and Chile to ward off the threat of Yankee conquest.[54]

MULTILATERAL APPROACHES AND MEXICO

The move toward political integration, meanwhile, achieved little progress. Indeed, Wilson himself occasioned something of a setback by issuing on his own authority an appeal to the contending Mexican factions on 2 June. Calling upon them to set aside their differences and to restore the peace "for the relief and redemption of their prostrate country," he cautioned that the people of the United States could not "indifferently" stand by and "do nothing to serve their neighbor" and might lend "active moral support to some man or group of men . . . who can rally the suffering people of Mexico." Wilson acted by himself in this instance out of conviction that a unilateral move would have the greatest effect. As he noted, Mexico was not accustomed to taking advice from Argentina, Brazil, and Chile. Ambassador Naón in turn approved of the initiative but hoped somewhat plaintively that, whenever the United States extended recognition, some unified action with the A.B.C. group would ensue. Bryan told him "it would be very nice" if something like that could take place.[55]

The crisis over the sinking of the *Lusitania* on 7 May 1915, in the interim, ripped official Washington and resulted in administrative changes. Among other things, it precipitated a final break between the president and his secretary of state. Rather than sign a strong note of protest because of deep disagreement over the anticipated consequences, Bryan resigned his position in the cabinet on 8 June. To replace him, Wilson settled on Robert Lansing, an experienced hand, the counselor of the State Department, and a recognized expert on international law. Perceived in the inner circle as dullish and unimaginative, Lansing impressed Colonel House as malleable yet technically adept. House advised Wilson that Lansing "could be used to better advantage than a stronger man." He would "do the details intelligently" without producing "the annoyance and anxiety that you have been under." Supposedly, Lansing would mind the shop without intruding upon the prerogatives of superiors.[56]

House rejoiced in Bryan's departure and anticipated brave new days. During his stay in Europe from January until June, House believed that sad conditions of disarray and confusion had beset the State Department for lack of leadership, and he held Bryan responsible. In a somewhat petulant diary entry, House recorded rumors that Bryan, upon resigning, had told the president with his voice aquiver, "Colonel House has been Secretary of State, not I, and I have never had your full confidence." House particularly blamed Bryan for the failure to advance the Pan American treaty. As he put it, the Great Commoner "had never done any serious work in his life . . . he was essentially a talker."[57] But House intended to set things right and proposed to consummate the project under his own direction. In a conference with Henry Fletcher on 18 June, he listened while the ambassador explained that any effort to proceed without Chile would disrupt Pan American solidarity and then bridled at the suggestion that a simple statement in support of the Monroe Doctrine would do as well. House upbraided

Fletcher for failing to grasp the full magnitude. "We desired to see the Americas knitted together so as to give the world a policy to be followed in the future." He insisted, moreover, upon the need for haste, since "the European war made the time opportune," and, if success did not come soon, "it might never do so." When Fletcher went back to Chile in July, he had instructions to do what he could to bring the country into line. House, optimistic, regarded him as "the best man we could get to help button up the South American matter."[58]

Mexico, meanwhile, required attention. Since Wilson's appeal for peace on 2 June had had no effect upon the warring factions, Colonel House concluded that conditions grew more dangerous every day. He wanted to keep in touch with the leading contenders and also to work closely with Lansing, "not only in the Mexican but the South American matter." Lansing, similarly agitated, suspected German machinations. He recorded in his diary on 11 July his impression "that the German Government is utterly hostile to all nations with democratic institutions. . . . Everywhere German agents are plotting and intriguing to accomplish the supreme purpose of their Government" in Mexico, Haiti, Santo Domingo, and "probably in other Latin American republics." While conceding that "The proof is not conclusive," he thought it, nevertheless, "sufficient to compel belief." In reaction, he recommended "The cultivation of a Pan American doctrine with the object of alienating the American republics from European influences, especially German influences," and also "The maintenance of friendly relations with Mexico," the accomplishment of which would require recognition of Carranza's faction, "the stronger." To implement the plan, he reckoned that "Union with other American republics will have a good effect," a view shared with John Barrett, who gave assurances in the middle of July of Latin America's friendship and goodwill and urged the importance of keeping the governments informed. He believed that "Pan Americanism is justifying the splendid support which the President has always given it." Colonel House, meanwhile, claimed credit on grounds that he had suggested the idea of A.B.C. mediation in the first place in January. Now he linked hands with Lansing and Barrett in advancing the proposal that "the A.B.C. Powers join us in composing the difficulties."[59]

The effort eventually enlisted six nations. Beginning on 5 August, the diplomatic representatives of Argentina, Brazil, and Chile, and also Bolivia, Guatemala, and Uruguay, initiated a series of "informal" and "advisory" discussions with the secretary of state. While seeking some solution to the Mexican imbroglio, Lansing showed delicate regard for the prerogatives of national sovereignty. He explained, making careful distinctions, that although "joint action" need not take place, a set of "independent" yet "identical" decisions among the six partners would have good effects. In the preliminary sessions, the diplomats agreed upon a strategy. They would issue a communication to the Mexican factions, inviting attendance at a conference of peace and conciliation, and then, if the gambit failed, work out some method for recognizing a government in Mexico.[60]

The Mexican rivals responded with different levels of interest. Villa and Zapata, now the weaker, expressed readiness to take part, perhaps seeing in the offer an opportunity to salvage something from a losing cause. Carranza and the Constitutionalists, in contrast, reacted with cold hostility, regarding the move as an unwarranted affront— indeed, a violation of national sovereignty constituting interference in Mexico's internal affairs. Carranza issued such complaints in letters to the presidents of Argentina, Brazil, and Chile and also instructed his agent in Washington, Eliseo Arredondo, to register protests. In spite of them, the United States and its associates set forth an appeal on 11 August, urging that the Mexicans set aside their feuds, agree to a process of compromise and conciliation, and take part in forming a provisional government. The tactic never had a chance. Carranza flatly refused the offer and insisted upon the recognition of his government or none at all. Acting out of a sense of military and political superiority, he required that the Pan American group choose him or endure further chaos. He allowed no alternative and in the end got his way. On 9 October, the United States and the other six countries bestowed de facto recognition upon him in the hope that he could henceforth maintain himself and the constitutional order. Lansing believed that the United States possessed no real choice in the matter. Although he expressed his wish that Carranza could retain "his supremacy over the semi-independent and jealous military chiefs on whose loyalty his power rests," he reasoned further that whatever the outcome, "We must not intervene in Mexican affairs" because "Germany wants us to do so."[61]

PURSUING THE PAN AMERICAN PACT

Leaders in the Wilson administration knew that putting the bet on Carranza entailed certain risks, yet they had managed to produce a decision by overcoming centrifugal tendencies within the Pan American group, and they had good reason for satisfaction. President Wilson hailed the outcome as a triumph, claiming in his annual message before the Congress on 7 December that "We have been put to the test in Mexico, and we have stood the test. . . . Her fortunes are in her own hands."[62] But the desired mechanism of regional cooperation in the future, the Pan American pact, still eluded success. Upon returning to the post in Santiago, Henry Fletcher pursued the cause by engaging officials in the Foreign Office in further conversations and persuaded himself that he saw signs of progress. On 9 September, he reported that some chance existed and wondered about the advisability of shifting the main talks to Chile's capital. But questions of protocol and prerogative blocked any such move. Ambassador Suárez would not relinguish control in Washington, D.C., and President Wilson, though "so exceedingly anxious to push this matter to an early settlement," hesitated to inflict a "discourtesy" upon the Chilean diplomat, even though "we have been able to do virtually nothing" while working with him.[63]

Colonel House, meanwhile, in a fit of urgency, put pressure on Lansing to hurry along the negotiations. On 14 October, the secretary revised the draft and addressed Chilean objections in two ways. First, to reduce concern over the guarantee of republican governmental forms, he allowed for the nullification of all commitments to defend any country abandoning them. The terms of the pact would simply no longer apply. In addition, he tried to calm fears of arbitration by muting the provisions in Article II. Substitution of the word "expeditious" for "prompt" would eliminate any implication of a definite time limit for the settling of boundary disputes. But his tinkering with the terminology angered House, who, aghast, thought Lansing obtusely oblivious to the real significance. In his diary, he recorded a conversation over a hypothetical instance. What if Germany should establish colonies in Brazil, gain control of the country, and then proclaim it a monarchy? Under Lansing's plan, no penalty would occur except exclusion from "the league," the very thing the Germans would want anyway. Lansing reportedly reasoned that it made little difference whether Brazil remained a republic or became a monarchy if the Germans obtained the power. But House demurred, recording his conviction that "Germany today would be inocuous [*sic*] and a satisfactory member of the society of nations if she were a republic." In a curious and convoluted passage, he wrote, "there was no objection whatever to the Germans going to South America in great numbers and getting peaceful control of the governments, and in continuing them under republican forms of government." Indeed, he averred, "it would probably be of benefit to the Americas rather than a detriment, for the German population would be in every way preferable to the population now in the majority of the South American countries." Such was his faith in the redemptive capacities of governmental institutions.[64] This odd amalgam of republicanism with racism subsequently contributed to a series of misjudgments on his part.

Faced with House's opposition, the State Department formulated still another draft and presented it to the Argentine ambassador on 20 October. This revision reinstated the phrase "under republican forms of government" and also called for the resolution of boundary problems within one year before resort to arbitration, both apparent attempts to brush aside Chilean misgivings. But when Naón then pressed the obvious concern over Chilean resistance, further deliberations and another round of discussions followed. From the Chilean capital, Henry Fletcher reported pessimistically that in the middle of September the Chilean parliament had endorsed Juan Luis Sanfuentes as the next president, but he would not take office until 20 December, and the interim government in all likelihood would refrain from any action. Fletcher foresaw little hope of progress without clarification of the impact on Tacna and Arica, what he called "the Scylla and Charybdis of Chilean diplomacy."[65]

Still another draft took shape in November. This one, mainly the work of Lansing and Naón, pursued an agreement by removing once again the time limit for settling boundary disputes while pledging good faith. A somewhat abbreviated rendition, it impressed Wilson as "the most satisfactory formulation . . . that we can hope to get adopted by all the parties." Following the president's lead, the secretary of state showed the revisions to the ambassadors of Brazil and Chile on 18 November and tried to persuade Suárez of the baselessness of his concerns. Lansing hoped for a quick endorsement so that Wilson could make the announcement in his annual message to the Congress, but the assent failed to materialize, and, indeed, new reasons for worry appeared. On 26 November, Ambassador Stimson in Buenos Aires transmitted from *La Prensa* an article attributed to Dr. Estanislao Zeballos, an old nemesis. His vociferous attack described Wilson's advocacy of Pan Americanism as a transparent attempt to flatter the self-esteem of South Americans and denounced it as a form of "mercantilism" designed to set Latin Americans against Europeans. According to Zeballos, the "paternal theory of protection" set forth by the Monroe Doctrine had as its analogue "the European protectorates in Africa."[66]

Undeterred by Chile's failure to respond, the president gave conspicuous attention to the Pan American theme in his presentation before the Congress on 7 December. In a frank admission, he stated candidly that "There was a time in the early days of our great nation . . . when the United States looked upon itself as . . . some sort of guardian of the republics to the south." But, he added, "it was always difficult to maintain such a role without offense to the pride of the [Latin

American] peoples." Taking the position that his country now had
outgrown such forms of behavior, Wilson applauded the obsolescence
of antiquated notions and the advent of "the new day in whose light we
now stand." Rather than seek "guardianship," the United States aspired to "a full and honorable association as of partners" and wanted to
advance "the independence and prosperity of the states of Central and
South America." In a rousing conclusion, he posited that all governments in the Americas possessed "genuine equality" and therefore
reasoned that Pan Americanism has "none of the spirit of empire. . . . It
is the embodiment . . . of the spirit of law and independence and liberty
and mutual service." The words delighted John Barrett, who expressed his "profound satisfaction" and regarded them as personal
vindication after "many years of disappointment, discouragement and
even ridicule." Unlike the predecessors, Roosevelt and Taft, Barrett
claimed, President Wilson had displayed "masterly statesmanship" and
understood "the immeasurable importance of promoting practical Pan
Americanism and advancing solidarity and comity among the American Republics."[67]

THE SECOND PAN AMERICAN SCIENTIFIC CONFERENCE

The Second Pan American Scientific Conference, succeeding the
first in Santiago in 1908, provided still another forum for the expression of high-minded sentiments. The formal sessions convened at the
Pan American Union on 27 December 1915, ran until 8 January 1916,
and attracted about 1,200 delegates, of which about 1,000 came from
the United States. The discussions aimed broadly at expanding "the
knowledge of things American" and took place within nine categories,
including anthropology, astronomy, natural resources, education, engineering, international law, metallurgy, public health, and economics.
Regional politics often intruded upon the considerations, and the Pan
American theme figured prominently in the celebratory speeches of
leaders, experts, and dignitaries. Secretary of the Treasury McAdoo,
for example, affirmed his conviction that the many changes necessi-
tated by the Great War would result in great improvements in the
conduct of international finance, and Professor Edwin W. Kemmerer,
an economist from Princeton, played the role of utopian by urging the
adoption of uniform currencies in the western hemisphere. In similar
fashion, James Brown Scott, the secretary of the Carnegie Endowment
for International Peace, and Elihu Root, the former secretary of state
and presently the president of the American Society of International
Law, extolled the American republics for their praiseworthy commit-

ments to peace and legality and pointed to the European horrors as dismaying counterexamples.[68]

The ceremonies culminated at Memorial Continental Hall on the evening of 6 January with an address by Woodrow Wilson. The president chose this occasion as the appropriate time to make public his plan for the negotiation of a Pan American pact. Buoyantly proclaiming his intention "to see to it that American friendship is founded on a rock," he promised that the guarantees contained in the proposed treaty would establish the peace upon "the principles of absolute political equality among the states" and upon "the solid, eternal foundations of justice and humanity." But the expectation turned into an illusion. Perhaps misled by Lansing's calculation that nine Latin American governments already had affirmed support for the plan, the president may have believed that he could now overcome Chilean hesitation. But Chile remained obstinate. According to Fletcher, the instability of political alignments made any commitment to the treaty impossible. Indeed, Fletcher's confidential message on 21 January reported that the Chilean Committee on Foreign Affairs had declared any such agreement out of the question because of the effects on Tacna and Arica. Eduardo Suárez Mújica, meanwhile, announced his decision to resign his position in a couple of months and aroused suspicions in the Wilson administration that he intended to return home and lead the opposition to the pact. Lansing, in frustration, recorded his conviction "that influences are at work to defeat the purposes of the treaty," conceivably, he added later, "some foreign power." His suspicions pointed toward Germany.[69]

To break up the deadlock, the president shifted his tactics, deciding that "it would be best to go forward . . . with or without the A.B.C. group." He proposed "to let them have a pretty plain hint that we mean to do so, earnestly as we desire their cooperation," and he wanted, further, to make them realize that "the whole fate of Pan-Americanism rests upon their attitude now at this critical turning point." Somewhat threateningly, he added, "we are in a position to make their isolation very pronounced and very unenviable." The State Department, accordingly, authorized diplomatic emissaries in Latin America on 24 January to invite their host countries to participate in negotiations leading to a treaty. Colonel House, meanwhile, somewhat quixotically sought leverage by enlisting British support. While in London, he broached the subject with Sir Edward Grey, the foreign secretary, and suggested that the United States would welcome a statement in the House of Commons in behalf of territorial guarantees in the western hemisphere. The overture produced something of an embarrassment. Though professedly inclined to favor the Pan American pact, Lord

Grey hesitated to do so in public and in opposition to Chile. House's maneuver came to nothing. The Brazilians then contributed to the confusion by advising that everything should await the next Pan American conference, "the American parliament," and, therefore, the proper body for such deliberations. House's anger seethed when he returned home late in March 1916 because the treaty had made no progress. Privately he blamed Lansing, but when he took over, the project became obstructed by other complexities.[70] Francisco Villa's raid on Columbus, New Mexico, had provoked a punitive expedition into Mexico, and the consequences proved inimical to House's aims.

COMMERCIAL EXPANSION AND THE WAR

In marked contrast with the treaty negotiations, the commercial contacts with Latin America expanded impressively in 1915 and 1916 and, from the United States' point of view, greatly enhanced the cause of economic integration. At the end of August 1915, the Department of Commerce reported that for the first time in history the nation's exports exceeded $3,000,000,000 during the preceding twelve months. As a result, the United States moved past Great Britain as the leader in the world. During the same time, the sales in South America also increased significantly over six-month periods from $38,751,000 in June 1914 to $52,263,000 in December 1914 to $60,573,000 in June 1915. As a further illustration, in the single month of June 1915, the export of agricultural implements to Argentina doubled; the sale of automobiles trebled, and the shipment of bituminous coal increased by ten times. The purchase of South American commodities in the United States also advanced from $105,477,000 for the six months ending in June 1914 to $144,074,000 in December 1914 to $153,043,000 in June 1915. Similar patterns existed throughout the entire region. According to the *Bulletin* of the P.A.U., "the fundamentally sound economic conditions" of the Latin American republics enabled them "to emerge with comparatively great rapidity" from the "state of industrial paralysis" at the beginning of the war.[71] To consolidate the gains, the leaders in the Wilson administration hoped for close cooperation by means of the International High Commission, but annoying difficulties got in the way. According to Frank L. Polk, the new counselor in the State Department, an assortment of "unavoidable delays" in choosing representatives in some of the other republics caused a postponement of the scheduled meeting in Buenos Aires from November 1915 until April 1916. The United States already had chosen a delegation consisting of Secretary of the Treasury William G. McAdoo, the chairman, John Bassett Moore, the vice-chairman, and nine others, including

Senator Duncan U. Fletcher, a Democrat from Florida and also the president of the Southern Commercial Congress, Samuel Untermyer, a Wall Street lawyer, Paul M. Warburg, a banker and member of the Federal Reserve Board, and Dr. Leo S. Rowe, the secretary general. In planning sessions before the Buenos Aires meeting, McAdoo ranked improvements in credit and transportation as "the paramount questions."[72]

Meanwhile, economic conditions in Argentina, Brazil, and Chile steadily improved. Although reductions in coal shipments from Great Britain caused problems in Argentina and Brazil, stockpiling and importation from the United States provided some measure of relief. In Brazil, a conversion to fuel oil from Mexico made power possible in mills and factories. In Argentina, the inauguration of a large, modern, meat-processing plant, the Frigorífico Armour de la Plata, a subsidiary of Armour and Company in the United States, occasioned public celebrations, and in Chile, the resumption of nitrate sales overseas for fertilizer and munitions dissipated much of the misery. Meanwhile, Eduardo Carrasco Buscañán, the head of the Chilean trade delegation in the United States, intended to stir up business and also some interest among North American capitalists in establishing a chain of hotels in Chile to improve living conditions for commercial travelers.[73]

The questions of credit and finance retained great importance, but improvements had occurred. In August 1915, the Department of Commerce reported that "the first sale of any importance of Chilean nitrate," some 4,000 tons, had taken place in which the producers accepted payment in New York exchange. Although London previously had ranked as "the preferred exchange in the nitrate fields," the Department explained, "The war . . . made possible the exchange of bills on New York in payment of some nitrate purchases." The Brazilians, meanwhile, initiated a courtship of United States bankers in the International Corporation, hoping to arrange for the negotiation of a $25,000,000 loan. Ambassador Edwin Morgan voiced support for the project, pointing out "the desirability," both from the standpoint of "consolidating American political and commercial influence" and "strengthening the interests of the International Corporation." A great deal depended upon the success of the venture. As Morgan remarked, "If American financiers wish to lay the foundation upon which further financial operations . . . can be built, they must prove that they had come to assist that Government and that in cooperation with it they are looking for something beyond high interest and sure guarantees."[74] Additional signs of progress appeared by the end of the summer of 1915 by which time the National City Bank of New York had installed branches in Montevideo, Buenos Aires, Rio de Janeiro, Santos, São

Paulo, and Havana, and had plans to move into Panama. Meanwhile, the Commercial City Bank of Washington, D.C., had established an office in Panama, and other enterprises anticipated expansion into the region in the near future. An optimistic survey published in the *Bulletin* of the P.A.U. observed, "it would seem that North American exporters interested in the Latin American field will soon have but little to complain of in connection with banking facilities, and that the day of 'dollar exchange' throughout the Americas has arrived."[75]

The inadequacies of shipping facilities remained acute and placed the United States at a disadvantage. For years, European carriers had hauled the trade, and now the war either diverted them to other, more remunerative routes or kept them tied up in port. According to Consul General Alfred L. M. Gottschalk, four steamship lines before the war maintained regular service between New York and Rio de Janeiro. Since August 1914, the German-owned Hamburg-American Line had discontinued service, and the United States and Brazil Steamship Line gave up carrying passengers, leaving only the British-owned Lamport and Holt Line and the Brazilian-owned Lloyd-Brasileiro Line, both of which had taken to operating irregularly and on short notice. As a remedy, Gottschalk advised the institution of fast, dependable transportation by United States companies. Soon after, in August 1915, the Caribbean and Southern Steamship Company announced a schedule of regular sailings between New Orleans and the major port cities in Brazil and Argentina, and in September, a vessel of the W. R. Grace Company traveled southward from San Francisco through the Panama Canal to the South American east coast, heralding the possibility of a permanent route. As part of the preparedness campaign, the Wilson administration endorsed a commitment to the construction of a merchant marine, capable of transporting the trade and averting unwanted dependencies on foreign nations. Before an audience in Cleveland late in January 1916, President Wilson lamented earlier failures to pursue a policy consonant with the nation's needs and pledged his support for a solution. Meanwhile, to illustrate the dimensions of the problem, Gottschalk put together a historical review, showing that, although the number of North American vessels visiting Rio de Janeiro had fallen from 245 in 1860 to fifty-one in 1900 to three in 1911, the figures increased markedly to 117 in 1915, consisting mainly of schooners carrying coal from Newport News and Norfolk, Virginia. Unhappily, he noted, a large share returned home in ballast because they lacked the capacity to transport coffee, and freighters avoided this route because they could obtain better returns elsewhere.[76]

Nevertheless, indications pointed toward steady expansion. In the middle of January 1916, a Brazilian executive decree bestowed preferential tariff treatment upon United States products and manufactures in return for similar concessions for Brazilian commodities. The news from Santiago suggested that Chilean consumers had acquired a compelling taste for United States goods, a point underscored significantly by the plans of the South American Steamship Company to institute weekly runs between Chilean ports and the Panama Canal; and in Argentina, farm implements made in the United States had displaced "nearly all" of the formerly dominant British and German models.[77]

When the International High Commission finally assembled for its first meeting on 3 April 1916 in Buenos Aires, the signs of economic recovery provided reason for taking heart. A seven-member United States delegation, headed by McAdoo, made the trip, departing from Hampton Roads on 7 March aboard the armored cruiser, U.S.S. *Tennessee*. The itinerary called for ceremonial stops along the way at Port au Prince, Rio de Janeiro, and Montevideo. In Buenos Aires, social functions and festive occasions consumed a great deal of time. As remarked by Mabel Stimson, the ambassador's wife, "Poor Mr. McAdoo has come down to work and so have the rest of his band and the Argentine idea is to give them a party every afternoon and every evening—which if they attended would leave no time for work." At the conclusion, they returned home by traveling north along the west coast to Santiago, to Lima, where they provoked adverse publicity by precipitously fleeing a rumored outbreak of plague, to Panama, and finally on 5 May to Hampton Roads.[78]

The meeting of the International High Commission, though certainly a sign of readiness to explore the feasibility of achieving closer commercial ties and more uniform laws and practices, had more symbolic than substantive importance. The discussions ranged over a variety of issues, many of them technical and complex—for example, customs regulations, patent and trademark laws, the rules for commercial travelers, and the arbitration of disputes. The main center of attention again fell on currency questions, finance, and transportation. The means of achieving more uniform currency exchange rates had occasioned sporadic conversations for twenty-five years. In this instance, the United States argued in favor of placing monies on account as the first step toward a stable system, while the Argentines, Bolivians, and Uruguayans more ambitiously preferred the creation of a common gold coin. These talks solved nothing and showed the difficulty of making much progress. The establishment of branch banks won endorsement with recommendations in favor of creating more of them.

In addition, the delegates agreed upon the need for better transportation but reasoned that only the United States had the resources for "the gigantic task" of providing carrying facilities independently of the Europeans and developing reliable service between ports in the United States and South America. As long-term goals, they expressed interest further in building a Pan American railway system and also in improving cable and telegraph communications everywhere in the western hemisphere.[79]

The meeting of the International High Commission marked the beginning of complex deliberations extending over the years into the 1930s. The advice and counsel handed down passed on to the participating governments but required no particular action. Nevertheless, this session captured some attention and prompted new visitations into Latin America by prominent groups of North American bankers and businessmen. In an effusive summary of the results, President Victorino de la Plaza of Argentina predicted as consequences "prolific . . . good for the nations of America" and stronger attachments to "the ties of race, sympathy and reciprocal interests that bind them and watch over the high destinies which human evolution has in store for the New World."[80]

THE DEMISE OF THE PAN AMERICAN PACT

The conversations over the proposed Pan American pact entered the final stage in the spring of 1916. Although the Wilson administration pressed hard, it achieved nothing, in large part because of difficulties with Carranza and dangers of war. Ironically, the Mexican problem first stimulated the interest in multilateral initiatives and then ruined it. The Chileans kept possibilities alive by responding at last to United States exhortations on 9 March with a note handed to Robert Lansing. They proposed to eliminate the problem of Tacna and Arica simply by omitting the second provision requiring arbitration. Coincidentally, early on the morning of the same day, Francisco Villa's attack across the border against Columbus, New Mexico, unsettled relations between the United States and Mexico and instilled an atmosphere of crisis. When the Wilson administration reacted by sending into Mexico military forces under the command of Brigadier General John J. Pershing, the consequences of reverting to unilateral act destroyed all hope for the successful negotiation of a treaty.[81]

The Chilean proposal dismayed the president and his aides. Rather than accept it, they prepared to go ahead without Chile but still hoped to bring the country around. Colonel House, meanwhile, attributed the failure to Lansing's ineptitude and to "the Germans and others interested in keeping the pact from materializing." Intending to take charge himself "regardless of Lansing's sensibilities," House called in Henry Fletcher for a special assignment. Recently retired from his post in Chile and newly designated as the ambassador to Mexico, Fletcher was well versed in the issue. He thought the real obstacle consisted of Eduardo Suárez Mújica, not the elected officials of Chile, and inadvertently reinforced some of House's misconceptions. House boasted in his diary, "When I first suggested the plan, I accomplished within a week nearly all the work that has been done so far. If I had had two weeks longer before going to Europe, and had not been handicapped by Bryan, I am reasonably sure it would have been finished by now." In a letter to Wilson, he claimed that able direction could produce the desired results within ten days.[82]

His assessment proved wrong. When after a week Fletcher could fashion no accord with the Chilean embassy, House wrote, "I read him the riot act" and insisted again upon the need for haste. In a note to Wilson, he conceded, "it would take longer than ten days, but that was the limit set for Fletcher." By the middle of April 1916, thirteen countries somewhat tentatively had expressed an interest in discussing the treaty, including Argentina and Brazil. Somewhat later, House learned that Brazil intended to aid in the cause by inducing Chile "to come into line." House grasped at straws, fantasizing in a conversation with Wilson that Lord Grey might provide the necessary boost by announcing his support of the Pan American pact. In reply, the president inquired how the proposed treaty could guarantee "under republican forms of government" the territorial possessions in the western hemisphere of the British monarchy? The presentation of still another draft on 27 April by the Brazilians kept negotiations going. After some modification, this version limited the guarantee of territorial integrity to "present undisputed territorial possessions" and the arbitration provision to "questions that may arise in the future." But even these terms went too far to suit the Chileans, and the Argentines also developed misgivings.[83] The reasons centered on Mexico.

The administration's hopes for a Pan American pact disintegrated in June 1916 because of complications brought on by the punitive expedition. During the early stages, the movement of Pershing's troops across the border set off a legalistic debate between the United States and Carranza's government over the right of "hot pursuit" and other measures for policing the border and maintaining security. At cross purposes, Carranza wanted Pershing out of Mexico as soon as possible, while Wilson could make no such move without assurances against future violations. He also used the promise of withdrawal as a means of exerting some leverage over the future course of the Mexican Revolution. If Carranza really wanted to remove Pershing, he would have to make some commitments about the rights of foreigners and the status of property in Mexico. The controversy turned ugly when a stalemate developed. On 12 April 1916, a shoot-out at Parral, Chihuahua, pitted Mexican soldiers against United States cavalry, and on 21 June another clash at Carrizal brought the two countries to the verge of war.[84]

Seeking to head off a calamity, Argentina again took the lead, hoping to arrange mediation. In this effort to replay the aftermath of Veracruz, Ambassador Naón informally inquired of Carranza whether he would welcome such an offer, and the First Chief in this instance responded that he would regard it as a sign of "friendly solidarity." Although abandoning his earlier position that any form of outside involvement in Mexican affairs would amount to intervention, he insisted, nevertheless, that the process must focus exclusively on the removal of Pershing's army, the only legitimate object. He would not permit mediation to extend to other subjects. Soon afterward, Peru, Honduras, El Salvador, and Costa Rica proffered their good offices, and Argentina, Brazil, Chile, Bolivia, and Ecuador participated in an attempt to organize joint action.[85] Leaders in the Wilson administration, meanwhile, nervously looked on, contemplating the prospect of full-scale intervention in stark recognition, as Lansing observed, that any such act would strike "all Latin America" as "extremely distasteful" and "might have a very bad effect upon our Pan-American program." If conditions should worsen, Lansing advised against using the term "intervention" and proposed instead to justify the broader use of force on defensive grounds. The United States would have to argue that Mexico's incapacity to control its side of the border had compelled protective measures.[86]

The Wilson administration on this occasion spurned the multilateral approach and chose instead to address the issues one-on-one with Mexico. In all likelihood, the leaders saw no clear advantage in accepting the mediation offer and may have feared that the involvement of other countries would divert and distract the United States and weaken its hand. Rather than run such risks in an election year, the president and his advisers put the blame for the crisis exclusively on Mexico and insisted that nothing in the circumstances warranted mediation by other powers. Mexico's failure to safeguard the border had required the United States to exercise the attributes of sovereignty and to do the job itself. The United States preferred bilateral negotiations while maintaining the punitive expedition in Mexico as an incentive and proposed not to retire the force prematurely. An opportunity to resolve the difficulty appeared when Carranza signaled his readiness by releasing the prisoners taken at Carrizal and then consenting to Secretary Lansing's proposal. The United States and Mexico would wrestle with the problem of border security and related matters through the creation of a joint Mexican-American commission.[87]

The ensuing deliberations dragged on for five months and accomplished little, except the avoidance of war. The fault resided in some measure with the United States for trying to broaden the discussions to include the future goals of the Mexican Revolution. Wilson wanted peace along the border and also guarantees and assurances about the fate of United States citizens and their interests in Mexico. When Carranza resisted, the talks bogged down, and the United States decided in the end simply to liquidate the undertaking by withdrawing the punitive force. Wilson did so on 5 February 1917 without demanding a quid pro quo and while retaining a free hand, thus reserving to himself in the future the freedom to act.[88]

The long wrangle with Mexico, nevertheless, had destructive effects upon the Pan American treaty by instilling an atmosphere of tension and uncertainty and by raising doubts about the president's good faith. The reversion to unilateral measures reinforced misgivings in Chile and provoked apprehension in Argentina, where the newly elected government of Hipólito Yrigoyen soon would take office. This nationalistic and idiosyncratic regime, as it turned out, had little interest in identifying too closely with the United States and preferred to keep its distance. Although Brazil still professed readiness to carry on with the negotiations, the country by itself wielded insufficient influence, and the United States for its part became less enthusiastic after the break with Germany.[89] The Pan American treaty died aborning, the victim of wishful thinking, miscalculation, and outright refusal to take Chilean objections very seriously. For leaders in the Wilson administration, the self-evident virtue of promoting natural harmonies ought to suffice in overcoming all resistance. For Latin Americans, in contrast, ambivalence over the consequences of too fond an embrace accounted for the reluctance. The implications for them never appeared quite so clear.

COMMERCIAL EXPECTATIONS:
THE PARIS ECONOMIC CONFERENCE AND AFTER

In spite of the political complexities, the economic effects of the war still favored the United States. The trade abroad had increased immensely, and observers wondered what would happen with the reestablishment of peace. In a speech on 25 May 1916 before the Southern Wholesale Grocers' Association in Memphis, Dr. E. E. Pratt, chief of the Bureau of Foreign and Domestic Trade, addressed the question and gave an optimistic response. He claimed that the real significance resided in the expansion of trade in countries outside the war zone. As he observed, "Our trade to Europe . . . has increased but it is more important . . . that our trade with countries only indirectly affected by the war has increased, and that that increase has been a very considerable one." Indeed, he proclaimed, the United States enjoyed an unprecedented prosperity and that the restoration of more normal conditions in Europe probably would not affect it too adversely.[90]

The statistical patterns in South America bore out his claim by showing impressive gains. Coal exports to Argentina got steadily larger, but a shortage of bottoms and high freight costs posed a problem. One consular report proposed a solution by urging that British vessels, rather than set out in ballast for Argentine ports to obtain grain, should first pick up coal in the United States and carry it southward in a triangular trade. Other reports showed large advances in selling machinery and machine tools. In Brazil, meanwhile, the incorporation of an American Chamber of Commerce in Rio de Janeiro with Ambassador Morgan as the honorary president testified to a persistent interest. Late in the summer, Brazilian leaders, still vexed by financial difficulties, announced their intention of seeking a $25,000,000 loan in the United States, where, conversely, the output of Brazilian manganese increasingly sparked attention. In Chile, the National City Bank of New York opened a branch in Valparaíso early in October; about the same time, the Guaranty Trust Company of New York closed a deal to buy $471,000 in bonds from the Water Board of the same city. The Commerce Department, meanwhile, confirmed that the value of United States foreign trade at the end of the fiscal year on 30 June 1926 indeed exceeded $6,500,000,000.[91]

A worrisome development then took place. At the Paris Economic Conference during 14–17 June 1916, Allied leaders laid plans for waging economic war against the Central Powers and for restoring the essentials of a mercantilist, state-directed system during the reconstruction period after the peace. Outright discrimination to deny commercial opportunities would characterize the treatment of the former enemies. Acting on the assumption that economic rivalries had contributed significantly to the onset of the war, the leadership among the Entente nations proposed to make sure that Germany and Austria-Hungary could not amass resources in preparation for any future war by substituting trade preferences and other restrictive measures for the unconditional, most-favored-nation policy that had typified European trade from 1870 until 1914. In part a reaction against the Central Powers' "*Mittel Europa*" plan of 1915 to consolidate the region

and exclude the British, French, and Russians, the Allies now called for
state subsidies, prohibitory practices, and other forms of direct involvement by governments in developing and maintaining foreign
markets. Pooling agreements, cooperative purchases of raw materials,
and concerted efforts to constrict the shipping of the defeated nations
could well become commonplaces in the postwar world.[92]

Although the Allies disclaimed any wish to damage neutral interests, including those of the United States, the Wilson administration,
nevertheless, reacted with concern over the possible ramifications.
Robert Lansing sounded the warning in a letter to President Wilson on
23 June, in which he reported that the Allies intended to employ drastic
measures against their antagonists during the war in an effort to
strangle commerce and industry, a legitimate aim, and also to prevent
recovery afterwards. The latter worried Lansing on the grounds that it
would make the negotiation of a satisfactory peace all the more difficult
and might even deter the Central Powers from entertaining the possibility. As for the neutrals "both now and after the war," Lansing
thought, "the intentions of the Allied Powers are disquieting and . . .
should receive very careful consideration." He cautioned, "We neutrals
. . . will have to face a commercial combination which has as its avowed
purpose preferential treatment for its members." Because of the in-
herent strength derived from "colonies and great merchant marines,"
Lansing feared the development of "a serious, if not critical, situation
for the nations outside the union by creating unusual and artificial
economic conditions." Since individual neutrals could do little in response, he advised united action, "some definite plan to meet the
proposed measure of the allies"; as he noted, "the best way to fight
combination is by combination."[93]

Others in the administration appraised the threat somewhat differently. In an address late in October before the annual meeting of the
American Manufacturers' Export Association, Dr. E. E. Pratt of the
Bureau of Foreign and Domestic Commerce anticipated the possibility
that each set of belligerents might constitute an economic bloc in the
postwar era, in which case "the neutral nations" would occupy "a
peculiar position." Although he expected that neither side would bestow most-favored-nation treatment upon the United States, he foresaw no blatant discrimination either. But still, he noted, "these
economic alliances and their possible effect upon the future trade of
the United States must be seriously considered." He wanted flexible
tariff schedules to function as "an aid in building trade" and to obtain
"the maximum advantage" in bargaining. He also wanted legislative
action to overcome confining antitrust laws and to permit "our manufacturers to combine for the purpose of developing foreign trade."

He calculated that "This will put our manufacturers on a basis similar to that of the manufacturers and exporters of other countries and will enable us perhaps more than any other one thing to meet effectively the growing centralization of economic resources in Europe."[94]

Taking up similar issues in the middle of November, Ambassador Henry Fletcher advised in favor of reaching some understanding with the South American republics, particularly the A.B.C. countries, in order to guarantee the gains since 1914. As he told Colonel House, he thought it imperative to hold "our market position in South America." Although Fletcher doubted very much whether "any European Economic alliance could be a workable arrangement," he thought it best, nevertheless, "to be on the safe side" and propagate the Pan American ideal as "a tangible, practical and vital thing." If the Allied nations should seek preferential tariff treatment "in the great consuming markets of South America" after the war, the United States then would have to arrange "with as many as possible of the American Republics mutually to protect our respective tariff positions." Fletcher estimated that the United States admitted 95 percent of the raw materials imported from South America duty free, including cocoa, coffee, rubber, hides, wool, copper, tin, and nitrate of soda. To conserve this "great and practically free market," he advised, if necessary, the creation of "an American Economic League for mutual protection."[95]

The Great World War became ascendant over the affairs of the western hemisphere in most things during the early months of 1917 when the United States first ruptured diplomatic ties with the German Empire and then issued a declaration of war. Henceforth, the Wilson administration largely would subordinate its aims and ambitions in Latin America to the exigencies of wartime demands. For the duration, the leaders wanted to avoid diversions and distractions at home and to keep things as quiet as possible among their neighbors. Consequently, political integration took on negative connotations, suggesting not so much a model for the Europeans after the war as a reprieve from police obligations so that the United States could work its will unhindered among the Europeans. Though political organization within the region remained an issue, the focus increasingly centered on how to achieve it within the larger context of a global system. Economic integration, in contrast, had advanced markedly between 1914 and 1917 but now confronted the Wilson administration with a dilemma. While seeking to cooperate in winning the war as an associated power with the Allied nations, the United States also intended to safeguard the trade in Latin America against any renewal of European competition in the future. The stresses and strains tugged at the Wilson administration until the armistice and beyond.

CHAPTER THREE

The Effects of Waging War

February 1917–November 1918

THE ENTRY OF THE UNITED STATES INTO THE GREAT WAR diverted primary attention away from Latin America but resulted in important effects within the western hemisphere. The leaders in the Wilson administration seized upon the opportunity to strengthen their position through consolidation. Regional integration remained a vital interest out of concern for short- and long-term purposes. The United States wanted no distractions while engaged in Europe and hoped to obtain the requisite forms of political and economic support. At the same time, officials in Washington never fully identified with the Allies' war aims and objectives and looked toward an independent role in determining the shape of the postwar world. To such ends, the president and his advisers attempted to cultivate a doctrine of Pan American solidarity, among other reasons to ward off any restoration of a large-scale European presence after the peace. The very nature of Great Power relationships facilitated such an aim during the war. The Europeans' preoccupation with the fighting weakened their strategic impact upon the New World and debilitated the traditional Latin American ploy of invoking continental influence as a counterpoise against the United States. Nevertheless, maneuvers and machinations all during the war maintained intimations of rivalry and cross purpose. Moreover, Mexico and Argentina flirted with Pan Hispanic alternatives, and Brazil, as a consequence, more than ever became the pivot of Wilson's policy in South America. The United States wanted a solid base from which to secure its hold in the future.

Five Battleships Ordered—A Few More Supports for the Nest. Reprinted from the *Philadelphia Inquirer*, 1903. Sentiments were similar in 1917.

THE BREAK IN DIPLOMATIC TIES

The break in diplomatic ties following the German resumption of unrestricted submarine warfare on 1 February 1917 emanated from profound miscalculations. By opting for a quick decision through the exercise of decisive boldness, German leaders under the spell of Field Marshall Paul von Hindenberg repudiated the more discreet prescriptions of Chancellor Theobald von Bethmann-Hollweg and ran a considered risk of confrontation with the United States. The revocation of the *Sussex* pledge of May 1916 meant that Allied merchant ships and passenger liners once again became the objects of attack. Even though President Wilson had warned against such measures, the Germans took the gamble, assuming that Great Britain would succumb before the onslaught more rapidly than any reaction by the United States could make a difference. In any event, they reasoned, the loans of private bankers already had created an informal alliance with the Entente nations, but, significantly, it lacked any foundation in military power, a fact demonstrated, presumably, by the abortive punitive expedition into Mexico. Such errors in estimate resulted in a faulty appraisal of the chances of success and the danger of driving the United States into intransigeance.[1]

Wilson severed diplomatic relations on 3 February 1917 more as an appeal for wisdom and rationality than as a preliminary for war. Hoping to give to the Germans some reason for sober pause, he wanted them to evaluate again the probable consequences of their acts. A State Department circular on the same day explained that the circumstances left "no alternative" except to persist in the course set forth in the note to the German government on 18 April 1916 during the *Sussex* crisis. The United States would terminate official relations but left open the possibility of an accommodation if the Germans should change their minds. The dispatch emphasized Wilson's unreadiness to believe that actual attacks against neutral commerce would take place but cautioned that the president, if necesssary, would "ask from Congress authority to use national power to protect American citizens engaged in peaceable and lawful errands on the high seas." To achieve full effect, the note also urged other neutrals to break relations in order to impress upon Germany the gravity of the decision upon which might depend "the peace of the world."[2]

The U-boat offensive also posed dilemmas for Latin American governments, requiring them to decide whether and to what extent they would follow Woodrow Wilson's lead in opposing the renunciation of the *Sussex* pledge. The first reactions in Latin America, though mixed, generally offered support in principle, especially among those countries with closest ties to the United States. Four of the protectorates—Cuba, Panama, Haiti, and Nicaragua—offered "cordial approval," "cooperation," and readiness to take more official responses whenever deemed "advisable" by the United States. Brazil similarly vowed to resist the German use of the submarine. Emphasizing that "Pan America must stand together," the government in Rio de Janeiro suggested that "concerted action" with "certain South-American powers" might have good effects. Elsewhere in South America, the authorities in Bolivia, Ecuador, Peru, and Venezuela condemned the German violation of neutral rights as illegal and illegitimate but hesitated to threaten a break in relations. Colombia, in contrast, still aggrieved over the loss of Panama, reportedly feared an invasion of its territory if the United States should feel compelled to safeguard the approach ways to the canal.[3]

The sense of mounting crisis necessarily heightened sensibilities within the Wilson administration over the possibility of German encroachments in the western hemisphere. Rumors and other unconfirmed reports of German submarines in the Caribbean particularly disturbed Robert Lansing, who issued a directive on 6 February 1917 urging upon diplomatic representatives the need for vigilance, accuracy, and verification. On the same day, President Wilson expressed concern over the security issue, reflecting upon the disconcerting nature of Cuban vulnerability. He wondered whether "It might be to Germany's advantage . . . to declare war on Cuba (or make it without declaring it) before taking action against us. A base for her submarines on this side of the sea would be most convenient." To avoid any pretext, Lansing advised the Cuban government against a rupture in diplomatic ties for the present. In the case of Panama, apprehensions also existed over the safety of the canal, but the government solemnly gave assurances "faithfully" of carrying out its obligations.[4]

During the next week, the State Department focused special attention as usual upon Argentina, Brazil, and Chile. Brazil, the most receptive, endorsed President Wilson's position as correct, refused to recognize the German submarine blockade as valid and effective, and placed upon Germany "the responsibility for all incidents" in violation of international law. The traditional "unwritten alliance" still held, providing a bond with the United States out of a sense of economic interdependence and the abiding mistrust of Argentina. The diplomatic dispatches out of Rio de Janeiro early in April indicated a large magnitude of friendly sentiment toward the United States—for example, as expressed by the formation of a patriotic organization known as the *Liga de Defensa Nacional*. The chargé d'affaires, Alexander Benson, counted upon it to mobilize political support. According to him, "The situation is . . . conducive to a strengthening of a pro-Ally, and naturally pro-American, feeling in Brazil, since it cannot be doubted that such a feeling is predominant among the better classes of this country." Sales and purchases established a network of links in which the United States also possessed a vital stake. As Robert Lansing observed, about 80 percent of the manganese used by his country in the manufacture of steel came from Brazil, and he urged special precautions from the government in defense of it. Produced in a region in Minas Gerais inhabited by Germans, the ore moved by railroad over three hundred miles of track susceptible to sabotage. Lansing would allow for no interruptions.[5]

The government of Chile also took a principled stand, affirming its commitments in defense of "the general rights of neutrality and the high purposes of world peace" but reticently eschewed threats and stridency. Chilean leaders wanted no trouble with either the Allies or the Central Powers. President Sanfuentes explained the matter forthrightly in a private conversation with the new ambassador, Joseph Shea, a former judge and a political appointment: Chile, a small country, had little importance in the geopolitics of the global struggle and little significance in the calculations of the Great Powers. According to the president, Chile favored international law and morality, but the country's very lack of stature dictated the necessity of remaining neutral. When Shea took exception, arguing the case that the defense of neutral rights required a break, Sanfuentes reminded him that Chile had no quarrel with Germany to warrant such a course. No Chilean vessels had come under attack, and Germany had made no promises to Chile about the conduct of submarine warfare. Shea later attributed Sanfuentes's extreme caution to the existence of German influence within the Chilean army and business community and cautioned the leaders in the Wilson administration against expecting too much.[6]

The Argentine government most ostentatiously spurned United States' recommendations. Early indications appeared on 5 February, when *La Prensa* printed an editorial, indeed, a manifesto, in which the former foreign minister, Estanislao S. Zeballos, exhorted the Argentines to recognize that recent developments in the Great War required them to act "with prudent vigilance, discretion, and tact in order to reconcile their rights and interests . . . with the duties of honorable and scrupulous neutrality." Advising against "sentimentality" and "fantasy," Zeballos insisted on "the greatest unity of action," while giving thanks for the failure of the Pan American Pact. Otherwise, he feared, Woodrow Wilson might have presented himself as the spokesman for the western hemisphere and insisted that the A.B.C. countries follow his lead in any impending declaration of war. Zeballos would not sanction such an outcome, since in his view the defense of commercial and mercantile interests, not neutral rights, had determined President Wilson's behavior, and Argentina possessed no reciprocal obligation to adhere.[7]

Uncertainty unsettled the United States embassy in Buenos Aires. During the preceding summer, the outgoing president, Victorino de la Plaza, had talked pointedly with Ambassador Stimson about the need for friendly relations, but the climate shifted with the inauguration of Hipólito Yrigoyen on 12 October 1916. Stimson complained of confusion and disorganization in the Foreign Office, especially early in February 1917 after the resignation of Foreign Minister Carlos Becú, regarded in some quarters as pro-German. Honorio Pueyrredón, the minister of agriculture, assumed the acting role. Though thought to be pro-British—he once had taken his family to England for the birth of a son—he showed no disposition to deviate from neutrality once established in the Foreign Office. As he explained, Argentina had lost neither lives nor cargos to the Germans and felt no need for strong measures. When Stimson suggested a forceful note of protest against submarine warfare, Pueyrredón held that such a move would appear unfriendly if carried out in concert with other neutrals. Mabel Stimson, the ambassador's wife, appraised official attitudes correctly, noting the uselessness of hoping that the Argentines would break off relations. "They need their German trade and it would be much to expect of them. There are so *many* influential Germans." Observing a personal dimension, she lamented the possibility of losing "about half of my Argentine friends for at least half are German by descent and sentiment and often they are the very nicest."[8]

To achieve clarification, Ambassador Stimson obtained an interview with Yrigoyen on 8 February. In an aide-mémoire presented in Spanish, Stimson explained the reasons for the United States' break in relations and then listened at some length while Yrigoyen expounded upon Argentine neutrality. As set forth on the following day in a note to Germany, the Argentine government felt distress over Germany's adoption of "extreme measures" but promised "as always" to behave in conformance with "the fundamental principles . . . of international law." Yrigoyen expressed no wish for a break in relations. Stimson, a prim Bostonian, somewhat ambivalently perceived Yrigoyen as an uncultured and unpredictable political curiosity. Other observers remarked that the president, though an adroit practitioner of mass politics, never gave speeches, and though appreciative of the title "Dr.," never finished his degree. His idiosyncrasies abounded. Reclusive and secluded in his habits, he acquired among his constituents an affectionate nickname, "El Peludo," referring to "a hairy kind of subterranean armadillo." Although he produced over a dozen children, he never married. Shortly before he took office as president. Stimson wondered whether he would dignify his station by taking a wife. On another occasion, Stimson compared him with Thomas Jefferson, claiming that "both in manners and in politics . . . he is distinctly a radical, and starts with the idea that everything should be changed." Pugnacious and parochial in his outlook, Yrigoyen preferred to hew to his own course independently of the United States.[9]

Also a neutral, Mexico caused special concern within the Wilson administration. Although the withdrawal of the Pershing punitive expedition on 5 February 1917 eliminated one source of trouble, the promulgation of a new constitution on the same day introduced another. This document, the Constitution of 1917, incorporated radical provisions, notably Article Twenty-Seven, and engendered a sense of profound threat among North Americans by authorizing the nationalization of mineral resources and the expropriation of private property. Since leaders in the Wilson administration would sanction neither claim, the issue ignited a long dispute over the status of foreign-owned petroleum lands in Mexico.[10] The Carranza regime's distaste for the United States also produced apprehension. As Robert Lansing recalled, Carranza's attitude manifested "suspicion and repressed hostility." Lansing characterized the Mexican president as "obstinate" and "defiant," ever ready to utilize "the popular antipathy for Americans as a politcal asset." Carranza refused "all overtures by this government to render him friendly assistance." Nevertheless, the Wilson administration bore the affronts. The involvement in the war meant that "it was no time for a break with this impossible old man." According to Lansing, "We had to swallow our pride to maintain as good relations as possible." The chance of a Mexican-German alignment worried them constantly, constituting, as Lansing noted, "a reasonable doubt" over the actuality of Mexican neutrality.[11]

A diplomatic initiative on 11 February 1917 created further distance from the United States. In a note "inspired by the most high humanitarian sentiments," Carranza called upon all of the neutrals to halt the European carnage through a collective offer of mediation. If the belligerent nations should refuse to take part, he proposed a resort to economic persuasion, specifically, an embargo on trade designed, among other things, to keep the conflagration from spreading. By refusing economic intercourse, he would deny to the warring nations, in Mexico's instance, the export of oil, and, to achieve the aim, he insisted upon unanimity. Since no single neutral possessed sufficient influence, he wanted broad participation by Argentina, Brazil, Chile, Spain, Sweden, Norway, and the United States.[12] Although the plan went beyond the bounds of Pan Americanism, it retained vestiges but differed markedly from Wilson's call for a break in relations.

Responses in Latin America indicated some measure of interest in following the Mexican proposal by sponsoring a conference among neutral states. The idea particularly took hold in Argentina, where newspaper editorials asked rhetorically why Argentines should "imitate" the United States, especially since Wilson had never asked them for any advice. As *La Razón* remarked, "We belonged to the lesser gods." When Ecuador suggested Montevideo as a possible site, the State Department reacted coolly, promising to give the notion "attentive consideration," but Wilson showed more favor. In an inquiry of Robert Lansing, he asked, "Might it not be a good thing (if not for the situation in the world at large, at least for the situation in the Americas) to acquiesce in the plan and take part in a conference such as is proposed?" By his reasoning, such a course might serve "to shoulder out any sinister influence now at work in Latin America. . . . It is the psychology of the thing, chiefly, that I have in mind, rather than any concrete result it might accomplish."[13] But other considerations came into play. On 3 March, Ambassador Stimson reported on the basis of "trustworthy information" that not much would come of a conference, probably nothing more than "the expression of a desire for peace." He detected little enthusiasm in Brazil and Chile. On 7 March, Robert Lansing emphatically recommended against taking part because, as he phrased it, "Conditions have materially changed." His words, in all likelihood, referred to the disclosure of the Zimmermann telegram. As he told Wilson, "Unless you feel there is something to be gained I will advise . . . that in view of present conditions the endorsement of the proposed Congress of Neutrals by this Government might be misinterpreted and cause division of opinion among American republics."[14]

The Zimmermann revelation raised disturbing questions and intensified fear of German ambitions in the western hemisphere. Rumors and allegations circulated constantly during the war years and unquestionably had some basis in fact. In the spring of 1915, for example, German agents engaged Victoriano Huerta in a conspiracy aimed at restoring the deposed leader to power in Mexico and provoking as much trouble for the United States as possible. Though agents of the Justice Department kept close watch and foiled the scheme late in June by taking Huerta into custody at Newman, New Mexico, the audacious display set sensitivities on edge. The Germans developed a compelling interest in using Mexico as a means of diverting United States' power and resources away from Europe. A war or an intervention on the southern flank could serve German purposes nicely by reducing or eliminating the United States' capacity to play a determining role in the Great War. Such a prospect animated enthusiasm once again early in 1917 when German leaders chose to set loose the U-boats. Foreign Minister Arthur Zimmermann especially wanted to occupy Wilson with Mexico. To such an end, a plan took shape for instigating a Mexican attack across the border, the consequences of which might tie down the United States indefinitely. Planners in the Foreign Office—for example, Hans Arthur Kemnitz, a Latin American specialist—believed that the failure of the punitive expedition illustrated the incapacities of the United States Army and allowed reasons for confidence. Mexican irregulars in the borderlands could provide more than an even match. Overall, the notion smacked of fantasy and delusion. It also implied a low appraisal of Carranza. Seen as impetuous and impulsive, the Mexican president presumably would take the bait once tempted, unable either to resist the lure or to calculate the risk when presented with an opportunity to regain Texas, Arizona, and New Mexico. Although the Germans wanted also to offer financial and military aid in support of the enterprise, they had neither the means nor the intention of providing it.[15]

False and arrogant assumptions resulted in a grand fiasco, the cause of much embarrassment for Germany and also graver difficulties with the United States. Contrary to expectations, Carranza showed no amenability toward manipulation. Indeed, he contrived his methods cunningly and displayed no willingness to put himself in service to the Germans without an equivalent advantage. To be sure, he had courted German support earlier in 1916, seeking a form of leverage while Pershing remained in Mexico. But with the departure, a primary incentive vanished, and Carranza, neither a fool nor a naif, wanted to give no excuse for inviting a return. The Germans also erred by failing to take into account the British secret service. The interception and decipherment of the Zimmermann telegram constitutes a classic spy story, told most fully and accurately by the historian Friedrich Katz.

Zimmermann's message, designated for transmission to Heinrich von Eckhardt, the German minister in Mexico City, contained both an announcement and offer and took final form in the Foreign Office on 15 January 1917:

WE INTEND TO BEGIN UNLIMITED U-BOAT WARFARE ON FEBRUARY 1. ATTEMPTS WILL NONETHELESS BE MADE TO KEEP AMERICA NEUTRAL.

IN THE EVENT THAT WE FAIL IN THIS EFFORT, WE PROPOSE AN ALLIANCE WITH MEXICO ON THE FOLLOWING BASIS: JOINT PURSUIT OF THE WAR, JOINT CONCLUSION OF PEACE. SUBSTANTIAL FINANCIAL SUPPORT AND AN AGREEMENT ON OUR PART FOR MEXICO TO RECONQUER ITS FORMER TERRITORIES IN TEXAS, NEW MEXICO, AND ARIZONA.

YOUR EXCELLENCY SHALL PRESENT THE ABOVE TO THE PRESIDENT IN THE STRICTEST SECRECY AS SOON AS WAR WITH THE UNITED STATES HAS BROKEN OUT, WITH THE ADDITIONAL SUGGESTION OF OFFERING JAPAN IMMEDIATE ENTRY TO THE ALLIANCE AND SIMULTANEOUSLY SERVING AS MEDIATORS BETWEEN US AND JAPAN.

PLEASE INFORM PRESIDENT THAT UNLIMITED USE OF OUR U-BOATS NOW OFFERS POSSIBILITY OF FORCING ENGLAND TO NEGOTIATE PEACE WITHIN A FEW MONTHS.

CONFIRM RECEIPT. ZIMMERMANN.[16]

The gambit miscarried in every aspect. The singular inclusion of Japan, for example, provoked derision in Tokyo, where, after the publication, the Japanese Foreign Office described the association as the product of German "mental delusions." Communications with Mexico City also posed a problem. Zimmermann initially intended to send the invitation aboard the U-boat *Deutschland*, but the Atlantic crossing required thirty days and would have delayed receipt until the middle of February, too late for the commencement of submarine warfare at the first of the month. Zimmermann, therefore, transmitted it in code by wireless from Nauen and also by telegraph through facilities acquired from the Swedish diplomatic service and the United

States Department of State. The message passed undetected through Washington, D.C., but not past British agents, who destroyed the intrigue by intercepting and decoding the transmissions and then turning over the information to Ambassador Walter Hines Page in London.

According to Friedrich Katz's most exact rendition, the traditional versions, first provided by Sir Reginald Hall, a principal actor as the chief intelligence officer in the Royal Navy, and later published by Burton J. Hendrick and Sir William James, contained some misleading inaccuracies. Katz corrects them by showing that the message originally went out from Berlin in a most secret code then unknown to the British. Fortuitously for them, Eckhard, the minister in Mexico, possessed no key, and Count Johann von Bernstorff, the ambassador in Washington, "had to decode and recode it in the old book," thereby permitting the British the means of solution. An agent in Mexico City picked up the relay in the old code from Washington, and, according to Katz's source, this intercept became "a kind of Rosetta Stone" for unlocking the puzzle. Good spy to the end, Sir Reginald Hall never revealed his knowledge of the whole truth.[17]

The publication of the telegram in the newspapers on 1 March 1917 produced a sensation in the United States. For Woodrow Wilson, it appeared as irrefutable proof of German duplicity and strengthened his resolve to deal firmly with the adversary. Already he had asked Congress for authority to arm merchant ships, but a problem emerged when critics, suspicious of a possible forgery, raised questions about the authenticity. Wilson could not tell them how he got the document without revealing to the Germans the capabilities of British intelligence, but then Zimmermann himself remarkably solved the difficulty by confessing to his act before the Reichstag on 3 March. To make matters worse, things also went awry in Mexico City. Although Carranza in all probability no longer seriously considered an alignment with Germany, the premature publicity must have dissipated any lingering hopes. For Carranza, an adroit practitioner of the diplomatic arts, the threat of lining up with Germany always had more utility vis-à-vis the United States than the actuality. Although the Germans persisted subsequently in pursuing an accord for several months, the Mexican president held back because of his primary interest in defending his nation against further interference by the United States.[18]

The Zimmermann episode nevertheless whetted a taste for conspiracy and machination, and apprehension abounded in the reports of the diplomats. Preston M. Goodwin, the United States minister in Venezuela, warned that Mexico "is very active in trying to stir up strife between the United States and Latin American Governments," and in Rome, Ambassador Thomas Nelson Page claimed that only firmness south of the border could counter German moves. For him, "the question is no longer confined within the limits of a local revolution but becomes one which may strike at the very base of the Monroe Doctrine." Page had become "profoundly convinced that Germany was working before the war to get a foothold in Mexico, as well as in other Southern Republics" and "that since the war broke out . . . has done everything in her power to carry out this work much more actively than before."[19]

Similar concerns centered attention on Cuba and Panama, both protectorates of the United States. On 26 March, Robert Lansing raised the question, asking what those countries should do in the event of a war declaration by the United States? Anticipating trouble if they remained neutral, he favored a hard line, reasoning that "we cannot permit Cuba to become a place for plots and intrigues not only against this country but against the peace of Cuba." He worried particularly about "the possibility of submarine bases, the organization of reservists, the use of cables . . . which would be . . . very serious and possibly disastrous." In addition, after recalling that United States Marines had gone into Cuba earlier that year, he pointed out, "if Cuba remained neutral, we could not use her ports for our war vessels and that might result in a renewal of the rebellious activities in the Island, which would be abetted by the Germans there." If the United States went to war, Lansing insisted, Cuba would have to follow, and "we ought to be prepared to tell them exactly what we want."[20]

Lansing wanted Panama to do the same. He could see no reason to let "Germans to be at liberty to go and come so near the Canal." Although he preferred to expel them, he recognized that the situation there "is not so easy to handle as the Government is less amenable." By whatever means, Panama would have to abandon neutrality, and President Wilson concurred in the view. As he remarked, "It is clear to me that the only thing we can prudently do is urge both Cuba and Panama to do just what we do." Worries over clandestine German activities persisted throughout the war. Indeed, when the United States became a participant, the State Department requested the aid of private businesses, notably W. R. Grace and Company, the International Banking Corporation, United States Steel Products Company, the National City Bank, the West Indian Oil Company, and the United Fruit Company. Reports in August 1917 showed that at least W. R. Grace cooperated by removing "from positions of responsibility and authority in several of their Houses . . . persons of German birth or sympathies, this to insure that the conduct of the business may be free from any influence possibly detrimental to the interests of the United States at this time."[21]

The possibility of a conference among neutral states, meanwhile, generated interest in Argentina and Mexico, and increasingly annoyed leaders in the Wilson administration. For some of them, Frederick Stimson bore the responsibility. Because of health problems with chronic bronchitis and other afflictions, Stimson had experienced difficulty keeping Yrigoyen in line. Lansing suspected that the ambassador had "broken down nervously" and suggested the possiblity of relieving him. But Brazil and then Chile provided reassurance by expressing their disinclination to go along with the Argentine initiative among the neutrals. On 12 March, da Gama told Frank Polk that his country would endorse the United States in a declaration of war. The State Department also withheld sanction from the Mexican call for mediation. On 16 March, Robert Lansing explained that German violations of law and morality and the Zimmermann outrage disallowed participation. A subsequent offer from Carranza "confidentially" and "unofficially" to employ Mexico's good offices in restoring diplomatic relations with Germany accomplished nothing. On 2 April 1917, President Wilson made the breach final by asking a joint session of Congress for a declaration of war. He obtained it four days later. For the remainder of his term in office, Latin America occupied a subordinate place in his conduct of foreign relations but retained important implications.[22]

THE ENTRY INTO THE WAR

The entry into the war precipitated sympathetic but diverse responses in Latin America. Most governments applauded the United States for defending neutral rights but, otherwise, reacted according to distinctive sets of concerns and aspirations. Within two weeks, ten countries declared neutrality, among them: Argentina, Chile, Colombia, Costa Rica, Mexico, Paraguay, Peru, El Salvador, Uruguay, and Venezuela. Seven nations broke relations: Bolivia, Brazil, the Dominican Republic, Ecuador, Guatemala, Haiti, and Honduras. Two declared war, Cuba and Panama, followed later in 1917 by Brazil, Costa Rica, Guatemala, Haiti, Honduras, and Nicaragua. Although John Barrett of the Pan American Union bravely asserted that "the public sentiment of Latin America as a whole is overwhelmingly with the United States," the actual policy decisions in each country entailed complicated calculations about relative advantage and the nature of the national interest.[23]

Brazil, among the first, severed diplomatic and commercial ties with Germany on 6 April 1917, an act provoked by an incident three days earlier. On 3 April, a German U-boat near Cherbourg attacked and sank without warning the Brazilian steamer *Paraná*. The ensuing public clamor directed criticism against Foreign Minister Lauro Müller for his German ancestry and resulted in some rioting. At Porto Alegre in Rio Grande do Sul, street crowds shouted "morras" (death) to Germany and fired gunshots into the Hotel Schmidt. The government, meanwhile, hewed closely to the United States and mounted a surprise in exhuming interest in the Pan American Pact. On 7 April, da Gama told of his government's readiness to sign, and Frank Polk, the counselor, reacted with favor. "In view of the very friendly attitude of Brazil and some other Latin American countries, it might be just as well to line up our friends at this time, and probably several of the governments not so friendly would sign rather than be left out." But Lansing perceived a danger. "It is just possible that the Brazilian Government would like to use the treaty as another excuse for declaring war against Germany." He doubted the efficacy of forming an alliance. Any such act would embarrass Argentina and might also draw some of the smaller republics into the conflict, an outcome he regarded as undesirable because "we might have to aid them." Mistrust of Argentina, no doubt, played a part in Brazil's move, and economic imperatives also held importance. Brazilian leaders feared economic isolation and further disruption of trade, onced the United States entered the war. To avert trouble, da Gama proposed a deal on 10 April, suggesting that Brazil guarantee 80 percent of the manganese production to the United States in return for coal and other necessary resources.[24]

The resurrection of the Pan American Treaty pleased President Wilson, but he wanted no embarrassment. Somewhat tentatively, he reasoned that "it would be well to go forward. . . . It might turn out to be the psychological moment, and the treaty might serve in part to show the European peoples a way to secure peace when the war is over." The idea of serving up a model retained appeal, but Wilson also wanted to consult with the Senate Foreign Relations Committee. The Brazilians then complicated the issue by adding more terms. In a proposed preamble to the pact, they wanted an affirmation of "common interest" among the American republics in maintaining "harmony and amity" for "the purpose of pledging mutual aid in the preservation of a continental system assuring them liberty, independence and autonomy in government." In addition, they wished to insert a four-point protocol. It would endorse as "a fundamental rule of conduct in international affairs" the principle of nonintervention in the political affairs of other states and also would stipulate that the guarantee of territorial

integrity and political independence should take effect only after a
formal request. The last two points upheld the de facto principle as the
guide in recognition policy and asked that the foregoing provisions
come under the ratification process.[25]

Brazil's aim in setting forth these amendments produced puzzlement and resistance. Frank Polk disliked them on grounds that acceptance would constrain the United States in its dealings with Mexico.
Moreover, he wondered, what could the United States do if another
country signed the treaty and then either openly or as an alleged
neutral sided with Germany? A similar issue concerned Robert Lansing. What if pro-Germans cut off the oil supply in Mexico or if German
nationals obtained bases in the western hemisphere? Lansing inquired
of Wilson, "Could we observe the territorial integrity of the nation
permitting this? Or could we do so if a Latin American country permitted its territory to become a refuge for Germans where they could
conspire and carry on their propaganda in this country and other
countries?" Possibly, he suggested, a limitation could reduce the danger by including in the pact only those nations willing to declare war,
sever relations, or adopt a benevolent neutrality toward the United
States, but he preferred to drop the matter altogether.[26]

President Wilson, in contrast, looked for ways to overcome the
obstacles. In answer to Lansing on 19 April, he argued that the existence of such a treaty would compel the United States to protect
alliance partners against the loss of independence or territory, even if
connected with Germany. As he noted, adherence to the Monroe
Doctrine would do the same thing. Conversely, if a country should
become a "base of operations against us, it would be acting in contra-
vention of the patent meaning of the pact and we would be free to act as
if there were no pact." The problem of German propaganda defied
solution. Wilson saw no hope of eliminating it in Latin America. Finally, he concluded, the negotiation of such formal arrangments would
not force the other signatories to follow the United States in a declaration of war because they would come "to our assistance with arms
only when our politcal independence and territorial integrity were
threatened."[27]

In the ensuing discussions. Lansing could anticipate no likelihood
of accepting the Brazilian terms, but Wilson remained ready to entertain the possibility. In defense of his earlier practices in Mexico, he
maintained that he had no objection to the nonintervention and de
facto principles, but the second provision in the protocol troubled him.
As he observed, to act only in response to a formal request would
amount to "a virtual repudiation of the Monroe Doctrine and could not
be accepted by us." Nevertheless, he wanted to proceed on the assump-

tion that Brazil "evidently desires very much to effect a definite rapprochement with us and her example would, in the present circumstances, be a very persuasive fact throughout Latin America." In order "to bring this great thing about," Wilson instructed Robert Lansing to organize "our diplomatic forces all along the line."[28]

Nothing ever came of the effort. The Pan American Pact still eluded success, as a result of centrifugal tendencies and cross purposes. Argentina, a principal distraction, acted independently of the United States and strove to bring about a conference of neutral states. Foreign Minister Honorio Pueyrredón explained that such an endeavor could result in "an agreement morally favoring the United States and Allies" and issued invitations on 22 April. The degree of German influence in Mexico also caused worry. On 21 April, Lansing instructed the new ambassador, Henry P. Fletcher, to impress upon Carranza the need for strict neutrality. Fletcher already had received assurances from Luis Cabrera, the minister of finance, that Mexico would not close down the oil shipments to the Allies. Indeed, according to Cabrera, Carranza genuinely wanted the friendship of the United States and would do whatever necessary to keep his country out of the war. Fletcher suggested that "the Mexican Government will take whatever advantage it can from the present situation" but believed that "our best policy is to help them, and to act as if we relied upon their friendly neutrality and good faith."[29]

The Chilean government, much less a concern, upheld a neutral policy and inclined toward a benevolent definition. The leaders would go no further. According to Ambassador Joseph Shea, they calculated that the costs of breaking relations would exceed the gains and that a declaration of war would have even worse effects. Mobilization of the army, for example, would entail large expenses and take men out of the nitrate fields. Shea reasoned, nevertheless, that "a great majority" of the Chilean people held pro-Ally views and would not participate in the Argentine plan for a conference among neutrals. The news promoted high hopes in the Latin American Affairs Division of the State Department, where some officials believed that "the opportune moment had arrived" for placing "the relationship between Chile and the United States on a more solid and satisfactory basis than has existed during the last decade." Jordan Stabler wanted an early resolution of the Tacna-Arica dispute with Peru to ease the way, elaborating further that "should Chile throw in her lot with the United States, any action on the part of Argentina would thereby be neutralized."[30]

In Buenos Aires, the interest in holding a conference prompted Foreign Minister Pueyrredón to bestow an explanation. He told Ambassador Stimson that he intended it to mobilize support among the neutrals for President Wilson. But strikingly different interpretations circulated in the newspapers. According to *La Razón,* "The Monroe Doctrine has been annulled by the intervention of the United States in the European conflict." Argentina, therefore, should take the lead in organizing the Latin American states, particularly for economic cooperation among producers of raw materials. The proposed gathering of neutrals presumably would have great utility toward such an end. *La Prensa* in turn reported growing support among other countries, depicted as a true manifestation of self-determination, and castigated the Chileans for lacking enthusiasm.[31]

Mexico, meanwhile, wanted to halt the war through neutral mediation. On 25 April, Carranza told Fletcher of his plan. If the Allies would formulate peace terms, the Latin American neutrals could transmit them to the Central Powers and exercise some useful influence. Fletcher in response warned of the consequences of an inconclusive peace that might leave "the military party in Germany as a standing menace to all nations who wished to work out their destinies in unarmed peace." After an hour of discussion, he felt confident that the Mexican president had acquired "a juster appreciation of the great issues and the effects on Mexico. . . . Mr. Carranza fully realizes the desirability and necessity of Mexico maintaining strictly its neutrality. His attitude was frank, cordial, and rather encouraging." Nevertheless, suspicions persisted all during the war, as Mexico and Argentina in particular sought ways of resisting the growing United States hegemony.[32]

THE BRAZIL CONNECTION

The quest for unanimity in the western hemisphere held special importance for United States' leaders during the war years. For example, John Barrett, the executive director of the Pan American Union, wanted to marshall the economic resources of the region and advised Robert Lansing of the need for special efforts. To succeed, such endeavors required political sensitivity. Because of the coolness of Argentina and Mexico and the reticence of Chile, the United States focused initiatives on Brazil. Although the attempted revival of the Pan American Pact accomplished nothing, the Brazilians inaugurated an eager courtship of the United States, first stating their opposition to a conference of neutrals and then instituting important changes in the Foreign Office. Foreign Minister Lauro Müller had come under criticism for many reasons, including alleged pro-German sympathies, dishonesty, and incompetency. His replacement, Dr. Nilo Peçanha, took over on 7 May and favorably impressed the United States chargé d'affaires in the Brazilian capital, Alexander Benson, who applauded his expression of "most cordial sentiments and friendship."[33]

The Brazilians made their ambitions more explicit on 15 May, when Domicio da Gama told Frank Polk of his wish for an understanding. According to the suggested terms, Brazil would enter the war and cooperate in the deployment of naval forces if the United States would reciprocate with favors. In Polk's words, "Brazil would give their moral, economic, and political support to the United States in exchange for some agreement, not necessarily a treaty, covering the attitude this Government would take in case Germany should consider Brazil an enemy." Da Gama also wanted economic assurances so that any embargo on exports in the future would not apply to Brazil and the country would retain access to the necessary ships for transport.[34]

Brazil's control of the manganese needed by the United States bestowed some bargaining leverage, and arrangements ensued. To operate the Central Railroad carrying the ore, the United States agreed to make coal available. Moreover, on 18 May, Polk gave assurance of assistance if trouble with Germany should occur. While addressing trade questions, he cautioned that some kind of rationing system might affect exports but that Brazil could earn "most favored nation treatment" by coming into the war. According to him, "we would be more liberal with countries assisting us than with neutrals." Da Gama in reply again affirmed Brazil's disinclination to take part in a conference of neutrals and raised a related question, asking whether an inter-American conference should assemble to discuss the allocation of resources and materials within the western hemisphere. Polk in reply put him off, asserting his preference for dealing individually with each country and directly with Brazil. He also wanted to drop further consideration of the Pan American Pact, explaining that concentration on fewer issues would avoid complications with the other South American countries.[35]

During the spring and summer of 1917, Brazil closely followed the United States' lead, edging ever closer to an actual break with Germany. In response to a submarine attack on the vessel *Tijuca* near Brest on 20 May, the government first obtained from the United States another assurance in defense of trade and territory, and then President Wenceslau Braz P. Gomes revoked the neutral policy of his country. Though not quite the equivalent of a declaration of war, the act served public notice of Brazil's decision to align with the United States. As the president explained before the national congress, reprehensible German practices and the traditional commitment to "continental solidarity" required such a move, and he won overwhelming endorsement in the Chamber of Deputies and the Senate. Ambassador da Gama later emphasized a similar point in a communication with Secretary Lansing when he stated that "one of the belligerents," the United States, "is a constituent portion of the American continent," and "we," the Brazilians, "are bound to that belligerent by traditional friendship and the same sentiment in the defense of the vital interests of America and the accepted international law." In a corollary move, Brazil also took possession of German merchant vessels in the nation's ports.[36]

The ambiguity of Chile's position, meanwhile, sparked worry. On 19 May, Ambassador Shea conveyed reports of German submarines off the southern coast, where, according to rumors, remote, sparsely populated islands might provide safe bases for attacks against nitrate shipments. As a safeguard, Shea instructed consular officials in Valparaíso to make an investigation, and the State Department broadly hinted that benevolent neutrality, possibly even a declaration of war, would solve the problem. When the Chilean ambassador asked Frank Polk on 12 June for elucidation of United States expectations, the counselor told him that Brazil's actions had gratified leaders in the Wilson administration. Polk rejected flatly a suggestion that neutrals might aid in arranging the peace, claiming that the more countries to wage war against Germany, the more quickly the war would end. In confirmation, Lansing already had gone on record, affirming the Department's position that a conference of neutrals could serve no useful purpose.[37]

By June 1917, most indications in Latin America suggested that neutral initiatives would not succeed. Much heartened by the failure, John Barrett issued a statement on 4 June in which he applauded Latin Americans for their responses and set forth a calculation. He thought it "not only possible but very probable" that "the whole Western Hemisphere will be directly engaged in the war before another year passes." By his estimation, "there is no question that . . . events would inevitably cause all [Latin American countries] to align themselves with the United States and its European allies and even take such steps as will be equal to a declaration of war." Indeed, the nations of Bolivia, Costa Rica, Haiti, Honduras, and Venezuela already had turned down invitations to attend the neutral conference; Peru, while accepting conditionally, had disavowed any intention of unfriendliness toward the United States, and Uruguay had opened its ports to North American warships. In response, Barrett proclaimed ebulliently, "Certain mighty irresistible but almost intangible forces and influences are . . . powerfully at work everywhere in Latin America and cannot be checked."[38]

Although Barrett overstated the inexorability of the process, the surge of sentiment in favor of the United States caused concern in Argentina over the prospect of diplomatic isolation. In this instance,

Estanislao S. Zeballos, the redoubtable editorialist, advised against undue apprehension. In an article in *La Prensa* on 30 May, he argued that Pan American doctrines had never implied any need for diplomatic and military solidarity, merely the exchange of ideas and goods. Moreover, he held, Argentina always pursued independence in foreign policy. In another essay on 8 June, he explained that "the whole Pan-American policy . . . has been undoubtedly commercial." While James G. Blaine had advocated "an American Zolverein," Woodrow Wilson had aspired to "a more formal system . . . designed to create commercial union between the states of the New World and to render them independent of European capital and manufacture." The latter ambition impressed him as ominous because the European powers, "including the very ones now allied with the United States," would react "with jealousy" to "the dangerous situation of their commerce in the New World against the powerful competition of the Great American Republic." Zeballos also attributed some measure of hypocrisy to Wilson, whose earlier calls for "brotherhood," "cordiality," and "moral and social progress" now ran counter to his opposition to a conference among neutrals.[39]

The nuances of Argentine behavior elicited various appraisals and explanations. On June, an analysis from United States Naval Intelligence posited the existence of aggressive designs upon Brazil and claimed, further, that German agents kept them stirred up in order to divert Brazil away from Europe. Reportedly, "Germany had fanned the embers with an idea of distracting the attention of Brazil and causing her to use all her resources in her own defense, so as to have nothing (especially in the line of food-stuffs) to furnish the Allies." Playing the double game, the Germans intended another incitement in the western hemisphere, but this agent, nevertheless, anticipated little prospect of a land invasion. Rather, "the danger" would come from the sea, where Argentina's capabilities exceeded Brazil's. As a recommendation in defense of Brazil, he called upon the United States to put on a show of naval force in the south Atlantic.[40]

Other reporters arrived at similar conclusions. On 20 June, Ambassador Edwin Morgan in Rio de Janeiro also attributed substantial influence to Germany in Argentina. He explained that Argentine neutrality followed from the promise of political and commercial favors after the war. Although he perceived little immediate threat to Brazil, even in the southern regions where pro-Ally demonstrations had silenced the German population, he had some apprehension. "Should the German fleet break through the British Naval cordon and effect a landing on this coast, or should the Argentine Government on some pretext or other declare war on Brazil, there is an element in the southern States which would prove of considerable assistance to the enemy." Since he regarded precautions as in order, he advised in favor of sending battleships to reassure the Brazilians and to impress the Argentines. Subsequently, Brazil requested permission to purchase three submarines in the United States.[41] During the war years, some degree of naval cooperation became a special feature of United States–Brazilian relations.

On 22 June, another report from Naval Intelligence provided a more benign interpretation. Claiming that "The great mass of Argentine people and also the leading circles, including the Cabinet, are pro-Ally, very decidedly," it affirmed that "Argentina is proud and dislikes to follow, especially when Brazil leads. This is the great reason why she hesitated, and not on account of any hostility for the U.S." Indeed, the German resort to submarine warfare came close to provoking a diplomatic break, and "Many prominent persons . . . have urged Mr. Stimson to ask for a visit of the fleet, guaranteeing an enthusiastic reception and saying it would have a good effect." With some subtlety, the author suggested that the proper attitude for the United States required the cultivation of "a polite aloofness, letting it be felt here in high quarters that we are very careful to heed the wishes of the President and not to embarrass him, and that we are too proud to go where there is the slightest doubt of our welcome by all the people."[42]

To display naval prowess, Admiral William B. Caperton and a contingent of the south Atlantic squadron visited the capitals of Brazil, Uruguay, and Argentina and were received with great festivals of enthusiasm. In response to a formal invitation, the warships *Pittsburgh*, *South Dakota*, *Frederick*, and *Puebla* spent almost two weeks from 26 June until 6 July in the harbor at Rio de Janeiro. From the moment of entry into the Bay of Guanabara, a holiday atmosphere of revelry and celebration occasioned a sequence of balls and receptions and even a joint military parade down the Avenida Rio-Branco on 4 July. According to the P.A.U. *Bulletin*, the affair vindicated "those idealists who have for years fostered the true spirit of Pan Americanism." In Montevideo, similarly, the naval presence elicited public excitement and strong statements of support for the United States from the Uruguayan government, technically a neutral. One eyewitness, Samuel Guy Inman, a Protestant missionary and Pan American advocate, felt heart-warmed at the sight of the United States sailors kissing babies and beaming at Uruguayan girls, a happy contrast, in his view, with the lamentable outcome when the U.S.S. *Baltimore* visited Valparaíso, Chile, in 1891. Equally spectacular, when the ships arrived at Buenos Aires on 25 July, a crowd of some 200,000 showed up to extend greetings and demonstrated thereby, according to the *Bulletin*, the true sentiments of the Argentine people.[43]

In part as a consequence of the excursion into the southern cone, the naval forces of Brazil, the United States, and the Allies developed new forms of cooperation during the war. An agreement worked out by Caperton and officials in the Ministry of Marine provided that Brazil would participate more actively in patrolling the east coast of the country and other designated areas in the south Atlantic, thereby freeing North American, British, and French vessels for more pressing tasks. Anticipating good things, Ambassador Morgan remarked, "It is unnecessary to point out the importance of the arrangement . . . and the effect it should have in developing the political relations between the United States and Brazil, in checking the devastation of German raiders, and in protecting the Brazilian coasts from attack."[44]

THE PURSUIT OF ECONOMIC INTEGRATION

The pursuit of economic integration still ranked high in the Wilson administration's agenda of goals and purposes. Access to the markets and resources of Latin America held significance both in the short and long terms and so intrigued Secretary of the Treasury William G. McAdoo late in 1916 that he asked the Senate for an appropriation of $50,000 to host a second Pan American Financial Conference. As justification, he claimed, "The results of the first . . . in improving the relations between the United States and the Republics of Latin America, cannot be overstated."[45] Although subsequently the entry into the war deferred implementation until the summer of 1919, the leaders hoped to build upon the achievement and actively to pursue an expansion of trade and investment.

The reduced capacity of the Europeans to compete stimulated mounting interest. In November 1916, the Bureau of Foreign and Domestic Commerce in the United States developed plans for an advertising campaign in South America, using films to make consumers aware of North American manufactures. In April 1917, the New Orleans Association of Commerce organized a Latin American Club for identical reasons, and, moreover, the Latin Americans appeared ready to reciprocate. The expenditure of millions of dollars for improvements of docking facilities at major South American ports appeared as evidence of good faith and an open invitation, but the dependency on British transports still rankled. While on leave in the United States late in 1916, Ambassador Frederick J. Stimson spoke of the subject before an audience at Dedham, Massachusetts, with a touch of hyperbole:

To talk about trade with Argentina . . . as the trade exists with Great
Britain, is like talking about trade with the Planet Mars. . . . There is
no American Line to Argentina. We are dependent entirely upon a
British Line which sailings are made uncertain by the war, and
who, though they do what they can to accommodate, will naturally
keep the interests of England first.[46]

Another warning issued from the Consul General's office in
Buenos Aires late in 1916. It complained that British interests had
engineered "a more or less organized campaign" against United States'
commerce and that "we should take some sort of concerted steps . . . to
protect and advance our position in the Latin-American trade war . . .
already well under way here with an ever-increasing seriousness." To
demonstrate the point, the report cited "an open attack on our trade,"
consisting of allegations and charges that "our manufacturers and
exporters failed to live up to their contracts and took advantage of cash
terms of sale and the general European conditions to swindle their
Argentine customers." Reportedly "to cripple American trade in this
market," the British circulated false accusations and misinformation,
but the Argentines, nevertheless, eagerly solicited trade and investment. Late in 1916, the New York investment firms Hallgarten and
Company and William A. Read and Company announced plans for a
joint loan of $100,000,000. In March 1917, Ambassador Naón told the
New Hampshire legislature that "the almost complete paralysis of
European imports" offered to the United States "an unsurpassed opportunity of increasing . . . its commercial field."[47]

The possibility of aiding in the financial reorganization of Brazil
late in 1916 also animated the interest of bankers and State Department officials. In November, the New York houses of William Morris
Imbrie and Company and the Equitable Trust Company took the lead
by loaning $5,500,000 to the city of São Paulo. According to Charles L.
Hoover, the United States consul, this "pioneer" transaction had succeeded against "the very strong group of foreign financial interests
which . . . have always regarded this part of Brazil as their private and
personal field of operations" and "will go a very long way toward
bringing about other financial operations in the future, and toward
diverting trade in general to the United States." Ambassador Morgan
endorsed this judgment by proclaiming, "The present opportunity
appears unusually favorable for American financiers to obtain a stake
in this country which will give them an influence which has hitherto
been wholly exercised by British or continental groups. The Secretary
of Commerce, William C. Redfield, noted simply, "Foreign loans are

. . . so essential a part of our own financial stability in the near future that we desire to encourage them within due reason."[48]

The same concern directed attention toward Chile. Indeed, the experience of wartime prosperity transformed the condition of the country, mainly the result of high demand and unprecedented prices for nitrates and copper. According to a set of statistics provided by the United States commercial attaché's office, the personal accounts in the National Savings Banks had increased by more than 11 percent in 1916, and, even more significant, the customary yearly deficit in the nation's finances had turned into a surplus. In May 1917, the estimates published in the P.A.U. *Bulletin* suggested that the sale of nitrates had earned for Chile no less than $200,000,000 in the previous year and that the United States had surpassed Germany as the best customer. In a parallel process, the United States' investment role in Chile had expanded significantly, but the figures were less exact.[49]

During 1917 and 1918, the United States developed special economic intimacies with Brazil, forging new and to some extent mutual forms of interdependency. A study published by the Department of Commerce in 1920 reviewed the course of events. Before August 1914, coffee and rubber, the agricultural mainstays, comprised over 80 percent of the foreign exports. With the onset of the war, Brazil lost the trade of the Central Powers, amounting to some 4,000,000 sacks at 132 pounds each year. Later, the circumstances worsened when the Allies restricted imports, thereby making Brazil more dependent than ever upon the United States. The reduction in demand drove prices down from $14.92 per sack in 1913 to $11.66 in 1914 to $9.18 in 1915, when the government in Rio de Janeiro revived a valorization scheme by which planters initially exchanged coffee as security for guaranteed loans and later sold it outright to federal authorities. The situation deteriorated further in 1917 when the United States placed coffee on the list of restricted imports. Meanwhile, the rubber industry also went into eclipse, though not quite so precipitously, the result of scarcities of new capital for developing land in Brazil and also emergent competition from Ceylon, Burma, Java, and the Malay Peninsula.

Brazil responded with attempts at diversifying agriculture and developing manufacturing. Although the Commerce Department report of 1920 stated that Brazil potentially "is capable of becoming one of the leading agricultural countries in the world," it noted too that the country would have to overcome "many obstacles," including serious inadequacies of labor, machinery, and transportation. The acquisition of manufacturing capability, though invigorated on a small scale by the war, suffered from disabilities, notably, an unskilled work force, the high cost of raw materials, and scarcities of investment capital. Nevertheless, according to a survey carried out by the Brazilian Foreign Ministry, some progress had taken place among small industries, particularly in meat-packing, textiles, shoemaking, tanning, and cereal cleaning. Indeed, the export of refrigerated meats expanded impressively from one metric ton in 1914 to 66,452 tons in 1917, mainly the work of big corporations based in the United States, such as the Armour, Swift, and Wilson Companies, all of which operated plants in Brazil or had them under construction. The Armour Company of Chicago and Buenos Aires had underway near São Paulo one of the largest facilities in South America. Running at full capacity, it could handle 2,000 cattle, 3,000 hogs, and 2,000 sheep each day and would employ 3,000 workers.[50]

To promote economic development and diversification, a resolution by the Brazilian Congress on 16 August 1917 directed the president to employ his authority of leadership and encouragement. The top priorities over the long term centered on the evolution of coal, iron, and steel industries, the construction of railroads, and the acquisition of ocean-going vessels. Others embraced the modernization of telegraphic and telephonic facilities and the enhancement of military and naval forces.[51] During the war years, Brazil's pursuit of these aims intersected with the United States' interests in several ways but particularly in the areas of cable communications, mineral resources, shipping and trade, and naval affairs.

The British domination of cable traffic with Brazil had always distressed the leaders in the Wilson administration, and they seized on opportunities to end it. On 13 August, the Central and South American Telegraph Company obtained a concession from the Brazilian government, establishing for the first time the right to lay lines between the United States and Brazil. Ambassador Morgan hailed it as "an event of considerable international importance" because it would break the British monopoly exercised for years by the Western Telegraphic Company. Since the decree forbade future monopolies, it invited participation by other United States corporations, and, according to Morgan, the Western Union Telegraph Company wanted very much to get into the game. Indeed, a representative, Nelson O'Shaughnessy, a former diplomat who had left the service after experiencing embarrassment in Mexico during the Huerta imbroglio, would soon arrive, intending to seek permission for running lines into the north to the West Indies and also into the south to Uruguay. Somewhat cryptically, Morgan remarked that "the Embassy is in a position to give the same assistance to the Western Union Co. that it has given to the Central and South America."[52] Obviously, he intended to capitalize upon the increase of United States influence in the country and the commensurate reduction of Great Britain's capacity to resist.

Another issue focused on manganese. For the United States, the difficulties of acquisition highlighted the transportation problems of Brazil. In the middle of August 1917, Morgan reported that the mines in Minas Gerais could turn out almost unlimited amounts of the vital resource but that sales ran low because the Central Railroad could not handle more than 50,000 tons of ore in a month. Labor unrest, riots, and the possibility of German sabotage posed another difficulty. Early in September, Roger Welles, an officer of United States Naval Intelligence, claimed to possess "specific information that German agents are working in the manganese mines . . . that the Germans have been the instigators of several of the strikes" and "that several German firms have offered to purchase many manganese mines." According to him, "The object, evidently is solely to tie up the working of these mines until after the war" and "to badly cripple the manganese production." Other observers saw the danger as less acute. Consul General Alfred L. M. Gottschalk anticipated ample cooperation from Brazilian leaders in securing protection, and Ambassador Morgan disparaged the notion that Germans had much influence around the mines. Lansing nevertheless called for an expansion of production to 60,000 tons a month and for appropriate safeguards to protect it.[53]

Questions of shipping and trade took on great importance and occasioned a divergence among Brazil, the United States, and the European Allies. When Brazil broke relations with Germany, the government requisitioned thirty-three German commercial vessels interned in port. Hoping to establish a merchant fleet, Brazilians wanted to retain the ships for their own use, but the other powers preferred to employ them more directly in trans-Atlantic routes. In July 1917, British diplomats in Rio de Janeiro pressed the matter, seeking to obtain the charter of no less than four of the German craft for service with the Royal Mail Steamship Company, two of whose passenger liners had suffered torpedo attacks, but Brazilian leaders resisted, planning to utilize the ships, once refurbished, in runs between Rio de Janeiro, Buenos Aires, and New York. As Morgan noted in his report, "There are several indications that British representatives do not favor the development of Brazil's merchant marine which is essential to the Nation's commercial expansion."[54] Secretary of the Navy Josephus Daniels's sense of priorities conformed more closely with the British than the Brazilian view, characterizing the former as "far wiser." When Brazil offered only small concessions to release Allied merchantmen from the Buenos Aires–New York and the Buenos Aires–Bordeaux routes, Daniels suggested as an incentive a kind of deal. If Brazil would

turn over the urgently needed vessels for immediate use in supplying
the Allies, the United States would guarantee a sufficient number of
bottoms for South America and also would build vessels for Brazil after
the war at fair prices. The French, meanwhile, offered to trade large
purchases of Brazilian coffee in return for access to the ships, but the
Brazilians claimed that, under the terms of the requisition decree, only
they could take possession of the German craft and utilize them under
their flag in the Lloyd Brazilian Mercantile fleet.[55]

A set of stop-gap measures later in the fall finally muted the
discussion and permitted various arrangements. Early in September,
Daniels settled upon a compromise as the means, affirming his support
for Brazil in establishing a commercial fleet, if at the same time the
country would allocate "as large a percentage as possible" of the interned vessels to the trans-Atlantic trade. After additional discussions,
the Brazilian Foreign Office announced plans in the middle of October
to organize the existing Lloyd Brazilian fleet and the interned German
ships, some fifty-eight vessels in all, under the Brazilian flag into three
trans-Atlantic lines. Two of them would run from ports in Brazil to the
United States and to Europe and a third between the United States and
Europe. Initially nineteen vessels, later twenty, would serve the third
route, mainly under the direction of the United States, while the British
and the French arranged independently for additional facilities. As
payment for the privilege, the United States consented to an annual fee
to Brazil of $14,000,000 and also to the purchase of two million bags of
coffee at $20,000,000. For Morgan, the long-term gains would more
than compensate for the initial costs. As he explained his understanding of the justification, "The Department will recognize the political
advantage of not allowing a European power, upon Brazil's entrance
into the war, to dominate her shipping situation and of not permitting
France to extend her influence over a Government and a people
already too much inclined to accept French leadership."[56]

After the reaffirmation of the unwritten alliance with the United
States, the Brazilian government formally entered the war on 26 October 1917, following a torpedo attack against the Lloyd Brazilian
steamer *Macão*, formerly the German *Palatia*. It marked the fourth
Brazilian ship sunk by German submarines and persuaded President
Wenceslau Braz that "we must face the situation and recognize at once
that a state of war is imposed upon us by Germany." In a show of
overwhelming agreement, the Brazilian Senate unanimously voted in
favor of a war declaration. Almost immediately, military and naval
questions took on new significance and intruded upon relations with
newly acquired allies. A resolution introduced into the Chamber of
Deputies on 4 November suggested the advisability of a French military

mission to provide training and instruction. Though, according to Ambassador Morgan, neither the officers nor the enlisted men in the Brazilian army inspired much confidence, the government had hitherto refrained from the use of foreign advisers, in large part in repudiation of the Argentine practice. Morgan believed in this instance that French help would improve Brazil's military competency and would not damage important United States interests. In contrast, he would not react favorably to the presence of British naval instructors because the Brazilian navy "is already too largely under the influence of British tradition and prestige." Instead, he wanted the United States Navy to undertake the obligation.[57]

Morgan elaborated upon the theme in subsequent dispatches. On 13 November, he warned of the implications for United States industry, cautioning that "A British naval mission would not only assure the construction in British shipyards of new units of the Brazilian Navy but would render it impossible for the Bethlehem Steel Company and similar American corporations to secure contracts for arsenals, dockyards and coast defense." In such an eventuality, he stated with chagrin, "Our manufacturers of military material would be entirely shut out." Morgan insisted that only direct exposure would have the desired effects. As he observed, "The influences which we have recently exerted over the Brazilian Navy" came about principally through "the effective teaching" of a few United States officers in the Brazilian Naval War College and "the favorable impressions" of young officers who served in Washington or with the fleet. Though "appreciative" of the United States, they had little authority. To reach the senior officers, Morgan would send a United States naval mission and also additional instructors to the Naval War College.[58]

The terms of the proposed collaboration became ever clearer in Morgan's mind. Although the Brazilian army could contribute little toward military victory, in part because of a strong, popular prejudice against putting ground troops into the battle lines, the leaders in the government hoped to benefit from the new relationship by purchasing arms and materials in the United States. Morgan advised a strict policy of reciprocity, obtaining "favors" and "advantages" while granting some of the requests. In contrast, he envisioned a more substantive degree of naval cooperation. By 1 December, he had obtained reasons to think that the Brazilian Marine Ministry intended to engage the service of five United States naval officers, two as professors in the Naval War College and the others as fire control instructors. In addition, Brazil in all likelihood would take part in naval maneuvers in south European waters by sending a squadron of four destroyers and two scouts. Morgan advised an invitation for the Brazilians to join

United States vessels patrolling between Gibraltar and the Azores, even if the actual advantages should prove "insignificant." He wanted a demonstration of solidarity which would appeal to "the poorest mind." He also advised in favor of selling to Brazil a late model Holland submarine by the Electric Boat Company. Otherwise, the competition from the French and Italian firms of Labeuf-Schneider and Fiat might capture the market and obtain the upper hand. Morgan warned solemnly against the ramifications of any such outcome. "As the responsibilities for the active prosecution of the war are thrust upon and assumed by the United States instead of the European Allies, it is evident . . . that European manufacturers will solicit and fill orders in South America," in which case, "The strides and conquests which American manufacturers have recently made in the Southern Hemisphere will be ephemeral unless they are alive to the fact and are prepared and allowed to actively continue their export business." Morgan feared, otherwise, that "Our foreign commerce will be handicapped to such a serious extent that at the close of the war the elimination of German and Austrian competition will not counterbalance the advantage which Britain and French importers have secured while the war was in progress." The "danger," he insisted, was "active and imminent."[59]

The prospect of cultivating closer relations with Chile also held promise. Early in July, Ambassador Joseph Shea claimed to detect "a more friendly attitude during the last few weeks." Although previously the government had bestowed too much concern upon German sensibilities, someone in the Foreign Ministry now suggested that Admiral Caperton and the south Atlantic squadron also pay a visit in Chile. Shea, accordingly, made a speculative leap, suggesting that "some high officials of the Government are giving serious consideration to the question of Chile's alignment with Brazil and the United States." But the expectation proved unwarranted and gave rise, instead, to controversy and instability within the Chilean cabinet. Indeed, a government under Ismael Tocornal, reportedly friendly toward the United States, had to resign after seven days early in August 1917 but could not leave office because the rival parties and factions would not agree on a replacement. Shea then reversed his estimate, noting "among many people an underlying feeling of prejudice and distrust" and expressing his apprehension that a stopover by the naval squadron would signify for many Chileans "an abandonment of neutrality."[60]

The acquisition of mineral resources also figured prominently and entailed special arrangements with the United States and the Allies. During the summer of 1917, an abrupt rise in the price of nitrates and the possibility of scarcities caused concern. According to Shea, much of the problem resulted from speculative ventures among Chileans and also from rival bidding among the Allies. To combat such practices, the British proposed early in September the creation of a cooperative program to end the competition and also to defeat alleged German interference with production and delivery. The British also recommended in favor of purchasing the entire Chilean production of nitrates in 1918, estimated at 3,500,000 tons, and of developing rational means of allocation among the Allies and the United States. The establishment of a joint commission to represent all parties in London would accomplish these goals.[61]

During the early fall, speculation persisted over Chile's ultimate course in the war. *El Mercurio*, a leading newspaper in Santiago, usually favored the Allied cause and applauded late in October when Brazil declared war. Presumably, the editor, Carlos Edwards, reflected the anglophilic sentiments of his brother, Augustín, the Chilean minister in London. Secretary of State Robert Lansing expressed similar preferences. During a meeting in Washington, he abruptly blurted out his wish for Chile also to take part. Various governmental agencies and departments, meanwhile, tentatively approved of the British plan for a Nitrate of Soda Executive, as long as apportionments met United States needs, and the Wilson administration informed London of its acceptance "in principle" on 16 November. The urgency of the circumstance accounted for the decision. As Rear Admiral Frank F. Fletcher observed, "a serious shortage" existed in the production of powder and high explosives and also in the supply of nitrates to produce them. But certain apprehensions also lingered. Before consenting to the final details, Lansing instructed United States diplomats in London "to insist upon utilization of existing American importing houses as purchasing agencies" because otherwise they would lose "their legitimate business advantages during the war" and "their position afterwards." To work with the Nitrate Executive, he designated W. R. Grace and Company, H. L. Wessel and G. L. Duval and Company, and Anthony Gibbs and Co., all of New York, and E. I. Dupont DeNemours and Company of Wilmington, Delaware.[62]

An expectation of eventual participation in the war also marked impressions of Argentina. After the visit of the south Atlantic squadron to Buenos Aires, Admiral Caperton recounted his view that "Popular feelings . . . generally . . . favor . . . the Allies." Though he realized that "President Yrigoyen has the rank and file" among the people, Caperton believed that "it is only a question of time" before Argentina would revoke the neutrality statute. Indeed, he reported, "Large numbers of people openly wonder when the break is coming." So far, Caperton attributed "the lack of initiative to a hatred of following where Brazil

leads," an aversion he interpreted as "racial." At the same time, he
attributed substantial importance to "a large German influence" in
Argentina and warned against affording "our enemies" in the country
"an excuse for directing the Argentine people against us."[63]

Seeking to turn the tables, the United States hoped to influence
Argentine public opinion against the Germans. Two incidents, the
sinkings of the *Toro* and *Monte Protegido* on 4 April and 22 June, irritated
Argentine sensibilities and caused tension, but the Germans prevented
an actual break by making accommodations. When they issued a statement of regret, agreed upon reparations, and promised to respect
Argentina's definition of freedom of the seas, President Yrigoyen
undertook a secret commitment to keep Argentine vessels out of the
war zone. Indiscretions in high places then produced more trouble. In
cablegrams to Berlin, the German minister, Count Karl von Luxburg,
advised in favor of sinking Argentine ships "without a trace" and also
characterized the acting foreign minister, Honorio Pueyrredón, unbe-
comingly as a "notorious ass and anglophile." In a small-scale replay of
the Zimmermann affair, the British secret service intercepted the dispatches and made them available for publication in the United States.[64]

The revelation stirred up adverse reactions in Buenos Aires and
resulted in Luxburg's dismissal from the country as *persona non grata*
but failed to precipitate a diplomatic break, presumably the State
Department's goal in making the information available. Yrigoyen, in all
likelihood, reasoned that the German diplomat, not his government,
bore responsibility for the affront. Nevertheless, calls for drastic measures emanated from the Congress and the press. Indeed, the Senate
and the Chamber of Deputies in the middle of September voted by
large margins to suspend relations with Germany, but the President
dismissed the counsel as meaningless on the intriguing grounds that it
had no relationship with public opinion. Robert Lansing then took his
frustration out on Frederick Stimson, chiding him for the alleged
inadequacy of his dispatches, probably out of annoyance with the
ambassador's inability to overcome Yrigoyen's commitment to neutrality. Stimson, suffering the effects of grippe and bronchitis, became a
scapegoat in the Luxburg incident. The acting foreign minister, in
contrast, became an object of mirth. According to Mabel Stimson, "The
whole of Argentina has screamed with laughter at poor Mr. Pueyrre-
don . . . being called a Notorious Ass by German Minister Luxburg."
The newspapers dubbed him "Notorio Honorio" and drew him in
cartoons with donkey ears.[65]

The debate over foreign policy set the Argentines at odds. As
Stimson simplistically characterized it, the respectable people favored
the Allies, whereas disreputable elements, "the poorest type of Spanish

and native strikers and anarchists," sided with Yrigoyen. When the government called for a conference among neutrals to assemble in Buenos Aires early in January 1918, United States observers leveled strong criticism. According to Naval Intelligence, Yrigoyen and the members of his party lacked skill and ability. His administration was "floundering deeper and deeper . . . giving a false impression of the country to the outside world . . . isolating itself and . . . losing its South American leadership." According to one report on 6 November, "The truth of the whole matter is that the President is not a big enough man for the present problems, and in addition he is obstinate and seems distinctly to lack proper judgment." Another on 14 November claimed that "The Argentine Republic is to-day to all intents and purposes, considered and treated by Germany as an Ally," an allegation presumably "born out by the fact that it is the only Nation whose ships are exempted by Germany from the submarine peril." Another on 19 November asserted that "A feeling of enmity to Brazil lies in the heart of every Argentine," but "discounted" the notion that "German influences" had much effect on Yrigoyen, except perhaps to flatter him into thinking that he is "the savior of the country." According to this view, the president maintained neutrality because of "that subconscious Argentine feeling" that the country must not appear to follow Brazil.[66] Among the countries of Latin America, only Mexico showed much support.

Economic dependencies, meanwhile, undercut Argentine neutrality. A study published by the United States Department of Commerce in 1920 explained that Argentina relied upon foreign countries "not only as markets for the disposal of yearly surplus agricultural and pastoral products, but also as the sources of the major portion of the manufactured goods needed to sustain economic life." Disruptive effects during the war—principally, the withdrawal of foreign capital and the isolation imposed by inadequate transportation—compelled upon Argentina "the necessity of doing without large quantities of essential commodities." Although the consequences resulted in "a degree of national self-sufficiency, which will doubtless have a lasting effect upon the national life," more significantly, "the limitation of imports forced by the war has also hampered industrial development, because many of the tools of industry must also be imported from overseas." Consular reports emphasized the latter effects with specifics and details. As scarcities drove up the cost of living, many ordinary goods became luxuries during the summer of 1917. The costs of freight and war insurance, the demands of the belligerent nations for foodstuffs, and inadequate transportation facilities also contributed. During the first nine months of 1917, some 479 fewer commercial vessels arrived in ports at Buenos Aires than during the same period in the previous year, and they carried 329,352 tons less in cargo.[67]

Wheat sales attracted special attention. In the fall of 1917, officials in the Division of Latin American Affairs expressed distress that Argentine exports of 85,000,000 bushels to Holland and to the Scandinavian neutrals exceeded actual needs by about half and that some of the surplus presumably found a way into Germany. To reduce the flow, Great Britain and France agreed to buy about 40,000,000 bushels but had trouble arranging the financing. Rather than transfer gold bullion, the Allies hoped to obtain credit in Argentina and to elicit from the Yrigoyen government a guarantee of the terms. The scheme presumed also the cooperation, if not the participation, of the United States, and Stimson worried about the ramifications. When the British Wheat Commission nominated six firms, one French and five British, to act as purchasing agents, he cautioned that the device "constitutes what amounts to a monopoly, and will doubtless prove of the utmost value for the promotion of British trade interests of this nature after the war, to the possible exclusion of the trade interests of other nations." The parts came together late in December 1917, when Argentina, France, and Great Britain signed an agreement providing for the purchase of 2,500,000 tons of surplus wheat and other cereals during the forthcoming year. It testified to the extent of economic dependency in Argentine foreign relations. In contrast, the Argentine plan for a conference of neutrals came to nought. Indeed, by the end of the year, informed opinion among diplomats in Latin America held that no such assembly would ever take place.[68]

ANTICIPATIONS OF PEACE

Anticipations of the coming peace, meanwhile, impelled a growing interest among leaders in the Wilson administration. To give it form and shape, the president called into existence a group of experts and specialists early in September 1917. Called the Inquiry, it consisted of academicians, primarily political and social scientists, and took as its charge the formulation of peace terms based upon investigations into history, geography, economics, and ethnography. Operating under the direction of Colonel House, prominent members included Sidney E. Mezes, Isaiah Bowman, David Hunter Miller, Walter Lippmann, and James T. Shotwell, The staff, numbering about 150 scholars, produced and collected nearly 2,000 reports and documents, focusing on every region of the world, including Latin America. More formally known as the American Commission to Negotiate Peace, the body prepared the way for the United States delegation at the peace conference.[69]

The recommendations for Latin America characteristically incorporated hegemonial assumptions about the United States. A document submitted by Henry Bruere on 13 October, "A Program for a Study of Latin American International Relations," affirmed simply, "It is apparent, therefore, in light of its historical position, and because of its special relation to all the nations of the western hemisphere, that the United States will have a dominating influence in peace discussions in so far as the Americas and Mexico are concerned." Bruere wanted to assemble "a comprehensive body of information regarding the political, commercial and economic status and conditions of the several Latin-American Republics" so that peace commissioners and the people of the United States could take part in discussions "with a full understanding of the needs and opportunities of the various nations" over which the United States has maintained "a political protectorate under the Monroe Doctrine."[70]

Colonel House, for his part, had strong convictions about the proper aims of peacemaking. On 27 October 1917, four years exactly after the Mobile address, House sent to the president a letter with important implications. House believed "very strongly that something should be done at the Peace Conference to end, as far as practicable, trade restrictions." He characterized them as "a menace to peace" and calculated, in contrast, that beneficent consequences would follow the adoption of free trade. "With tariff barriers broken, with subsidies by common consent eliminated, and with real freedom of the seas, both in peace and in time of war, the world could look with confidence to the future." In a foreshadow of the Fourteen Points, he insisted, "There should be no monopoly by any nation of raw materials, or the essentials for food and clothing." House then recalled "your Mobile speech" and "the doctrine that no territory should ever again be acquired by aggression." Expressing his wish to incorporate it into peace agreements as a central feature, he averred, "this doctrine is now recognized throughout the world." House exhorted Wilson to use his "commanding position to bring to the fore this other doctrine which is so fundamental to peace" and assured him that "you will have done more for mankind than any other ruler that has lived." House hoped, too that the overthrow of autocratic and imperial institutions in Germany would facilitate the emergence of a representative government. Otherwise, he feared, the process "would inevitably lead to economic warfare afterwards—a warfare in which by force of circumstances this Government would be compelled to take part." To realize the better alternative, House wanted to build peace in the future around the principles of free

trade and nonaggression and the institutions of representative democracy. He concluded with a prayerful acknowledgment to Wilson that
"you are the one hope left to this torn and distracted world. Without
your leadership God alone knows how long we will wander in the
wilderness."[71]

On a more prosaic plane, the problem of achieving further
economic integration between the United States and Latin America
preoccupied the members of the International High Commission. This
body, established in 1915, also looked toward peace but centered its
attention on commercial and financial questions in the western hemisphere. The main agenda in 1918 included specific items, such as the
drafts of treaties calling for an international gold clearance fund and
defining the treatment of commercial travelers and their supplies, the
promotion of negotiable instruments legislation, including bills of exchange, checks, bills of lading, and warehouse receipts, the proper
procedure for the arbitration of commercial disputes, and the complete ratification of trademark, copyright, and patent conventions of
1910, particularly out of concern for establishing trademark registration bureaus in Havana and Rio de Janeiro. Although Secretary of the
Treasury McAdoo in his report to the president at the end of the year
indicated no unqualified successes in any one of the areas, he emphasized an overall impression of progress in painstakingly complex
sets of negotiations and a readiness on the part of most participants to
locate areas of common interest.[72]

During the early stages of the peace planning, the leaders in the
Wilson administration wanted to delve into Latin American issues
without drawing attention, thereby giving little reason to patriots,
nationalists, and other critics to kick up old controversies or to raise
new antagonisms. When Dr. Sidney E. Mezes, the Director of the
Division of Territorial, Economic, and Political Intelligence within the
Inquiry, asked in November 1917 for the terms of the proposed Pan
American Treaty, Robert Lansing sent along a copy with instructions
that "you understand that this is of a most confidential nature and for
the present I prefer you not to show it to anyone else and certainly not
without having discussed the matter with me."[73] Lansing wanted to stir
up no further complications; but then, in violation of Lansing's wishes,
John Barrett of the Pan American Union maladroitly set off an alterca-
tion, exactly of the sort the secretary had hoped to avoid.

In the middle of November 1917, Barrett gave publicity to a plan
for promoting broader forms of Latin American support in the war. In
a memorandum widely distributed to leaders in the administration and
the Congress and also to major newspapers, Barrett called for the
creation of a special Pan American committee to achieve coordination

and mobilization in the western hemisphere. The participants would cooperate in resisting German influences, obtaining food and raw materials for the Allies, taking part in combat, and defining the peace terms. Though Barrett explained that he had no wish to involve the neutrals, an eventuality he described as "contrary to the true principles of Pan Americanism and harmful to the Pan American Union," he wanted, at the same time, to devise "a practical means" of enlisting more formally the aid of the others and necessarily introduced questions about the propriety of his role.[74]

Barrett's blunder particularly elicited criticism from Chile and Argentina. Both neutrals, these countries wondered why the executive director of the Pan American Union, an organization representing many nations with diverse views, should put himself in service purely to United States interests, and Latin American diplomatic representatives in Washington, D.C., objected strenuously to such displays of tactlessness and incompetency. Brazil, though less emphatically, also voiced concern. Lansing, meanwhile, reprimanded Barrett for causing an embarrassment. Claiming that "publicity given to the proposal . . . nullified from that moment any element of good which it possessed," the secretary of state chastised him for confusing private and public concerns. "In spite of your assertion that your expressed views were personal and not official I do not think you could divorce yourself from your international character, and I am convinced that the members of the Pan American Union cannot but look upon your suggestion as indiscreet, if not highly improper by reason of your official position." Bluntly, Lansing charged, "a proposal on the part of the Director General of the Union to organize a council will be construed by neutral governments as an attempt to influence them in their international policy, and may very probably be attributed to this Government's influence." Particularly angered by stories in the Washington *Post*, he added, "you seriously weakened your influence in the Pan American Union . . . very materially increased the difficulties of this Government in dealing with other American Governments, and . . . undoubtedly created the impression that the Pan American Union is partisan and dominated by a desire to aid this country in the war." Barrett responded characteristically with verbose self-justifications but failed to overcome the negative effects.[75] Although he managed to hold on to his position for a while, his stature and influence waned until his resignation in the spring of 1920.

The prevalence of divisiveness and rivalry produced adverse commentary at the end of the year. *El Mercurio*, the pro-Ally newspaper in Santiago, remarked that Pan Americanism had not matured in 1917 and expressed regret that the A.B.C. countries and the United

States had failed to establish common policies toward Germany. Aggrieved for different reasons, the United States' consul general's office in Buenos Aires raised the alarm early in 1918 over the magnitude and intensity of European competition in the western hemisphere, particularly over the allegedly "intolerable" practices of Great Britain. Claiming that the British habitually engaged in manipulation and deft maneuver in pursuit of their trade aims, the document complained, "It scarcely seems conducive to the best harmony in our political and military relations that we should have a commercial war of this sort waged against us in Argentina for what seems such small and selfish reasons under the international circumstances."[76]

Other considerations blunted the impact. In Brazil, still the focal point, Ambassador Morgan anticipated a favorable response if the United States would send officers to the Naval War College and endorsed as "a basic principle of our South American policy" the notion that "all American navies as much as possible should be brought under the influence of the navy of the United States." He included among the advantages "the future construction in our shipyards of their naval vessels and of orders for naval materials being placed with our steel works" and also "the development and standardizing of an American continental type of naval science." In Argentina, Ambassador Stimson identified a positive public reaction to the wheat convention and a greater inclination by President Yrigoyen "toward a rapprochement with the United States," and in Chile Ambassador Shea learned of an official anxiousness to expand nitrate production and a willingness to take over the properties of German firms. He looked optimistically toward resolution of "the delicate political situation."[77] Early in 1918, the vital concerns of the United States appeared in good order.

FOR THE DURATION

For the duration of the Great War until the armistice on 11 November 1918, the details of economic relations and the preparations for restoring the peace dominated the international affairs of the western hemisphere. For the United States, these tasks meant the consolidation of an already strong position—as J. G. Lay of the Latin American Affairs Division remarked, the need to do "something more" to cultivate the Latin Americans and to brace against resumed European competition.[78] Brazil, Argentina, and Chile, meanwhile, angled for advantages, and rumors of British machinations caused trepidation.

Relations with Brazil turned somewhat sour early in 1918 because of difficulties over transportation facilities. The Allies retained an interest in the interned German vessels and requested the use of thirteen more of them. The United States, in turn, experienced trouble in maintaining access to the manganese resources of Minas Gerais. In the middle of January 1918, the Brazilian government closed down the Central Railway over which the ore traveled, claiming that it could not guarantee operation until the United States granted export licenses for 600,000 tons of coal destined for Brazil, and the Wilson administration retaliated by refusing to do so until France obtained leases on the desired German ships.[79]

In other areas, particularly military and naval affairs, various means permitted the maintenance of cordial ties. Although some United States officials worried that Brazil intended an arms buildup against Argentina, the cultivation of military and naval cooperation more characteristically impressed them as a reliable method of collaboration. As Josephus Daniels told Robert Lansing early in 1918, "I appreciate fully the importance of military and naval commissions to South American states on account of the marked political and commercial effect that these commissions have produced in the interest of nations sending them in the past and which they may well produce in the future." Daniels wanted to take full advantage and authorized a short while later the sale of a submarine to Brazil. He explained that "everything possible should be done to foster the relations now existing between Brazil and this country."[80]

Ambassador Morgan, meanwhile, bridled over Brazilian high-handedness, characterizing the suspension of manganese shipments over the Central Railway as "a lack of international courtesy and of loyalty to the Allies . . . seldom equalled." Nevertheless, plans for enlisting Brazilian naval forces into Allied patrol operations proceeded. The cruisers *Rio Grande do Sul* and *Bahia* and four destroyers soon would rendezvous with Allied warships near Gibraltar, and Morgan hoped very much to attach them to a United States squadron. Otherwise, he warned, the British "would undermine our naval and political position in this country," and "British naval science and practice would obtain an unusual opportunity to fix itself upon the Brazilian navy." According to him, high commercial and political stakes required that "a continental standard shall be established for naval construction, armament, tactics, and discipline," and it should conform with North American procedures.[81]

In pursuit of such ends, the Navy Department ordered three officers to Rio de Janeiro in February 1918 to serve in the Naval War College and also as instructors in gunnery and aviation. Meanwhile, other agreements resolved the transportation imbroglio by reopening the Central Railway, providing for coal shipments to Brazil, and allowing to the French greater use of the interned German vessels. They also introduced the possibility of a $50,000,000 loan from the United

States government to Brazil. As further evidence of growing influence, the emissary Nelson O'Shaughnessay obtained permission for the Western Union Telegraph Company to lay cable lines to the north and the south, an event regarded as especially significant "strategically and commercially . . . in the coming competition" with Great Britain. The Brazilian presidential elections in March 1918 confirmed the prospect of friendly relations by endorsing the status quo. They resulted in the selection of Dr. Francisco de Paula Rodrígues, a solid representative of the established elite from São Paulo who previously had served a term as president from 1902 to 1906. Although, as it turned out, he became too sick ever to assume the office and died within a few months, occasioning a special election in 1919, the initial outcome provided reassurance. For the remainder of the war, the "unwritten alliance" with Brazil held strong, although suspicions still surfaced within the Wilson administration that Brazil's real incentive in waging war on Germany resulted from the ongoing rivalry with Argentina. As observed by a naval intelligence report late in March, "By her declaration of war against Germany, Brazil automatically acquired the United States as an ally and thus checkmated Argentina."[82]

In Argentina, Ambassador Frederick Stimson observed less intransigeance within the Yrigoyen administration and widespread approval among the people of the recent wheat convention. Indeed, he regarded the transaction as "most satisfactory . . . both to the Allies and the United States." Although it maintained "an economic alliance with the Argentine which binds that country more closely to the interests of the Allies in the war," he thought the United States also would benefit from more favorable attitudes. The failure of the Argentine plan for a conference of neutrals also gave reason for satisfaction. Mexico alone responded to the call in January 1918 by sending a delegation headed by Luis Cabrera, a Constitutionalist leader and adviser of Carranza, but nothing came of the venture. Although, according to United States naval intelligence, some elements in "local German circles" speculated that a defensive treaty linking Mexico and Argentina against the United States and Brazil might have taken shape, the office of the naval attaché regarded such reports as "absurd." Stimson, in apparent concurrence, reported later on, after meeting with Cabrera, that the envoy wished to speak only of his recent trip to Paraguay and avoided the subject of the neutral conference altogether.[83]

An effort to align Argentina economically more intimately with the United States and the Allies provoked puzzlement and uncertainty in February 1918. The instigator, Ambassador Rómulo S. Naón, had taken an extended leave from Washington, feeling out of touch with his country and government because of his long absence. Upon his return to Buenos Aires, he tried to exert influence over Argentine foreign policy by undertaking an initiative, presumably on his own. Late in February, he approached an officer in the United States embassy, Warren D. Robbins, and suggested a plan of action. Noting that the war had created a treacherous economic environment over which Argentina had no control, Naón proposed to remedy the circumstance through negotiated agreements with the United States and the Entente powers. According to Robbins, he wanted to address "in a permanent way" Argentina's economic and commercial ties with those nations on the presumption that "reciprocal cooperation . . . would permit the Allied Powers on the one side to dispose of their products and Argentina on the other side to make use of the products of the Allies which she may need in the development of her industries." Naón explained further that such an approach should define clearly Argentina's international position so that, in Robbins's words, "she would then appear before the world as definitely a friend of the Allies," and "a political atmosphere . . . propitious in future developments" might come into existence. To safeguard long-term interests, Naón saw no alternative, because Yrigoyen and the Argentine people regarded an open break with Germany as out of the question.[84]

Naón's frankness elicited surprise in the State Department, and the officers in charge advised against any public comments without fuller information and further instructions. Early in March, Naón elaborated upon his thoughts in conversations with Stimson and sweetened the offer. Notably, Argentina should invite sales in Allied countries by extending unlimited credit and also by allotting the German ships interned in Argentine ports. But then, in all likelihood, difficulties developed in winning over Yrigoyen, and the scheme bogged down until later in the month, when Stimson received a lengthy draft in translation. It set forth terms less agreeable to the Allies and more agreeable to the Argentine government. Essentially, the proposal called on the United States, Great Britain, France, and Italy to support and sustain Argentina's commercial and industrial development by providing exports, transport, and loans. Argentina, in return, would encourage the sale of raw materials in the United States and western Europe and do whatever possible to facilitate the financing. Naón hoped to incorporate the provisions into a treaty among the five parties, but Stimson gave him little reason for hope, responding with "no comment whatever," except to assure prompt consideration by the State Department.[85]

Economic issues also dominated relations with Chile but occasioned diminishing cause for worry. Late in January 1918, Ambassador Joseph Shea remarked upon his impression that "the attitude of Chile toward the Allied Cause is better than it has been at any time since our entrance into the war." Although he perceived small chance of a break with Germany, he anticipated no alignment with the enemy either. Within Chile, a ripple of opposition against the creation of the Nitrate of Soda Executive had developed, but Shea attributed it to the resentment of speculators and not to "the thoughtful people of the country," who understood the wishes of the Allies and the United States to expand nitrate production, not to contract it. Indeed, other observers commented that Chileans had "grave concern" over future markets for this product once the war ended and that the French had a deal in mind. If Chile would hand over the 329,000 tons of interned ships in Chilean ports, the Allies and the United States should commit themselves to buy the entire production of nitrates for the next five years. Persistent shortages still caused concern. Indeed, the problem became one of the "pressing questions" before the Supreme War Council late in February 1918 and also worried Robert Lansing, who fretted about "the possible stoppage of production" through sabotage or labor disturbances. In March, he requested immediate "precautionary measures."[86]

As the year advanced, the process of peacemaking and peace-keeping and Latin America's role in it compelled ever more attention. Beginning in the spring, crucial questions raised the issue henceforth of relationships between large and small powers in the conduct of international relations. An unsigned memorandum produced within the Inquiry in April asked, "Will the League of Nations consist of the Great Powers only? If not, what other nations shall be admitted and *how* shall they function?" Another matter focused more specifically on the readiness of Latin American countries to cooperate with the United States and the Allies. A résumé prepared by the Inquiry in the same month presented hopeful expectations. Argentina, though neutral, had made accommodations. Although alarmists still worried about pro-German influences, some even suggesting the possibility of a war against Brazil or Uruguay and the creation of a pro-German federation of states in South America, this report disparaged such notions, pointing out realistically that "These are not probabilities, but merely conceivable perils." In Brazil, the tradition of friendship boded well for the future, even though Ambassador Morgan worried about British and French wiles, and, in Chile, the leaders increasingly recognized a compatibility of interest with the United States and the Allies. The document also emphasized the continued importance of raw materials and resources.[87]

To achieve consolidation, plans within the State Department called for concerted moves. Undersecretary of State William Phillips, for example, drew attention to the west coast of South America, where, according to him, the United States occupied a weak position in need of strengthening, because the region "will play a very important factor in Latin American politics." To accomplish the aim, he proposed shifting around diplomatic appointments in the embassies and legations, putting "the most capable and best trained men whom we have in Latin America, in the strategic ... and most difficult posts." Part of the care in this instance developed from anxiety over the well-being of Ambassador Shea in Chile. An allegation attributed a habit of excessive drinking to him, and when President Wilson responded by suggesting his removal, Phillips advanced a defense based on mitigating circumstances. According to Phillips, "when Judge Shea arrived at his post he had never seen a cock-tail ... the Judge was as delighted with them as a child with a new toy and even grew to like them before breakfast." In Phillips's opinion, "the delight in a new thing rather than any tendency to drunkenness . . . was at the bottom of the trouble."[88]

Robert Lansing also advised close scrutiny of Latin America. In a letter to Dr. Sidney E. Mezes, a leader in the Inquiry, he attributed special importance to Central and South America, particularly "in view of the uncertainty as to the scope of the [peace] conference which will take up world affairs." While recognizing that Latin American issues might not come under consideration at all, Lansing insisted that "as a matter of precaution we should give as careful study to them as to the countries of Europe and Asia, following the same general treatment along historical, ethnological, geographic and economic lines." Lansing worried, "It would be most unfortunate to be without a preparation if these countries become subjects of discussion." Mezes in reply noted budgetary constraints but expressed an intention of taking up Latin America after the other work had advanced further, particularly if facilitated by additional appropriations.[89]

A British mission to South America in the spring of 1918 underscored the intricacy of the issue and intensified the apprehension over economic competition after the war. Under the leadership of Sir Maurice de Bunsen, a special ambassador, the delegation consisting of eight men gave representation to military, naval, political, and commercial interests and departed from Devonport for Rio de Janeiro on 20 April. As a charge, the group had instructions to cultivate goodwill among the countries sympathetic to the Allies in Latin America, to explore "various delicate economic questions," and to improve communications with British diplomats. According to Maurice de Bunsen's own understanding, the mission amounted to "a visible sign of our intention to maintain and even largely develop [sic], both politically and economically, our pre-war position in the South American continent."

"To this end," he remarked, "we must draw closer to the principal countries of South America and strive to convince their Governments that their true interest lies in the triumph of the cause for which the Allies are contending in the war."[90]

An extensive undertaking, the journey took the travelers from Brazil in the middle of May to Uruguay, Argentina, Paraguay, Chile, Peru, Ecuador, Colombia, Venezuela, Cuba, and Washington, D.C., before the return voyage home to London in the fall. Although official pronouncements emphasized friendship, cordiality, and solidarity of purpose with the United States, the visitation distressed United States' observers and possessed more than ritualistic significance. The real issues bore on trade and finance. To nullify any newly won British advantage, the State Department considered for a time in May sending its own expedition, headed by William Howard Taft, on grounds that the Latin Americans would feel flattered by a visit from the portly, former president.[91] But nothing came of it, and other moves ensued.

Ambitious arrangements at the end of May 1918 called upon Brazil to negotiate large loans with United States' bankers, as much as $50,000,000, in a process to be facilitated by guarantees of 250–350,000 tons of manganese each year. Officers in the Treasury Department considered such a deal advantageous to all parties in that Brazil would get capital, the steel industry access to a vital resource, and the United States government assurances of friendly relations. But presumptions over a growing threat of British competition heightened the anxiety. According to some observers, the British aimed at obstructing the operations of United States cable companies in South America. Even worse, other reports in the summer of 1918 suggested that the British firms Sir W. B. Armstrong, Whitford and Company, Ltd., and Vickers, Ltd., had offered to construct in Brazil a marine arsenal with works for the manufacture of arms, ammunition, and steel plate. According to Morgan, the consummation of any such courtship "would close the open door to many foreign products," because Brazil would have "to place orders with British concessionaries" in order to pay the interest. Although interpreting the impending danger as a tribute to de Bunsen's successes, Morgan described it as "a conclusive proof of the commercial and industrial purpose which animated that mission" and "of the intensity, directness and persistence of the present Brazilian drive, not only to secure a fair share for Britain of Brazilian commercial business but to establish monopolies," the outcome of which "would jeopardize the commercial opportunities of other nations."[92]

Other considerations muted the threat. As Morgan recognized, the prospects under incoming president, Rodrígues Alves, gave reason for optimism. According to Morgan, "There is every indication that the

President-elect is a strong Pan-Americanist, believes in continental solidarity and in the influence which the United States should and does exercise over the American continent." In spite of his advanced age and physical frailty, Morgan expected him to exert vigorous leadership. As a sign of goodwill, Frank Polk of the State Department wanted to send a special ambassador to represent the United States at the inauguration, a task carried out later by Rear Admiral William B. Caperton on 15 November. Nevertheless, within the Latin American division of the United States Department of Commerce, the chief, Dr. Julius Klein, grumbled about "rumors . . . of unfortunate friction between British and American agents and trade representatives in various South American cities" and affirmed his wish to keep the rivalry upon "a frank and above-board basis."[93]

In the summer of 1918, the Argentine plan for an economic alliance with the Allies and the United States surfaced again. Upon returning to the United States early in July, Ambassador Rómulo S. Naón bore a second title, that of high financial commissioner, charged with the responsibility of devising the new relationship. Seeking to advance his aim of obtaining greater access to manufactured goods for importation into Argentina, he confided in Frank Polk, claiming as his real desire a wish to bring Argentina into the war, but Yrigoyen, characterized as a provincial who regarded his country as the center of the earth, would never permit it. Therefore, the next best choice required close economic and financial affiliation, preferably by means of a treaty. But the prospective negotiating partner reacted coolly, seeing little point in exchanging large favors for small advantages.[94] Indeed, late in August 1918, Warren D. Robbins, the chargé d' affaires in Buenos Aires, reported that an impressive extension of United States commerce in Argentina already had taken place during the preceding six months. In March 1918, the W. R. Grace Company, Argentina, Sociedad Anónima, acquired permission to carry on a general trade with capital fixed at $500,000 in Argentine gold. Robbins noted that the business had commenced on a large scale and no doubt would figure prominently in the sale of North American machinery and automobiles. In May, a contract established ties between the Beaver Export Corporation of New York and the Argentine State Railways for purchases of heavy equipment exceeding $1,500,00. Moreover, the Pan American Wireless Telegraph and Telephone Company had secured property for the construction of a powerful station near Buenos Aires; the Central and South American Telegraph Company had petitioned for permission to lay cables between the Argentine capital and Uruguay, and the Compañía Swift Internacional and the Frigorífico Armour had expanded upon their meat-packing enterprises. Finally, as concluding indications, the Rohm Hass Company of Wilmington, Delaware, and the Dearborn Chemical Company of Chicago, Illinois, had inaugurated sales; the J. F. Mosser Company of Boston had begun buying Argentine wools and hides, and the Manufacturer's Agents Company of New York had opened a branch in Buenos Aires for the sale of all manner of United States merchandise. But in spite of it, Robbins remarked upon commensurate gains for the British and anticipated an intense struggle for the Argentine market after the war.[95]

Nitrate sales and pessimistic expectations for the future dominated relations with Chile. An Inquiry study in June 1918 by Verne L. Havens, a former commercial attaché in Santiago, observed that the war had so disorganized Chilean foreign trade that "normal data is not available for any year after 1913." Nevertheless, the available information suggested grim prospects. After the fighting, an increase in demand for nitrates in fertilizer would compensate partially for the reduced use in explosives but not enough to avoid a sharp fall in national income. To ward off this "source of great danger," Chilean leaders hoped to increase overseas sales of copper and iron, since in 1916 the country derived more than 50 percent of its revenues from the export tax. The Chileans, meanwhile, lamented their fate. *La Nación* anticipated "distress almost impossible to imagine," and *El Mercurio* called upon the government to inaugurate a campaign for expanded trade with the United States, a course increasingly perceived as the route to rescue. Early in October, Ambassador Shea reported that an emerging concensus supported it.[96]

While economic networks with Argentina, Brazil, and Chile took on increasing importance in the summer and fall of 1918, relations with Mexico deteriorated precipitously. Although the Mexican Constitution of 5 February 1917 had introduced a source of enduring acrimony, the Wilson administration had chosen to avoid forcing the issue until the conclusion of the war in Europe. The provisions in Article Twenty-Seven legitimating the nationalization of mineral resources and the expropriation of foreign-owned petroleum lands particularly caused trouble. Oilmen in the United States attributed a confiscatory intent to them and won the diplomatic support of their government in efforts to delay implementation. The Carranza regime, meanwhile, kept the issue alive by calling for the registration of petroleum lands with federal authorities and the validation of foreign-held concessions, thereby eliciting a sequence of protests from the United States.[97]

The controversy took on alarming proportions in the summer of 1918 in response to an effusive address by President Wilson before a delegation of visiting the Mexican newspapermen. After affirming his "sincere friendship" for the Mexican people, he described his sentiment as "not merely the sort of friendship which prompts one not to do his neighbor any harm, but the sort of friendship which earnestly desires to do his neighbor service." He claimed that, properly understood, the principle of nonintervention had always underlain his policy toward Mexico, in elaboration asserting that "the internal settlement of the affairs of Mexico was none of our business. . . . When we sent troops into Mexico, our sincere desire was nothing else than to assist you to get rid of a man who was making the settlement of your affairs for the time being impossible." He then resurrected the defunct Pan American Treaty and issued an appeal.

> Some time ago, as you probably all know, I proposed a sort of Pan American agreement. I had perceived that one of the difficulties of our relationship with Latin America was this: The famous Monroe Doctrine was adopted without your consent, without the consent of any of the Central or South American States. . . . Very well, let us make an arrangement by which we will give bond. Let us have a common guaranty, that all of us will sign, of political independence and territorial integrity. Let us agree that if anyone of us, the United States included, violates the political independence or the territorial integrity of any of the others, all the others will jump on her.[98]

Wilson's expression of goodwill unexpectedly precipitated a storm of criticism in Mexico. Newspaper attacks, probably officially inspired, assailed the president for duplicity and hypocrisy, a charge growing from the alleged incompatibility of his words with the official position of his government in the controversy over Article Twenty-Seven of the Mexican Constitution. On 2 April 1918, Ambassador Henry P. Fletcher had filed a formal protest against an apparent "intention" to separate the ownership of surface lands from the mineral resources beneath, to allow the present owners "a mere preference" in the process of validating rights, and also to levy exorbitant taxes. Though he disclaimed any wish to obstruct policies carried out "for sound reasons of public utility" and with "just compensation," his government would not sanction any procedure "resulting in confiscation of private property and arbitrary deprivation of vested rights." Since Mexican practices implied "a trend in that direction," Fletcher emphasized "the necessity" which may impel the United States "to protect the property of its citizens in Mexico divested or injuriously affected."[99]

The disparity supposedly suggested a likelihood of interference or intervention, and Mexicans reacted with outrage. Under the headline "President Wilson Threatens Mexico," *El Pueblo* on 14 June compared

Wilson's speech with Fletcher's note. The former, "theatrical" and "sonorous," a public show of "benevolence, disinterestedness, and nobility," contrasted unfavorably with the latter, "secret . . . hard . . . threatening . . . an eloquent indication of what the powerful neighbor is capable of doing to protect the property of its citizens in Mexico." According to *El Pueblo*, "Each gives the lie to the other," another example of "a double game" played by the United States for seventy years. The paper warned that such affirmations of peace and friendship historically preceded fresh acts of aggression.

In subsequent editorials, *El Pueblo* articulated an interpretation of the nature of national sovereignty and a ringing defense, characterized as the Carranza Doctrine. According to this rendition, the promulgation of petroleum legislation, an attribute of national sovereignty, allowed no grounds for diplomatic protest and hence rendered the United States' position unacceptable. Elaborations later extended the claim. On 29 June, under the headline "The Monroe Doctrine Annulled by the Carranza Doctrine," *El Pueblo* published extracts from the First Chief's speech at San Luis Potosí on 26 December 1915 and presented them as universal principles by which to govern the conduct of international relations. As a result of Mexico's recent experience with the United States, Carranza called upon all nations to join in absolute adherence to the principle of nonintervention. He wanted particularly for the countries of Latin America to side with Mexico in "the establishment of Justice and Right," the abolition of foreign privileges, the abandonment of force in defense of private economic interests, the respect of the strong for the weak, and the ascendancy of national sovereignty. On the following day, *El Pueblo* expressly repudiated the Monroe Doctrine. Claiming that the Mexican government no longer concurred in the supervision of its "foreign or interior affairs" by the United States, the Carranza Doctrine required "a policy of close union and real solidarity with Latin America" so that the republics of Central and South America could participate in the true defense of national equality and self-determination. A similar emphasis marked Carranza's address before the Mexican Congress on 1 September 1918.[100]

Carranza's invocation of the Pan Hispanic alternative dismayed Henry Fletcher and other United States officials. Fletcher initially attributed it to a deliberate attempt "to prove . . . insincerity and to destroy the good effect" of President Wilson's commitment to Pan Americanism. Later he ascribed more sinister intentions, claiming that "Carranza aims, not only at the elimination of the financial, economic, and political influence of the United States in Mexico, but also hopes by alliance with a strong European and Asiatic power and treaties with other Latin-American States, to isolate the United States and destroy its influence in this hemisphere." He also anticipated a Mexican readiness to force a "showdown." As Fletcher explained, "Under the shibboleth of this new Carranza Doctrine," Mexico would seek "to enforce Article 27 of the Constitution and justify its disregard of the elemental principles of justice and fair dealings in its treatment of foreigners" on grounds that "its action affects nationals and foreigners alike and that foreigners therefore have no right to complain."[101]

The implications had far-reaching significance for the process of peacemaking and after. At the very least, the Mexican advocacy threatened to diminish the cohesiveness of relations among the nations in the western hemisphere and to undercut the political and economic prerequisites upon which Wilson calculated his plans for after the war. A condition of such disarray, further, might invite more powerful forms of European competition and even confront the president with an international alignment of foreign states directed against the exercise of United States influence. These disturbing prospects called for strong responses. Boaz Long, an official in the State Department, unblinkingly assessed some possibilities and set forth widely shared views in August 1918. While recognizing that "The European war now commands our first attention," rendering "Everything else . . . secondary," even "a policy of temporization" in Mexico, he reasoned that "The logical and natural thing" compelled the Wilson administration "to contemplate . . . a settlement of the Mexican situation immediately after the conclusion of the European peace." Since "the rehabilitation of Mexico is an American problem, and . . . European nations will not be welcomed to assist," the responsibility for "reintroducing peace and prosperity in Mexico" would fall uniquely upon the United States.[102] The problem of arranging the peace while retaining the prerogative of managing the affairs of the western hemisphere held special significance for after the war.

Room for All Under the New Umbrella, by Cartoonist Charles L. "Bart" Bartholomew. Reprinted from the *Minneapolis News*, with permission.

CHAPTER FOUR

The Consequences of Making Peace

November 1918—March 1921

AT THE END OF THE GREAT WAR on 11 November 1918, the United. States possessed the dominant influence in the western hemisphere and ambitious plans in other regions. For leaders in the Wilson administration, the process of making peace required a creative involvement by the United States. As a basic strategy, President Wilson intended to act as the arbiter, imposing the terms and procedures upon both sets of belligerents, the Central Powers and the Entente nations. To bring about the necessary reform and rehabilitation, he would purge the European system of militarism, colonialism, and autocracy, the presumed causes of the war, and institute a new era of peace, characterized by the institutions of free trade, representative democracy, and international cooperation. His preferred methods, the devices of self-determination, collective security, and the League of Nations, drew on his experiences with Latin America and incorporated the supposition of natural harmonies. Nevertheless, Latin Americans played an inconsequential role at the peace conference, overshadowed always by the interests of the Great Powers and the special relationship with the United States. While Wilson professed his aim for a just and lasting peace among equals, his critics in Latin America wondered how he would reconcile hegemonial assumptions in the New World with his opposition to such conditions in the Old. Could the Monroe Doctrine coexist logically with the Fourteen Points? A tendency to relegate Latin American concerns to a lesser plane produced dismay and disquietude over prospects for the future.

POSSESSING THE DOMINANT INFLUENCE

The commanding position of the United States over trade and investment in Latin America at the end of the war expressed one form of dominating influence. The raw figures showed dramatic changes. According to the published statistics, the volume of commerce with the twenty republics had expanded significantly between 1 July 1914 and 30 June 1917, showing an increase of 105 percent for United States imports from Latin America and 109 percent for exports. At the end of June 1918 a year later, the numbers showed that aggregates had grown 133 percent larger than in 1914, and that the dollar totals amounted to $1,741,892,128 in comparison with $747,308,215.[1]

Such sums invited close scrutiny and admonitions in behalf of careful interpretation. A study prepared for the Inquiry by John Barrett and W. C. Wells, the chief statistician of the Pan American Union, manipulated the figures revealingly. As they observed, the published statistics during the four war years showed that United States imports from Latin America had expanded by 118 percent and exports by 157 percent but failed to represent accurately "a true index of the increases in volume." Rather, the numbers reflected inflationary trends and marked "to a very considerable extent the advance in prices" since the onset of the war. Another problem resulted from the insufficiency of data in all countries to render more accurate computations. Barrett and Wells estimated that the figures actually ran low, an understatement of 15–20 percent for imports from Latin America and 10–12 percent for exports. Taking into account this correction, they calculated the real trade for the year ending 30 June 1914 at $857,000,000 and for 30 June 1918 at $1,998,000,000.

Further refinements and adjustments demonstrated that the true growth amounted to 46.5 percent in imports, 42.1 percent in exports, and 44.9 percent for the whole. Moreover, Barrett and Wells affirmed, it signified an enlargement of an old trade, not necessarily a new one. The imports brought into the United States "alimentary substances" and the "so-called raw products used in the industries upon which the country is dependent to a very large extent." These included copper, gold, silver, zinc, lead, sisal, wool, rubber, hides, skins, nitrates, sugar, and coffee. To be sure, these items comprised the "chief" imports from around the world, but, according to this report, "the most significant thing about the list is that Latin America is for the United States the principal, in many cases, the only, market outside its own territory within which to secure these commodities so necessary to our industry." Similarly, the majority of United States exports into Latin America, though much broader in range than usually understood, comprising "practically every line of manufacture," represented an enlargement of an already established trade, accentuated by the reduced capabilities of the British, French, and Germans to compete. By the day of the armistice, the United States had taken over about 90 percent of Latin America's import trade with the outside world, and, according to Barrett and Wells, the tendency would persist for some time. Comparative efficiencies would establish the key. As long as United States manufacturers sold better goods at cheaper prices than European competitors, they could retain their dominance within the market. In addition, the development and utilization of new commercial agencies, including ships and banks, would provide immeasurable advantages.[2]

Appraisals of the future generally expressed optimistic expectations. The *Bulletin* of the Pan American Union affirmed the view in a sequence of published articles. An assessment of "the probable course of trade after the war" in January 1918 predicted a continued expansion. It explained, "the increases in United States trade are greatest where this trade was most firmly established before the war." It claimed too that "the building of the new trade is not accidental, as many believe, but is the legitimate outgrowth of a trade that before the war had already in a large measure displaced German and British trade," and the story took pains to rebut the false belief "fostered by German propaganda" that "the large increase in United States exports to Latin America has no other foundation than the present inability of Latin America to import from Europe, particularly Germany." In October 1918, the *Bulletin* heralded the new day, declaring that "a great awakening throughout all America" had taken place. "America is coming to know itself. No part thereof need longer consider itself as an appendage, culturally, industrially, or commercially, of any part of Europe." Although conceding that "The European trade with America will revive after the war, no one doubts that," the *Bulletin* asserted, nevertheless, that "it will never occupy the predominating position in . . . Latin America it did occupy before the war."[3]

During the war years, the Commerce Department issued periodic warnings of British, French, and German preparations for resuming economic competition after the war. To underscore the point, Ambassador Shea in Santiago emphasized the effects of the Bunsen mission to South America, affirming that "British business interests in Chile have been very active in an effort to recover trade which has been diverted from the European countries to the United States during the war." But in spite of such premonitions, the degree of United States preponderance never came seriously under challenge. The figures during the first nine months of 1919 showed that United States' trade with Latin America exceeded Great Britain's by a substantial margin, with exports valued at $630,950,122 in comparison with $168,569,280, and the

imports at $931,946,714 to $520,465,195. The Europeans never succeeded in reversing the trend.[4]

Part of the reason had to do with the construction of a merchant
fleet. An achievement attained during the war years, the aim had
animated interest in the Wilson administration from the beginning. As
the P.A.U. *Bulletin* reported in September 1918, "America is engaged
in the upbuilding of the greatest merchant marine ever owned by any
nation." According to the prevailing estimates, "Of the 25,000,000 tons
of ocean-going tonnage which the United States Shipping Board plans
to have completed by 1920 upwards of 8,000,000 tons will be available
for South American commerce." The productive capacities of United
States industry had worked miracles during the war. According to the
Bulletin, shipbuilders recently had launched a 5,000-ton collier a mere
twenty-seven days after laying the keel and on another occasion had
turned out ninety-five ships in a single day. As observed by Edward N.
Hurley, the chairman of the Shipping Board, the United States had
constructed "the vast tonnage . . . for the defense of civilization; for the
hurrying of troops and their supplies to the battle lines of the allies."
But, Hurley emphasized, "with the coming of peace there will be this
new-made fleet in full readiness to carry to all markets the merchandise
that has been congesting in terminals for lack of transportation." Hurley calculated that "with the advent of peace South America should
come into an era of unprecedented prosperity, provided ships are
available," and "can count it something more than fortunate that her
great sister of the north will be in a position to carry all the exports she
wishes to freight to foreign ports and to bring in all the imports which
her merchants need." A special emphasis would cater to the needs of
Argentina, Brazil, and Chile, allocating an estimated 2,500,000 –
3,000,000 deadweight tons to each.[5]

Another article in the *Bulletin* in February 1919 reviewed the
course of the naval war in Latin America and evaluated some of the
consequences. At the beginning of the conflict, German and Austrian
warships and merchant vessels took refuge in their own harbors or
sought internment in neutral ports in order to escape destruction by
the Royal British Navy. Subsequently, a few German raiders caused
sporadic trouble, but the submarines posed the gravest danger to
Allied commerce. During 1916 and 1917, the U-boats sank ships at
rates more rapid than the Allies could construct them. When Wilson
entered into the war, the United States took over as the chief ship-
builder, and its merchant flag quickly, if uncharacteristically, became
"a familiar sight wherever ships sailed." In calculating the needs for
after the fighting, the Shipping Board anticipated the utilization of 431
vessels in plying the Latin American trade, including the West Indies,
of which 238 would possess United States registry.[6]

The establishment of branch banks in Latin America also facilitated the extension of United States commerce. By the end of the war, the National City Bank of New York City had facilities in the major cities, including the capitals of Argentina, Brazil, Chile, Cuba, Peru, Venezuela, and Uruguay. Moreover, the Commercial Bank of Boston, the American Foreign Banking Corporation of New York, and the Mercantile Bank of the Americas had founded others. Though the advocates of trade expansion still wanted more, the Commerce Department affirmed, "Progress in these directions during the last year has been continuous, and the outlook is now more promising than it has been for some time." This particular publication concluded with the satisfying assurance that such attainments would "insure the United States its due share in the development of the world's business."[7]

Changing investment patterns also showed the extent of the predominating influence of the United States. Although the available figures also lack precision, the published statistics allowed some appreciation for the magnitude of the shift from 1913 during the war years and into the 1920s. According to the analysis presented by Max Winkler, direct United States investments of Latin America in 1913, amounting to $1,242,000,000, rose to $5,587,494,100 in 1929. For Great Britain, in contrast, the 1913 total of $4,983,320,000 had expanded only to $5,889,353,000 in 1929. A detailed Department of Commerce study published in 1918 illuminated the process. As a premise, it claimed "One of the outstanding facts in the foreign commerce of the great exporting nations has been the way in which such trade has been enlarged and stimulated by the investment of capital in the countries to which the goods are sold." Indeed, according to this analysis, "the willingness of foreign capitalists to assist in the development of a country's resources creates a favorable attitude on the part of that country's citizens and a receptivity toward other business propositions." It averred, moreover, "Before the war the commanding position of European nations in certain Latin-American markets was due in large measure to their great investment there."[8]

The introductory sections characterized the South American continent as a region with "extensive areas of undeveloped and partly developed territories" and as "a magnet for the investment of considerable amounts of foreign capital." Before the war, "Great Britain, France, Germany, Belgium, the Netherlands, and to a less extent, perhaps, the United States . . . investigated opportunities in the southern continent" and "successfully developed railways and public utilities, mines and manufactures, farms and cattle ranches, have purchased Government, State, and municipal bonds, and have otherwise made investments in the field." But with the onset of the First World War, "an immediate change" took place. "The conservation of the resources of the warring countries and their neighbors immediately stopped the exportation of capital from Europe, and the Latin American republics became dependent on the United States for their needs financially." The document explained that, before the war, "the interests of the United States in South America, other than in mines and the packing industry, were negligible." But after 1914, since the Europeans no longer possessed the wherewithal, North American bankers developed interests in floating loans and purchasing bonds. Their attention centered particularly on railroads, mining, petroleum, nitrates, manganese, and "other forms of enterprise." The details constituted the body of this substantial 544-page compendium, laying out the information on a country-by-country basis, particularly in regard to government, state, and municipal loans, banks, railways, public utilities, insurance companies, manufactures, mines, shipping, forest products, and agriculture. The influx of capital established a large stake for United States investors.[9]

PEACE PRELIMINARIES

In the preliminaries to the peace conference, Latin America and its affairs figured only peripherally. For the planners, the traumatic effects of war and revolution created profound urgencies out of concern for what remained of established order. To address them, President Wilson intended to lead the United States delegation in Paris and to restore the world. In comparison with the European wreckage, the most compelling questions in Latin America faded in intensity. Nevertheless, to achieve adequate preparation, the Latin American divisions of the State Department and the Inquiry launched a cooperative venture through the collaborative efforts of their respective chiefs, Jordan H. Stabler and Dr. Bailey Willis.

The ensuing investigations of Latin American affairs covered a broad range of questions. Though prominent concerns centered on historical and geographical issues, the central ones focused on complicated boundary disputes, pitting in one instance or another almost all of the countries of South America against a neighbor. In this context, the Tacna-Arica controversy retained special importance. Other matters entailed Latin America's future role in the economic and political systems to emerge from the peace, notably, the capacity to contribute to "the World's Raw Materials," and the "Status of so-called Latin American 'Republics' among the democracies of the World." On these points, paternalistic preconceptions framed the issues for scholars in the Inquiry. In an extraordinary expression, one document anticipated the classification of nations "as mature, immature or criminal" and the development of tests "to determine whether they are yet ready to be allowed to conduct their own affairs in a world to be governed by reason and justice in accordance with the principles of democracy." Further, it put forth the questions, "how will they affect the Latin-American nations [?] How many Cubas are there?"[10]

In another appraisal, Professor Bailey Willis of the Inquiry established similar themes. According to him, the questions most likely to come under discussion at the peace conference addressed the likelihood of war over territorial disputes, the role of Latin America in world trade, the capability of the governments to behave with responsibility, and the capacity of volatile and racially mixed peoples to practice self-determination. In the ensuing studies, the members of the Inquiry expended less effort and money than for other portions of the globe. Dr. Sidney Mezes told Lansing that he could probably wrap up the Latin American segment without exhausting the allocated budget of $6,000. In any case, he worried that "the results would hardly bear on the peace conference and should be judged on the basis of their possible utility to the Department of State," for which purpose Lansing authorized a three-month continuation of the cooperative effort between the Inquiry and the Latin American Affairs Division.[11]

An interest more inportant than the conduct of Latin American affairs concerned the extent to which the traditions of United States' statecraft in the western hemisphere might serve the Europeans in the future as a model and a guide. No less an authority than Woodrow Wilson observed an analogous relationship and presented the essentials of his thoughts before the Senate on 22 January 1917 in his famous "peace without victory" speech. While putting a charge before the inhabitants of the United States, asking that they play a conspicuous part "in that great enterprise" of devising anew "the foundations of peace among the nations," he proposed to attain conditions of order and justice by instituting "a peace between equals" and incorporating "the principle that governments derive all their just powers from the consent of the governed." Joint measures with "the other civilized nations of the world" would guarantee "peace, equality, and cooperation," and the prescribed means should draw upon the unique experiences of the United States in the western hemisphere. The full passage provided an explicit invocation:

> I am proposing . . . that the nations should with one accord adopt the doctrine of President Monroe as the doctrine of the world: that no nation should seek to extend its polity over any other nation or people, but that every people should be left free to determine its own polity, its own way of development, unhindered, unthreatened, unafraid, the little along with the great and powerful.

> I am proposing that all nations henceforth avoid entangling
> alliances which would draw them into competitions of power; catch
> them in a net of intrigue and selfish rivalry and disturb their own
> affairs with influences from without. There is no entangling al-
> liance in a concert of power. When all unite to act in the same sense
> and with the same purpose all act in the common interest and are
> free to live their own lives under a common protection.[12]

The timeless wisdom of the Founding Fathers, thus rendered
universal in applicability, inspired the vision for later extrapolation.
The most important rendition, the Fourteen Points, first articulated
before the Congress on 8 January 1918, set forth a fuller version in
richer detail. Exclaiming at the first that "we entered this war because
violations of right had occurred . . . and made the life of our people
impossible," Wilson intended to provide a correction and to bring into
existence a world "made fit and safe to live in." The initial five points set
forth general principles: "Open convenants of peace, openly arrived
at" to avert the pitfalls of secret diplomacy; "Absolute freedom of
navigation upon the seas" to overcome the peril of the submarine;
"The removal, so far as possible, of all economic barriers and the
establishment of an equality of trade conditions among nations" to
prevent the division of the world into economic blocs; the reduction of
"national armaments" to diminish the risk of war, and "a free, open-
minded and absolutely impartial adjustment of all colonial claims" to
assure just treatment for all people. The next eight points advanced
solutions to specific territorial questions, all based on the right to
self-determination, and the last, the most momentous, called forth "A
general association of nations . . . formed under specific covenants for
the purpose of affording mutual guarantees of political independence
and territorial integrity to great and small states alike."[13] The Four-
teenth Point had descended directly from the earlier Pan American
Pact.

Public discussions in the United States provoked sharp differences
over the wisdom and desirability of Wilson's peace plan. Republicans
by and large disliked it, in part because they had no hand in fashioning
it, and also because they mistrusted some of the implications. The
League, collective security, and the effects on national sovereignty
caused concern, and so did the impact on the traditional structure of
relations in the western hemisphere. Would membership in a suprana-
tional organization unwork regional arrangements, such as the Monroe Doctrine? One authority on the subject, Professor John H. Latané
of Johns Hopkins University, a diplomatic historian who wrote one of
the first comprehensive accounts of relations with Latin America, disparaged the apprehension and endorsed Wilson's view, claiming that

the methods of statecraft in the western hemisphere, indeed, held the key to peace in the future. As he wrote in July 1917, "The Monroe Doctrine is a guarantee of the *status quo*, the only principle on which the peace of the world can securely rest." To overcome the European practices of alliance systems and balances of power, the United States must seek "universal recognition" of Monroe's declaration "in favor of guaranteeing to free states the right of self development" and join with the Europeans in "some form of world confederation" in defense of peace and democracy. Arriving at quite different conclusions, Senator Henry Cabot Lodge of Massachusetts, Wilson's great antagonist in the debate over the treaty, suggested "the possibility of arranging for two Leagues,—one in Europe and the other America with the United States in control under the Monroe Doctrine, the two Leagues to cooperate if the need arose," As the historian William C. Widenor noted, although such an approach conformed more closely with the traditions and prejudices of the populace and might haved edged them closer to acceptance of the internationalist position, it had no chance of winning over Woodrow Wilson.[14]

John Barrett, too, saw many parallels and campaigned indefatigably in behalf of Wilson's peace plan. When the war ended in November 1918, he assessed the impact, claiming that it had done more than anything since the declaration of the Monroe Doctrine "to develop both practical and ideal Pan-American solidarity." The American peoples in the various republics had come to "a mutual realization of their interdependence." Barrett advised close scrutiny in the workings of the Pan American Union and depicted it in his writings as "A working Prototype of a World League of Nations." This particular analysis went out to members of the United States peace delegation in Paris and eulogized the Pan American Union for "preserving and enlarging the principles of practical Pan Americanism, the Doctrine of Monroe, and the right of a group of nations with mutual political and economic interests and geographic propinquity to act and stand together for their own good and that of the world." In another essay entitled "Practical Pan Americanism—Past, Present and Future," Barrett asserted that "Pan Americanism has experienced a remarkable development during the last ten years" and "should show a far greater record of achievement" in the decade to come. He had no doubt that peacemakers would benefit from the precedent.[15]

More mundane procedural questions preoccupied the conference organizers, particularly over the role of the lesser powers. On 15 November 1918, Brazil raised the issue, inquiring whether to seek representation at the preliminary meetings scheduled to take place at Versailles. Domicio da Gama, now the Foreign Minister, also wanted to know when the actual peace conference would get underway and whether protocol required that he lead the Brazilian delegation. When the State Department put him off, responding that no need existed for sending anyone yet, the representatives in the Brazilian Chamber of Deputies wanted to know how and by what means the participants would receive invitations. The United States later made certain that Brazil would take the most active part among the Latin American states, thereby affirming once again the dictates of the unwritten alliance, in part, perhaps, because of some uncertainty over Brazilian politics. A severe illness prevented the president-elect, Rodríguez Alves, from taking office on inauguration day, 15 November 1918, putting Dr. Delfim Moreira into the acting role. Later, Rodríguez Alves's death from a heart attack on 16 January 1919 compelled a special election and brought forth the candidacy of Ruy Barbosa, a critic of Brazil's attachment to the United States and Pan Americanism. A victory for him might produce unwanted changes, but Captain C. T. Vogelgesang, U.S.N., upon his return to the United States after serving as a naval instructor in Brazil, saw little likelihood. According to him, the Brazilians favored "the solidarity of the Western Hemisphere." They "crave a closer relationship with us . . . and know it will come with closer trade relations."[16]

On the morning of 4 December 1918, President Woodrow Wilson departed New York City for Paris aboard the *George Washington* as the head of the United States Peace Commission, which also included Colonel House, Secretary Lansing, Henry White, a career diplomat, and General Tasker Bliss, formerly of the Supreme War Council. At this point, procedural ambiguities still abounded, and various Latin American governments pressed for a definition of their proposed roles, particularly, as with Uruguay, if a break in relations with Germany had taken place. After Colonel House reported from Paris that "considerable opposition" existed "to bringing into the preliminary conferences [any] but the great Allied powers and the United States," observers in the State Department and the Inquiry tried to anticipate what to expect. Various reports and studies reviewed the behavior and attitudes of Latin American countries during the war and concluded that among the belligerent nations, Cuba, Haiti, Guatemala, Honduras, Nicaragua, Costa Rica, Panama, and Brazil, the majority had contributed nothing at all to the German defeat and therefore deserved no consideration at all for any kind of a reward. The exceptions, Cuba, Panama, and Brazil, in contrast, had cooperated closely with the United States and had grounds for legitimate claims. Brazil, for example, might want to keep the interned German vessels and also to obtain loans in support of economic development. Among the nonbelligerents severing ties with Germany, Uruguay and Peru might seek support from the United States in various territorial disputes, most notably the Tacna and Arica question, while the others, Ecuador, Bolivia, and Santo Domingo, warranted nothing for having done nothing. The remainder, Argentina, Chile, Colombia, Mexico, El Salvador, and Venezuela, had stayed neutral, and, according to Stabler and Willis, "are not entitled to consideration at the Peace Conference."[17]

Some measure of clarification came about by the end of the year when the United States decided to support Central and South American countries in their aspiration to attend the conference if the governments in question either had declared war or broken relations. Informally, Lansing encouraged that they send a delegate or two, "in case they are to be accorded representation," but, apparently convinced that they would count for little, he included no Latin American specialists among his technical advisers. Argentina, meanwhile, mounted a campaign, wishing also to take part, affirming friendly sentiments toward the Allies and the United States, in spite of neutrality, and also a profound wish to become part of the League of Nations. But Frank Polk in the State Department stood in opposition, insisting that wartime attitudes provided the grounds for disqualification.[18]

The Great Powers finally agreed upon a tripartite approach for allocating representation. Within the first rank, the great belligerent nations with general interests in the peace settlement would attend all sessions and take part in all commissions and committee assignments charged with specific tasks and responsibilities. These included the United States, Great Britain, France, Italy, and Japan. Within the second rank, the belligerent countries with special interests, notably Belgium, Brazil, the British Dominions, India, China, Cuba, Greece, Guatemala, Haiti, the Hedjaz, Honduras, Liberia, Nicaragua, Panama, Poland, Portugal, Rumania, Serbia, Siam, and Czechoslovakia, would take selective part, participating in those proceedings focused on questions of special significance to them. Last, neutral states and newly formed governments might appear in response to invitations from the Great Powers. Eleven Latin American countries sent formal missions, among them Bolivia, Brazil, Cuba, Ecuador, Guatemala, Haiti, Honduras, Nicaragua, Panama, Peru, and Uruguay. In addition, Mexico sent an envoy, Alberto J. Pani. Though never officially received, he lobbied against interventionist pressures in Mexico and kept his government informed.[19]

TACNA AND ARICA

While momentous global issues absorbed the attention of leaders among the Great Powers, a provincial concern in South America suddenly flared into prominence. The difficulty over Tacna and Arica

developed soon after the armistice, the result of Peruvian demonstrations in behalf of self-determination. During the war, Peru followed
the United States' lead by severing diplomatic relations with Germany,
but the country refrained from a declaration of war, according to
President José Pardo, on grounds that it lacked the means to fight an
adversary some eight thousand miles away. At the conclusion of the
peace, Peruvian nationalists in and around Tacna and Arica seized the
opportunity publicly to champion the rights of small nations and provoked countermeasures and mob violence. In November and December, notably in Iquique, Peruvian banking and commercial houses
came under assault, and Peruvian nationals experienced threats, in-
timidation, and even physical expulsion. Levels of trepidation ran
high. Indeed, according to one United States observer, the unrest
introduced a "virtual reign of terror" and resulted in a decision by the
Peruvian government to withdraw consular representation from Chilean cities.[20]

The region under dispute, containing a populace of 38,000 in a
territory a little larger than Massachusetts, also sparked the interest of
land-locked Bolivia. Seeking to unwork the inequities of history, the
Bolivian government in November set forth a set of claims to a port on
the sea and also to the cession of all of Arica. Comparing themselves
with the Serbians, the Bolivians claimed that an interposition of their
authority between the Chileans and Peruvians would serve in the long
run the cause of peace. They also affirmed their intention of sending a
delegation to Paris to address the matter, unless the United States
initiated immediate procedures for procuring a settlement. The possibility of utilizing the international forum in forcing resolution of local
disputes held some attraction.[21]

The State Department responded by attempting to exercise restraint and calm. On 4 December, Frank Polk sent identical statements
to the presidents of Peru and Chile, affirming that his government
viewed the severance of consular relations "with the gravest apprehension." Polk exclaimed, "Any agitation tending to lessen the prospect for
permanent peace throughout the world, particularly on the eve of the
convoking of the Peace Conference in Paris" could have "disastrous"
implications. To ward them off, he advised that "the Government of
the United States stands ready to tender alone, or in conjunction with
the other countries of the hemisphere, all possible assistance to bring
about an equitable solution of the matter." On the same day, Polk tried
to enlist the support of Argentina and Brazil, urging them to use their
influence with Chile and Peru in behalf of moderation. But the de-
marche collapsed amidst the ensuing confusion and misinterpreta-
tion.[22]

Perhaps in a conscious effort to bring in the United States, the Peruvian government misconstrued the offer and announced on 9 December its acceptance of mediation proceedings, calculating in all likelihood that the interjection of outside authority would work as an advantage. On the same day, other reports indicated that Argentina also had extended to Chile a similar proposition, all of which surprised and dismayed Counselor Frank Polk. Seeking clarification on 11 December, he inquired whether President Wilson really intended to suggest something as formal as mediation or merely to make available "all possible assistance" in bringing about a resolution "to the present difficulties" in Iquique. Polk preferred the more limited aim. Chile, meanwhile, responded to the initial communication on 9 December by acknowledging receipt and affirming pacific intentions but then, two days later, expressed uncertainty over the Argentine bid, claiming correctly that it went well beyond President Wilson's stated intention. Chile wanted a more precise definition of the scope. The Argentine Foreign Ministry, in response, professed ignorance, explaining that it had offered "good offices," not "mediation," and that an error in transmission or transcription must have occurred. From Paris, Lansing tried to overcome the mix-up by denying on 18 December that President Wilson had intended to convey a formal offer but hoped only to facilitate some kind of settlement "at a time when the whole world is looking toward the avoidance of force in the adjustment of international controversies." Lansing also wanted to contain the dispute within the western hemisphere and to avoid putting it before the peace conference.[23]

In a letter to Wilson on 28 December, Lansing characterized the wrangle over Tacna and Arica as "a vexatious one," rendered all the more complex by the Bolivian intrusion, in which he found "a mixture of justice and reason" but thought it unlikely to stimulate much sympathy in Chile or Peru. If the United States should support the Bolivian desire for a seaport, President Wilson could count on winning the animosity of both Chile and Peru. A formal involvement in mediation or arbitration, similarly, would entail difficulties, because any decision, "however just," would provoke resentment from one or the other. As Lansing observed, "The whole situation is charged with trouble which it will be hard to avoid."[24]

Addressing the same issue at the end of the year, two technical advisers with the Inquiry, James Brown Scott and David Hunter Miller, provided an assessment. Characterizing the issue as "frankly diplomatic" and "not judicial," Scott and Miller recommended against any attempt to seek a "comprehensive solution . . . at this time." A variety of conditions and the complexity and scope of the controversy militated against any such approach. Since for them the "great concern of the United States" resided more in preventing "a resort to force" than in achieving an immediate settlement, the proper means invited negotiation and delay to head off war, possibly by invoking William Jennings Bryan's "cooling off" treaties of 1915. Frank Polk, in disagreement, perceived greater need for urgency. Lacking "a definite settlement," disturbances over Tacna and Arica could take place at any time and might draw in other nations. But Polk understood the difficulty. Chile, in all likelihood, would resist requirements imposed from the outside, and, if the United States should succeed in bringing about mediation or arbitration, it would elicit unhappiness in Peru or in Chile or in both. Polk now intimated that the best approach might set the Tacna-Arica issue before whatever peacekeeping machinery should emerge from the peace conference, but he knew too that such an expedient might appear to critics in the United States as a violation of the Monroe Doctrine.[25]

The two authorities with the Inquiry, David Hunter Miller and James Brown Scott, took seriously the latter danger and warned against "any possible prejudice to the American views and interests relating to the Monroe Doctrine." Indeed, they suggested the utility of encouraging direct negotiations between the two countries and won over Robert Lansing. On 16 January 1919, he characterized the dispute as "purely American" and advised against submission to the peace conference, where Peru, in any event, might enjoy an advantage for having broken relations with Germany. For Lansing, a diplomatic rather than a juridical solution also set forth the proper aim. But the Peruvians, more ambitious and disinclined to go along, served notice on 23 January of their desire to pursue a settlement at Paris. Hoping to dissuade them, Polk argued the case that territorial questions in the New World always should come first under the jurisdiction of the Pan American powers, but he failed to establish the point. The Tacna and Arica controversy still defied solution when the peace delegations seriously got down to business.[26]

THE CONFERENCE PROCEEDINGS

The conference proceedings formally convened on 12 January 1919, and the distribution of responsibility and authority posed an immediate problem. With hundreds of participants and observers in attendance from the twenty allied and associated powers at war with Germany, the vast clutter of people impeded the conduct of business in plenary sessions. According to plans, various commissions and committees would investigate the principal questions, assemble the germane information, and make appropriate recommendations to the larger body. The limited number of seats available made them the object of rivalry, especially among the lesser states. During the early stages, the Supreme Council, or the Council of Ten, took charge. It consisted of the two ranking delegates, the head of state and the foreign minister, from each of the five Great Powers, Great Britain, France, Italy, Japan, and the United States, but it too functioned awkwardly, and in March 1919 the Council of Four became the center of power. For the duration, Prime Minister David Lloyd George of Great Britain, Premier Georges Clemenceau of France, Premier Vittorio Orlando of Italy, and President Woodrow Wilson of the United States assumed the responsibility of determining the fate of the world.[27]

The urgency bore heavily upon them and required immediate measures. For the Europeans, the ruination of their continent, the collapsed political and economic systems, and the specter of Bolshevism demanded first attention, followed by other efforts to address the German question, the disposition of German colonies, the arrangement of complex territorial issues, and the definition of continental security for the future. But Wilson, the outsider, inverted the order of priorities and insisted upon the creation of a League of Nations as the first consideration. When he presented the details before the conference by reading the text of the League Covenant on 14 February 1919, he declared, "A living thing is born." The task of translating the Fourteen Points into specific peace terms still remained.[28]

For Latin Americans, the dominance of the Big Powers caused contention and bitterness. Though Robert Lansing remedied an earlier oversight by summoning to the conference an expert on Latin America, Jordan H. Stabler of the Division of Latin American Affairs in the State Department, the Latin American delegations, nevertheless, bridled over the peripheral roles assigned to them and the exclusion from the centers of decision-making capability. On 25 January 1919, Pandía Calogeras of Brazil complained, "It is with some surprise that I constantly hear it said: 'This has been decided, that has been decided.' Who has taken a decision? We are a sovereign assembly, a sovereign court. It seems to me that the proper body to take a decision is the Conference itself."[29] He disliked especially the insufficiency of representation for the smaller states, particularly on the commission drawing up specifications for the League of Nations.

The disenchantment proliferated among the Latin Americans. On 1 March, Jordan Stabler observed, "I find that they have been left alone too much and have been having Latin American Conferences among themselves." He noted too that only Brazil occupied a seat on the

League of Nations commission and Uruguay on International Waterways. The failure to include any Latin American governments on the Economic and Financial commission produced particular dissatisfaction. Though initially allocated five seats on each commission by the Council of Ten, the smaller states issued complaints and requested more. Upon obtaining them, they could not agree among themselves. In this case, when the Latin American countries, supported by China and Siam, lined up against the Europeans and obtained a majority, the Council of Ten aroused more unhappiness by refusing to sanction the outcome.[30]

According to members of the United States delegation, the decision to restore the seats to the lesser European states resulted in "very hard feelings against the Great Powers." Consequently, House, Lansing, White, and Bliss advised a statement disavowing any intention of treating the Latin Americans "in an arbitrary manner." As they observed, "The actual importance to the lesser Latin American nations of having representation on either Commission is probably very slight, but the pride of various governments seems to have been hurt." Moreover, since the United States held membership on the Council of Ten, "it comes in for its share of the resentment against the Great Powers and our relations with Latin America may be seriously impaired if we do not do all in our power to better the situation." The task fell to Jordan H. Stabler, who complained of "having a very difficult time with the Latin Americans" over the allegedly "arbitrary action and oppression" of the Great Powers. He anticipated bad effects, remarking in a memorandum to Lansing, "A tempest in a teapot you may say, but I for one think tea leaves are rather bitter and do not want the U.S. to have to drink any."[31]

Latin American states performed inconspicuously at Paris and wielded little influence over the deliberations, although, to be sure, they clamored to become members of the League of Nations as a mark of standing. In similar fashion, Latin American affairs intruded only tangentially upon the main concerns of the peacemakers and then constituted mainly diversions. The most prominent centered on Tacna and Arica, Mexico, and the Monroe Doctrine.

The Chilean attitude toward Tacna and Arica underwent some moderation early in 1919 and may have reflected a sense of growing crisis within the nitrate industry. At the end of the war, an abrupt contraction of demand aroused apprehension over future sales and possibly encouraged Chileans to cultivate the most important customers, Great Britain and the United States, with a show of goodwill and reasonability. In any case, the leaders indicated readiness to address the issue through mediation. Indeed, if such a process came about,

Augustín Edwards, the minister in London, invited His Majesty's government to take part. Subsequently, the chiefs in the Wilson administration also took an interest in participating on the condition that France similarly become involved. Later in March 1919, Edwards went further, explaining to Shea in Santiago his regret that his government had not accepted Wilson's offer of assistance in the previous December. He regarded the lapse as a mistake but now proposed to rectify it by suggesting as possible terms separate plebiscites in Tacna and Arica and the creation of a customs-free port for Bolivia. But in this particular rendition, he put off the United States by stipulating that Wilson serve as the mediator.[32]

At the end of April, President Wilson concluded that submission of the dispute to arbitration procedures under the League of Nations would best serve the cause of peace. Peru already had attained membership by acceding in the League convenant. But then more hitches developed. Polk raised the question whether such methods might not actually deter the Chileans from joining out of concern for an adverse judgment. Moreover, he pointed to the likelihood of bad effects upon United States public opinion. The Senate had not yet ratified the Treaty of Versailles to bring the United States into the League of Nations. How could the administration advise recourse to an international body for which it lacked approval? Would not referral to the League also violate the Monroe Doctrine? The president, once apprised, reversed himself, citing his "instinct" as the reason for his decision in this instance to await acceptance of the League.[33]

Mexico also attracted attention at the Paris Peace Conference. Though uninvited, the Mexican government sent Alberto J. Pani as a delegate. He traveled to France early in January 1919 aboard the *George Washington* with officials from the United States but encountered a rude reception upon his arrival in Europe. Neither the British nor the French would receive him. Pani attributed the slights to resentment over Article Twenty-Seven, Carranza's presumed pro-German sympathies during the war, and Mexico's failure to make good on foreign debts. Nevertheless, he stayed through the spring, observing the goings-on and lobbying against any effort by the international oil interests to act against the Mexican Constitution of 1917. In the middle of February 1919, he told Carranza that Edward L. Doheny, a United States citizen with large interests in Mexican petroleum, had arrived in the French capital for just such a purpose.[34]

A related issue also caused a stir. At the insistence of the United States, Article Twenty-One of the proposed treaty formally recognized the Monroe Doctrine, stating that "Nothing in this Covenant shall be deemed to affect the validity of international engagements, such as treaties of arbitration or regional understandings . . . for securing the maintenance of peace." Pani objected to the implications and voiced strong criticism. He feared that "imperialists" in the United States would use the provision as justification for new interventions in Mexico, especially if the more bellicose Republicans won control of the presidency in the election of 1920. He calculated too that the treaty generally served the interests of the Great Powers at the expense of the lesser.[35]

In Mexico, meanwhile, Carranza assailed the Monroe Doctrine. On 25 April, the Mexican government served notice on the State Department that it "has not recognized nor will it recognize that doctrine, nor any other which attacks the sovereignty and independence of Mexico." A short while later in an interview on 8 May 1919 with a New York *World* correspondent, Robert H. Murray, the Mexican president elaborated upon his views, characterizing the traditional policy of the United States as "an arbitrary measure which seeks to impose and does impose upon independent nations a protectorate which they do not ask for and which they do not require." Carranza denounced it as "a species of tutelage" with no possible justification.[36]

The Mexican question increasingly nettled administration leaders during the spring of 1919. In a memorandum to President Wilson on 1 March, Henry P. Fletcher, the United States ambassador then on assignment in Washington, depicted horrific conditions. Among other outrages, he charged, "Article 27 of the new Constitution practically closes the door to foreign investments and threatens those already made in the country," "Carranza is virtually a dictator," and "The attitude of the Mexican Government toward a League of Nations" would express "entirely . . . selfish considerations." In response, Fletcher advised, the Wilson administration either could "let matters drift in their present unsatisfactory condition" or "call upon the recognized Government of Mexico to perform its duties as a government . . . or to confess its inability so to do and accept disinterested assistance from the United States or of an international commission to restore order and credit." As a preferred choice, Fletcher opted for the last course.[37]

The pressure to reorient policy along harder lines became ever stronger when business leaders in the Oil Producers Association and the National Association for the Protection of American Rights in Mexico made common cause with Republican political partisans in opposition to Carranza. To overturn the Mexican Constitution, they devised a strategy for withdrawing diplomatic recognition from Carranza and precipitating a revolt of more pliable Mexicans against him. One critic, William Gates, summarized the complaints. "We want Pan-

Americanism and the Monroe Doctrine in its true meaning; and not in Mexico a center of international Bolshevism, Pan-Latinism as an international menace to us, with antagonistic foreign alliances to support it." Though expressed in disarranged syntax, Gates' position held that the best alternative required cooperation with "the better Mexicans" in order "to rehabilitate the country with our aid."[38]

The clamor in the United States put Mexican leaders on edge. Foreign Minister Cándido Aguilar perceived "a criminal intention to intervene in our country" and later warned that foreign petroleum interests in the United States had engaged in various intrigues to promote the use of violence against Mexico. General Heriberto Jara worried, meanwhile, that Carranza had played into his enemies' hands with his denunciation of the Monroe Doctrine. But the Mexican president, undeterred, proceeded with plans to rally Latin American opinion in his behalf by publishing in his own defense *La Doctrina Carranza y El Acercamiento Indo-Latino*, a polemical justification of the Pan Hispanic approach, and *Labor Internacional de la Revolución Constitucional*, a documentary compilation pertaining particularly to relations with the United States.[39]

Within the State Department, Henry P. Fletcher kept harping on the issue, calling upon the Wilson administration to consider "a radical change in policy with regard to Mexico," and finally obtained a hearing. On 4 August, Wilson admitted that he had carried Fletcher's earlier communication of 1 March "across the water . . . and brought it back without reading it until yesterday." He now wondered whether Fletcher would make the same analysis and recommendations, to which Fletcher allowed flatly, "Conditions have rather deteriorated." The ambassador still wanted to call upon the Mexican government to perform its duty. Otherwise, he feared "a gradual drifting until by some sudden emergency, intervention is forced upon us." Within the United States Senate, meanwhile, Albert B. Fall, a Republican from New Mexico, launched an investigation into Mexican affairs on 8 August and constituted a forum for critics unfriendly toward the Carranza regime. The proceeding contributed substantially to the uproar and put additional pressure on the Wilson administration. As General Pablo Gonzáles told the Mexican president on 18 August, "The present hour is more grave than is generally believed." For Mexico, the possibility of intervention persisted all during the fall until the denouement in December 1919.[40]

In comparison, a measure of serenity marked relations with Argentina. Although Ambassador Rómulo S. Naón's resignation soon after the armistice aroused suspicions of pro-German machinations in the Foreign Office, the event turned out to signify little. Economic

imperatives by and large governed Argentine foreign policy, and the
government after the war courted the Allies and the United States,
hoping to obtain loans and also a renewal of the Wheat Convention as a
guarantee of overseas sales. Argentina also served notice of eagerness
to accept membership in the League of Nations. Though criticism of
the Monroe Doctrine still showed up on occasion in the newspapers,
the country's official position emphasized the similarity of purpose and
aspiration with the United States.[41]

Similar concerns dominated relations with Brazil. Two weeks after
the armistice, Ambassador Morgan reiterated familiar themes. Better
transportation facilities would secure many advantages, and preferential freight rates could ward off the effects of European competition.
Morgan retained a consuming interest in developing military and naval
aid and assistance programs and worried that British contracts would
deprive Bethlehem Steel and other North American firms. As he
observed early in February, the extension of British influence would
result in orders for naval equipment in British shipyards and would not
prove advantageous "to our political and commercial interests."[42]

Politics also attracted attention. In the special presidential election
in the middle of April 1919, Epitacio da Silva Pessôa, the leader of the
Brazilian delegation to the peace conference, ran against Ruy Barbosa,
a perennial candidate in opposition and a critic of Pan Americanism.
Morgan put his stamp on the former, describing Pessôa as "a safe
although not a brilliant selection." By Morgan's account, "His experience as a practicing lawyer, a judge on the Supreme Court and a
senator as well as his association at Paris with the leading statesmen in
the world will fit him for the position he will fill." When Pessôa turned
out the winner, Barbosa charged that Morgan had plotted against his
candidacy and intended to transform Brazil into a United States protectorate. Domicio da Gama, the acting foreign minister, too, complained that politics had engendered "a very delicate state of affairs,"
particularly over the claim that the United States had become "our
liege." He thanked Robert Lansing, nevertheless, "for the help you
gave us . . . at the Conference . . . supporting our claims." To "the great
majority of the people with common sense," da Gama affirmed, "your
attitude toward us" testified as "one effective manifestation of our old
mutual friendship."[43]

FOR THE REMAINDER OF THE TERM

For the remainder of the term, the Wilson administration persisted
in efforts to pursue the cause of regional integration within the western
hemisphere and to achieve further consolidation, thereby taking full

advantage of propitious circumstances. At the same time, the president intended to blend the newly established position of economic hegemony in the New World into a global system of free trade in which all the participants would enjoy the ensuing opportunities and rewards. Again, a conception of natural harmonies underlay his notion of an international division of labor. Wilson's message to the Congress on 2 December 1918 asserted the theme and presented an affirmation. In a salute to his own peace plan, the president exclaimed,

> No policy of isolation will satisfy the growing needs and opportunities of America. The provincial standards and policies of the past, which have held American business as if in a strait-jacket, must yield and give way to the needs and exigencies of the new day in which we live, a day full of hope and promise for American business, if we will but take advantage of the opportunities that are ours for the asking.

In elaboration, he explained, "The recent war has ended our isolation and thrown upon us a great duty and responsibility. The United States must share the expanding world market." But as a qualification, he stipulated, "The United States desires for itself only equal opportunity with the other nations of the world, and that through the process of friendly cooperation and fair competition the legitimate interests of the nations concerned may be successfully and equitably adjusted." This classic defense of free-trade theory and open-door ideology set forth the essentials of Wilson's convictions.[44]

Within the western hemisphere, the Wilson administration relied on tried and tested methods to encourage the flow of trade by working particularly through the Pan American Union and the International High Commission. Public assemblies and more intimate forms of diplomacy constituted the means. Representing the former, the Second Pan American Commercial Conference convened at the Pan American Building in Washington, D.C., on 2 July 1919. Conceived as a follow-up to the first such meeting in February 1911, this notable endeavor provided "another informal but comprehensive exchange of views and information between the official and unofficial commercial representatives, trade experts, businessmen and other interested parties of North and South America." Some 1,181 delegates attended, including 200 from Latin America. According to the P.A.U. *Bulletin*, the five days of discussion and exchange marked another "new epoch in Pan American commercial relations."

The conference provided full opportunities for the ritualistic affirmations of friendship and good intentions, but the main concerns centered on trade, investment, and loans. In the end, the participants set forth twelve specific recommendations, calling for many of the customary things. The delegates wanted better transportation and communication facilities, more reciprocity and cooperation in trading practices, improved means of extending credit, and greater appreciation mutually of history, language, and culture. The endorsement also supported a plan to hold a Second Pan American Financial Conference in January 1920. In an enthusiastic summary of the achievements, the *Bulletin* explained the significance as a mark of impressive change. To underscore the point, it reported that at the first such meeting in 1911, North Americans without knowledge or experience had asked, "Tell us how we may trade with Latin America?" At the second, they observed the new circumstances and inquired, "What shall we do to hold the trade we have and to increase it?"[45]

The International High Commission played an important role in following the latter aim and planning the conduct of diplomacy. One United States representative, Dr. Leo S. Rowe, complained in November 1919 of "a notable lack of coordination in some matters between our Departments in Washington" and looked toward the proposed Second Pan American Financial Conference as a remedy, hoping to elicit specific statements from Central and South American republics about "the practical needs." Another, John H. Fahey, thought it would enhance greatly the interest in Latin American financial development and the sale of securities in the United States. In anticipation of the event, the new secretary of the treasury, the former congressman from Virginia, Carter Glass, observed that the first Pan American Financial Conference came about in 1915 in response to a "great danger which threatened to paralyze the commerce and finance of all nations of this Hemisphere" and gave rise to "various organizations and movements calculated to stimulate closer and more enduring financial and commercial relations." The next such conference would build upon those achievements by addressing "questions of public debt, taxation and other matters bearing directly upon the nature and extent of public and private credit." Glass intended to put greater emphasis upon "subjects involving the fiscal policy of governments and their attitude towards the development of commerce and industry." As he remarked, "the creation of markets for the public and private securities of Latin America cannot be undertaken unless there is generated a wholesome atmosphere of confidence in the stability and healthy functioning of Latin American Governments."[46]

The United States delegation to the International High Commission took charge of the preparations. The body in 1919 consisted of Secretary of the Treasury Glass, John Barrett Moore, the vice-chairman, Leo S. Rowe, the secretary general, Senator Duncan U. Fletcher of Florida, and a group of bankers and financiers, Andrew J.

Peters, Paul M. Warburg, Samuel Untermyer, John H. Fahey, and John H. Wigmore. They defined their principal task directly as determining how the United States could best provide the necessary capital and credit facilities to meet the needs of Latin America. Preliminary reports pointed to the ongoing want for additional United States branch banks in South America and possibly too for the extension of South American banks into the United States. An observation in one of the documents put the point this way: To promote "closer commercial relations . . . it is desirable to encourage connections and intercourse between the established financial institutions of the South American countries and those of the United States, so that each may avail itself of the acquired experience of the others." The proposed agenda enumerated six issues of central importance:

1. The effect of the war on the commerce and industry, manufacturing and mining, agriculture and public utilities of the American republics. 2. Methods to generate capital and credit facilities. 3. National credit, and the factors affecting it. 4. The effect of the war on transportation facilities. 5. Measures to facilitate commercial intercourse among the American republics. 6. The development of uniformity of legislation regarding commercial intercourse.[47]

The proceedings began on 17 January 1920 and continued for seven days. At the opening session, sixty delegates from the twenty Latin American republics and about 250 from the United States, mainly business leaders and members of advisory committees, heard Secretary of the Treasury Glass, the presiding officer, extend greetings, but Dr. Leo S. Rowe, the secretary general of the International High Commission, carried out the organizational work. The published accounts characterized the gathering as a grand achievement. According to the *Bulletin*, "It was a worthy successor of the first conference of this kind," and "It will rank among other Pan American gatherings which have assembled in Washington." The adopted resolutions also won applause on grounds that they looked "to a great future of cooperative Pan American effort which should give practical Pan Americanism a firmer foundation and more lasting essential success than it has ever enjoyed before." The endorsed recommendations, numbering eighteen specifics in all, ran the gamut, calling for better transportation, communication, and banking facilities, and advised also to change the name of the sponsoring agency to the Inter-American High Commission, thereby indicating more clearly "the constituency and scope of work."[48]

In the annual report at the end of 1920, the Secretary of the Treasury also bestowed high marks. Among other things, the republics of the western hemisphere had concurred in the International Trade Mark Convention and planned to establish registration bureaus in Havana and Rio de Janeiro. Moreover, they ratified the Commercial Travelers' Convention first proposed in Buenos Aires in 1916, providing more simple and uniform rules for the treatment of salesmen and their wares, and they manifested a growing interest in formal machinery for the arbitration of commercial disputes. While the United States representatives hoped further to facilitate the transaction of commercial exchanges through more homogeneous practices, Secretary Glass expressed a personal wish for the creation of an inter-American tribunal to settle all manner of business controversies.[49] The institutional requirements of promoting trade preoccupied leaders in the Wilson administration until the end.

The president, meanwhile, attempted to restore purpose and direction within the government after suffering a series of hammer blows. The Republican revolt in the Senate against the Treaty of Versailles and the League of Nations constituted one source of trauma and ultimately shattered Wilson's health and hopes. While seeking to rally public opinion in his favor, the president collapsed on 25 September 1919 after a speech at Pueblo, Colorado, and then suffered a cerebral thrombosis upon his return to the capital. For no less than six weeks, he languished, the victim of illness at a critical time. His incapacity denied to his advocates the requisite qualities of prestige and leadership so necessary in the struggle, and the effects of his ordeal later may have intensified a temperamental disposition toward stubbornness. Though he attained partial recovery, he steadfastly refused the concessions required to bring about some kind of treaty and rigidly insisted that his adversary, Senator Lodge, make the compromise. By his own act, he doomed his progeny, and committed, in Thomas A. Bailey's memorable phrase, "the supreme infanticide."[50] When he left office on 4 March 1921, he bore with him the effects of a broken heart.

Though less devastatng in outcome, the Mexican question also caused trouble. During the autumn of 1919, a coalition of disgruntled businessmen and political partisans subjected President Wilson's established policy to a barrage of abuse. Under Senator Fall's direction, they demanded a greater show of toughness, eventuating, if necessary, in the ouster of Carranza and the installation of a new regime consisting of Mexicans more willing to work with and to safeguard foreign investors. To such ends, they cooperated with Carranza's enemies, notably, Félix Díaz, the nephew of the former dictator, seeking to remove Carranza by means of a revolt against him; they also may have favored military intervention as a last resort.[51]

The so-called "plot against Mexico" drew in members of the Wilson administration in November 1919 because of Cerranza's repeated attempts to enforce Article Twenty-Seven of the Constitution of 1917 and his alleged disregard for the safety of foreigners and their interests. The kidnapping of a United States citizen, William O. Jenkins, a consular agent in Puebla, underscored the charge. In response, Henry Fletcher and Robert Lansing gave the appearance of falling in with Wilson's domestic opponents by urging strong demands. Because of Wilson's illness, Lansing assumed leadership within the cabinet and took a threatening stance, demanding immediate redress. At the same time early in December, Albert Fall called for a Senate resolution to authorize a break in diplomatic relations, but no one had consulted with President Wilson. Since his breakdown in September, wild rumors had abounded, suggesting an assortment of terrible things, even a mindless lunatic held captive in the White House by his keepers. To obtain some idea of the president's preferences and also the degree of his incapacitation, Senate leaders arranged for an audience for two of the members, Gilbert M. Hitchcock, a Democrat from Nebraska, and Albert B. Fall, a Republican from New Mexico. When they entered the sickroom on the morning of 5 December, Wilson greeted them with cheerful alertness. When Fall remarked, "Well, Mr. President, we have all been praying for you," Wilson shot back, "Which way, Senator?" The second Mrs. Wilson, Edith Bolling Galt, believed that Fall and the Republicans intended to drive Wilson from office with evidence of mental disability but could not find it. They also failed to obtain the president's consent to a break in relations, in part because Carranza made timely concessions. The president's posture meant that no abrupt change in policy would disturb relations with Mexico until the overthrow and assassination of President Venustiano Carranza during the course of a military revolt in the spring of 1920.[52]

Though Wilson rode out the difficulty, the effects put his administration in disarray. A falling-out at Paris and the mistrust of Edith Bolling Wilson removed Colonel House from the centers of power. After the Mexican blowup in December 1919, Henry Fletcher, one of the original Latin American hands, found himself irretrievably at odds over fundamentals and resigned from the diplomatic corps within a month. Later in the spring, Frank Polk departed the State Department for reasons of ill health, and John Barrett, now something of an embarrassment, returned to private life. Significantly, Robert Lansing also took his leave. Already compromised by differences at Paris, Lansing's behavior during the Mexican crisis ruined him in the president's eyes by raising questions of usurpation of authority. When the president asked for his resignation, the secretary responded early in February 1920.[53]

To replace him, the president settled on a curious choice. Bainbridge Colby, a New York lawyer and Progressive politician, had no experience in the diplomatic arts but had supported the Democratic ticket in 1916 and must have impressed Wilson as an agreeable subordinate. Able and adroit, Colby served out the remainder of the term as secretary of state in a creditable fashion without challenging the president's privileges and prerogatives. He also designated Latin America as a region requiring special attention. Indeed, one historian, Daniel M. Smith, depicted him as a precursor and progenitor of the Good Neighbor policy later adoped in the 1930s by Franklin D. Roosevelt. Though something of an overstatement, surely an exaggeration of Colby's actual, creative involvement with the policy-making process, the view points correctly to his more subtle appreciation of United States interests in Latin America. According to Smith, Colby moderated the prevailing practices in the Caribbean protectorates and looked forward to a time when military withdrawal might take place. His goodwill tour into South America later in 1920 also won acclaim as another marker indicating the advent of a new era in Pan Americanism.[54]

The conspiratorial suspicions so characteristic of the First World War lingered in some circles for a time in the postwar period. In 1920, a remarkable, unsigned document produced by United States naval intelligence anticipated an alarming array of threats confronting the United States in Latin America. Running over one hundred pages, the typescript elaborated upon a most dismaying thesis. Foreign elements had unified their capabilities in order to nullify recent gains. Seeking "to combat North American influences in Latin America and to further their own political, economical and secret causes in these countries," a variety of aliens, including "the Japanese, Germans, Mexicans and Italians," have combined "all of their secret forces operating in Latin America and are conducting a gigantic campaign hostile to the United States of North America." So "massive" and "active" an organization posed an acute threat to the Monroe Doctrine and required determined countermeasures. To compound the matter, "Germany, Japan, Italy, and Spain are desirous of increasing their influences in Latin America" and wish "to further their own territorial ambitions in this direction." Indeed, Germany and Japan intended "to colonize Latin America" and would support an "anti-American League of Latins" as part and parcel of the plot.[55]

Though such sensational allegations may have stirred trepidation among policymakers late at night, the official records of the State Department suggest little sense of undue danger over obsessional concerns. To the contrary, the summary statements set forth in March 1920 by Bainbridge Colby revealed much more placid expectations. Late in the month, he averred, "No questions of any importance are now pending between Argentina and the United States." On the same day, he affirmed, "There are no questions of importance now pending between the governments of the United States and Brazil." Somewhat earlier, he had recognized that Chile and the Tacna-Arica question still posed a problem, but overall, his estimation pointed to the existence of orderly and routine conditions within the conduct of international relations in much of the western hemisphere.[56]

The prospects for loans, trade, and cable communications dominated relations with Argentina and Brazil. Though the outflow of gold from the United States into Argentina disturbed Treasury Department officials for a time in the spring of 1920, the expectation of favorable balances and steady expansion buoyed hopes for the future. From Brazil, meanwhile, Ambassador Morgan transmitted the good news that the firms Armstrong, Vickers, and Bethlehem Steel had formed a ⅓-⅓-⅓ combination to build a naval arsenal and had avoided thereby his worst apprehensions. The Tacna and Arica controversy, in contrast, defied solution and, indeed, sparked another war scare in the summer of 1920, when Bolivia threatened a resort to the use of force. The issue exasperated Secretary Colby and frustrated Wilson, who admitted in April 1920, "I am somewhat at a loss what judgment to form." Whether to submit the matter to the League of Nations and risk the criticism for violating the Monroe Doctrine caused agitation. Unhappily for them, the dispute eluded resolution, but they managed to contain it within the bounds of statecraft. Direct negotiations, encouraged by United States mediation, finally produced a settlement in 1929.[57]

The Colby voyage to South America at the end of 1920 held symbolic meaning and underscored the Wilson administration's enduring commitment to Pan American initiatives. Described by the historian Daniel M. Smith as "a major endeavor to reduce Latin American suspicions and to cement better relations," the trip originated in a wartime request from Brazil to send a mission, following up Secretary of State Elihu Root's highly publicized tour in 1906. Though the administration considered for a time the possibility of designating General John J. Pershing to lead the undertaking, the chiefs decided later that the secretary of state should head an official state visit. The itinerary consisted of Brazil, Uruguay, and Argentina. The arrivals in Rio de Janeiro on 21 December and Montevideo a week later set off friendly public demonstrations and effusions of stylized rhetoric. The reception in Buenos Aires on New Year's Day, though somewhat cooler, featured a cordial interview with President Yrigoyen and appropriate displays. In an appraisal of the consequences, Leo S. Rowe, the new director general of the Pan American Union, applauded Colby for his "great service" in behalf of unity within the western hemi-sphere.[58] The secretary of state provided a more prosaic justification a few days before leaving office in a speech at the New Willard Hotel in Washington, D.C. Recalling Wilson's themes from the campaign in 1912, he exclaimed, "Good trade with South America presupposes good relations with South America. The former is the outgrowth of the latter. You will not buy from a merchant whom you dislike nor employ a man whom you do not wish to meet." By his account, the Pan American formula would narrow the breach and sustain the essentials of the regional system.[59] The faith ran constant and animated the leaders in the Wilson administration throughout the eight years.

FINAL CONSIDERATIONS

The drive for regional integration constituted a central thrust in Woodrow Wilson's conduct of policy toward Latin America and af-firmed his most coherent vision of proper relationships within the western hemisphere. His conception of a functioning, regional system, in which the constituent parts would cooperate in the pursuit of the common good, conveyed an essential attribute of his approach to statecraft. Natural harmonies and ultimate compatibilities of interest and aspiration would bind the nations together in a common purpose and would elevate the conduct of international relations to a higher, more edified plane. His convictions sustained the integrity of the ambi-tion throughout the eight years and, in spite of contradictions and inconsistencies, retained sufficient hold to form the model for his plan for peace at the end of the Great War. The enduring legacies persist until the present day.

The economic and political components in Wilson's scheme of things set forth compelling assumptions about the behavior of modern nation states. Commercial intercourse, carried out freely, could take on adhesive qualities, forming networks of mutual interest in prosperity and peace. In Latin America, Wilson served notice in the Mobile address of his wish to break up the old system of concessions and special privileges. The tenets of free trade, translated literally into practice, would open the doors of opportunity, roll back the European presence, and establish new connections between the United States and Latin America. Similarly, the cultivation of political ties would forge new bonds. By joining with the stable countries in the exercise of an inter-national police power, the United States could escape the onus of unilateral action and achieve some measure of legitimacy through the utilization of multilateral forms. Wilson, to be sure, desired means of upholding national sovereignty and territorial integrity, but before recognizing any nation's unqualified right to self-determination, he insisted upon proper observance for the rules of civilized order. The proposed Pan American Pact would have overcome the improvisational characteristics of the prevailing interventionist practices and would have constituted a reliable system, providing for joint measures whenever the need arose.

Wilson failed to obtain the desired devices to bring about political collaboration, in large measure because he underestimated the degree of Latin American mistrust and also because he could not overcome parochial responses. The Tacna and Arica controversy particularly got in the way. Latin American nationalists feared the effects of too warm in embrace, reasoning that manipulation and control by the United States might occur if they acceded too much. In the more particular case, Chile wanted no outside interference in the dispute with Peru. Nevertheless, the magnitude of United States influence expanded appreciably, both in the economic and political realms, in part because of skillful planning and careful execution, and also because of the very dynamics of the war. The enormity of the effort in Europe necessarily reduced the capability of the continental powers to retain positions of strength and influence in the New World. By the armistice in November 1918, Wilson had attained many of the aims put forth at Mobile and reigned dominant over the western hemisphere, though, admittedly, by less formal political means than the president had desired.

For Latin Americans, the extension of the North American presence under the auspices of Pan Americanism held mixed implications. Though the governing elites by and large favored an increase of trade and investment in order to promote growth, they preferred a situation in which the European nations would compete with the United States for sales and purchases. With the exception of Brazil, Latin American countries also shied away politically, choosing oftentimes to invoke the European powers as counterbalances against the United States. The effects of the Great War wrecked for a time the utility of the traditional ploy and required that Latin Americans face up to the burgeoning regional power of the northern colossus. To a large extent, it bound them in, constricting the range of options by compelling submission to an overweening economic might.

Though Wilson presumed beneficent results from a thriving trade and thereby anticipated the views of advocates of the "diffusion" model of development in the present day, the Latin Americans more characteristically recognized the extent of their dependency upon the United States but saw little alternative to it. The need for markets, capital, and manufactured goods left them little room to maneuver. While Argentina and Chile tried to obtain maximum advantage by arranging wheat conventions and nitrate deals with the United States and the Allies, the bargaining leverage clearly resided with the other side, especially when the war ended. The stark realization compelled Argentina and Chile, though to a lesser extent, to emulate Brazil's example by affirming a greater measure of political solidarity with the United States. As Rómulo S. Naón pointed out toward the end of the war, South American countries, dependent on the sale of agricultural commodities and raw materials, had to exist in a perfidious economic environment over which they exerted no control. He understood intuitively the precepts of modern-day dependency theory and sought unsuccessfully to moderate the dilemma by appealing to the generosity of the Great Powers.

The ramifications extended to the central features of Wilson's preferred plan for peace. Though newly arrived as the controlling economic power within the New World, the United States proposed to amalgamate its commanding position into a global system based on the principles of free trade. Competitive advantages over war-wrecked rivals would allow North American manufacturers to retain the markets they possessed and also to obtain new outlets in other regions after which they aspired. In Wilson's world, they could have their cake and eat it too. But the political problem escaped solution. While calling for acceptance of the treaty and the League, Wilson envisioned an international system of multilateral cooperation to keep the peace, but in asking the people of the United States to undertake political obligations in areas beyond their borders, he aroused both a partisan and a principled opposition. The central question asked, to what extent should the United States accept prior commitments to the defense of other countries? In this instance, the United States Senate under Republican leadership played a role analogous to the Chilean part in the discussion over the Pan American Pact. The Treaty of Versailles also went down to defeat. Now, throughout the world, much as in the western hemisphere, the United States would engage in economic expansion without formal statements of any corollary political obligations and responsibilities. Wilson's world, half formed, left room for incalculable uncertainty in the unformed part.

Chapter Notes

ABBREVIATIONS

CR   U.S. Dept. of Commerce. Bureau of Foreign and Domestic Commerce. *Commerce Reports*. Washington: Govt. Printing Office, 1915–18.

DCTR   U.S. Dept. of Commerce. Bureau of Foreign and Domestic Commerce. *Daily Consular and Trade Reports*. Washington: Govt. Printing Office, 1913–14.

EMHP   Edward M. House Papers. Yale University. New Haven, Conn.

FR 1913–21 U.S. Dept. of State. *Papers Relating to the Foreign Relations of the United States, 1913–21*. Washington: Govt. Printing Office, 1920–36.

FRLP   U.S. Dept. of State. *Papers Relating to the Foreign Relations of the United States, The Lansing Papers, 1914–1920*. Washington: Govt. Printing Office, 1939.

FRPPC   U.S. Dept. of State, *Papers Relating to the Foreign Relations of the United States, 1919, The Paris Peace Conference*. Washington: Govt. Printing Office, 1942–1947.

HPFP   Henry P. Fletcher Papers, Library of Congress, Washington, D.C.

JBP   John Barrett Papers, Library of Congress, Washington, D.C.

PAUB   Pan American Union. *Bulletin*.

PWW   Link, Arthur S., et al., eds. *The Papers of Woodrow Wilson*. Princeton: Princeton Univ. Press, 1966 ff.

RDS   Record Group 59 (unless otherwise noted). Records of the U.S. Dept. of State. National Archives. Washington, D.C.

RLP   Robert Lansing Papers. Library of Congress, Washington, D.C.

WWP   Woodrow Wilson Papers. Library of Congress, Washington, D.C.

NOTES TO THE PREFACE

1. Arthur P. Whitaker, *The Western Hemisphere Idea: Its Rise and Decline* (Ithaca: Cornell Univ. Press, 1954).
2. Thomas L. Karnes, "Pan-Americanism," in *Encyclopedia of American Foreign Relations, Studies of the Principal Movements and Ideas*, ed. Alexander De Conde (New York: Charles Scribner's Sons), vol. 2, pp. 730–32.

3. Hernán Ramírez Nicochea, *Historia del Imperialismo en Chile* (Santiago: Empresa Editora Austral Ltda., 1960), p. 191.

4. Introductions to the literature are found in Ronald H. Chilcote and Joel C. Eldelstein, eds., *Latin America: The Struggle with Dependency and Beyond* (New York: John Wiley & Sons, 1974); André Gunder Frank, *Latin America: Underdevelopment or Revolution, Essays on the Development of Underdevelopment and the Immediate Enemy* (New York: Monthly Review Press, 1969); Fernando Henrique Cardoso and Enzo Faletto, *Dependency and Development in Latin America*, tr. Marjory Mattingly Urquidi (Berkeley: Univ. of California Press, 1979); Abraham F. Lowenthal, "'Liberal,' 'Radical,' and 'Bureaucratic' Perspectives on U.S. Latin American Policy: The Alliance for Progress in Retrospect," in *Latin America and the United States: The Changing Political Realities*, eds. Julio Cotler and Richard R. Fagen (Stanford: Stanford Univ. Press, 1974), pp. 212−35; Jorge I. Domínguez, "Concensus and Divergence: The State of the Literature on Inter-American Relations in the 1970s," *Latin American Research Review* 13 (no. 1, 1977), pp. 87−126; and Tony Smith, *The Pattern of Imperialism, The United States, Great Britain, and the Late-Industrializing World since 1815* (Cambridge: The University Press, 1981).

5. Steven W. Hughes and Kenneth J. Mijeski, "Contemporary Paradigms in the Study of Inter-American Relations," in *Latin America, the United States, and the Inter-American System*, eds, John D. Martz and Lars Schoultz (Boulder: Westview Press, 1980), p. 36.

NOTES TO CHAPTER 1

1. Walter LaFeber, *The Panama Canal, The Crisis in Historical Perspective* (New York: Oxford Univ. Press, 1978); David G. McCullough, *The Path Between the Seas: The Creation of the Panama Canal, 1870−1914* (New York: Simon and Schuster, 1977).

2. William Appleman Williams, *The Tragedy of American Diplomacy*, 2d ed. rev. (New York: Dell Publishing Co., Inc., 1972), chap. 2; William Diamond, *The Economic Thought of Woodrow Wilson, The Johns Hopkins University Studies in Historical and Political Science*, vol. 61, no. 4 (Baltimore, 1943); Sidney Bell, *Righteous Conquest, Woodrow Wilson and the Evolution of the New Diplomacy* (Port Washington, N.Y.: Kennikat Press, 1972), chaps. 1−3.

3. *PWW*, 25:38.

4. *PWW*, 24:33−36.

5. Quoted in *PAUB*, 36 (April 1913), p. 615; Salvatore Prisco III, *John Barrett, Progressive Era Diplomat: A Study of a Commercial Expansionist, 1887−1920* (University: The Univ. of Alabama Press, 1973).

6. Burton I. Kaufman, *Expansion and Efficiency, Foreign Trade Organization in the Wilson Administration, 1913−1921* (Westport, Conn.: Greenwood Press, 1974), pp. 3−4.

7. *PAUB*, 39 (Dec. 1914), pp. 975−82.

8. *PAUB*, 39 (Dec. 1914), pp. 978−79, 981−82.

9. Quoted in *PAUB*, 36 (Feb. 1913), pp. 278−81; *DCTR*, no. 39, 15 Feb. 1913, pp. 817−22.

10. William H. Becker, *The Dynamics of Business-Government Relations, 1893−1921* (Chicago: Univ. of Chicago Press, 1982), pp. 116−23; *DCTR*, no. 62, 17 March 1913, pp. 1313−14.

11. *PAUB*, 37 (Aug., Nov. 1913), pp. 230−35, 713, 38 (Jan. 1914), p. 102, 41 (Nov. 1915), pp. 659−62.

12. *PAUB*, 36 (Apr. 1913), p. 615; 37 (Nov. 1913), p. 703, 38 (Feb. 1914), p. 240; Resolutions, 28 Feb. 1913, 710.11/107, RDS.

13. John T. Reid, *Spanish American Images of the United States, 1790−1960* (Gainesville: Univ. Presses of Florida, 1977).

14. James W. Gantenbein, ed., *The Evolution of Our Latin American Policy: A Documentary Record* (New York: Octagon Books, 1971), pp. 348, 362; Gordon Connell-Smith, *The United States and Latin America, An Historical Analysis of Inter-American Relations* (New York: John Wiley & Sons, n.d.).

15. Charles DeBenedetti, *The Peace Reform in American History* (Bloomington: Univ. of Indiana Press, 1980), chap. 5; C. Roland Marchand, *The American Peace Movement and Social Reform, 1898 −1918* (Princeton: Princeton Univ. Press, 1972), chap. 2; David S. Patterson, *Toward a Warless World: The Travail of the American Peace Movement, 1887 −1914* (Bloomington: Univ. of Indiana, 1976), chap. 11.

16. Marchand, *Peace Movements*, p. 65; Reprint of "A Pan American Court of Justice" by Joseph Wheless, spring 1913, 710.11/148 1/2, RDS; Paolo E. Coletta, *William Jennings Bryan*, vol. 2: *Progressive Politician and Moral Statesman, 1909 −1915* (Lincoln: Univ. of Nebraska Press, 1969), p. 208.

17. *PWW*, 25:503; Arthur S. Link, *Woodrow Wilson, Revolution, War, and Peace* (Arlington Heights, Ill.: AHM Publishing Corp., 1979), chap. 1.

18. Ray Stannard Baker, ed., *Woodrow Wilson: Life and Letters* (Garden City, N.Y.: Doubleday, Doran and Co., 1931), vol. 4, p. 55; the best book on the early years is John M. Mulder, *Woodrow Wilson, The Years of Preparation* (Princeton: Princeton Univ. Press, 1978).

19. Eleanor Wilson McAdoo, *The Woodrow Wilsons* (New York: Macmillan and Co., 1937), pp. 135−36.

20. *PWW*, 27:335.

21. *PWW*, 25:24−25.

22. Straight to Henry P. Fletcher, 10 Oct., 21, Nov. 1912, 18 March 1913, Willard Straight Papers, Cornell University, Ithaca, N.Y.

23. Rachel West, O.S.F., *The Department of State on the Eve of the First World War* (Athens: Univ. of Georgia Press, 1978), esp. chaps. 3, 4, 5; Coletta, *Bryan*, 2: chaps. 6−7; Kendrick A. Clements, *William Jennings Bryan, Missionary Isolationist* (Knoxville: Univ. of Tennessee Press, 1982), chaps. 4−5; Kaufman, *Efficiency and Expansion*, pp. 68−71, 95−103; Becker, *Dynamics of Business-Government Relations*, pp. 123−30; Alexander L. and Juliette L. George, *Woodrow Wilson and Colonel House, A Personality Study* (New York: Dover Publications, Inc., 1964, fp. 1956), chaps. 5, 6; Diary, 22 Jan. 1913, EMHP.

24. *La Prensa*, 4 March 1913; E. David Cronon, ed., *The Cabinet Diaries of Josephus Daniels, 1913−1921* (Lincoln: Univ. of Nebraska Press, 1963), pp. 6−7.

25. *PWW*, 27:172−73.

26. Enclosure, George Lorillard to Bryan, 17 March 1913, 710. 11/124, RDS.

27. Charles C. Cumberland, *Mexican Revolution, Genesis under Madero*; and *The Constitutionalist Years* (Austin, Univ. of Texas Press, 1952, 1972); Stanley R. Ross, *Francisco I. Madero, Apostle of Mexican Democracy* (New York: Columbia Univ. Press, 1955); Michael C. Meyer, *Huerta, A Political Portrait* (Lincoln: Univ. of Nebraska Press, 1972); Douglas W. Richmond, *Venustiano Carranza's Nationalist Struggle, 1893 −1920* (Lincoln: Univ. of Nebraska Press, 1983).

28. Kenneth J. Grieb, *The United States and Huerta* (Lincoln: Univ. of Nebraska Press, 1969), chaps. 5, 6; Larry D. Hill, *Emissaries to a Revolution, Woodrow Wilson's Executive Agents in Mexico* (Baton Rouge: Louisiana State Univ. Press, 1973), chap. 4.

29. Paolo E. Coletta, "Secretary of State William Jennings Bryan and 'Deserving Democrats,'" *Mid-America* 48 (April 1966), pp. 75−98; and *Bryan*, 2:112−19; Clements, *Bryan*, pp. 60−64; West, *Department of State*, chaps. 7, 8.

30. Straight to Fletcher, 21 Nov. 1912, Fletcher to McAdoo, 1 Feb. 1913, Fletcher to his father, 13 Oct. 1913, box 3, HPFP.

31. Coletta, *Bryan*, 2:239−49; Cronon, ed., *Cabinet Diaries*, pp. 26−27.

32. Coletta, *Bryan*, 2:244−46.

33. Clements, *Bryan*, chap. 5; Coletta, *Bryan*, 2: chap: 7, pp. 183, 189; Hans Schmidt, *The United States Occupation of Haiti, 1915 −1934* (New Brunswick: Rutgers Univ. Press, 1972), p. 48.

34. Gresham to Wilson, 25 Feb. 1913, 710. 11/101, Stafford to Wilson, 22 Feb. 1913, 710. 11/105, RDS; Roland G. Usher, *Pan-Americanism: A Forecast of the Inevitable Clash Between the United States and Europe's Victor* (New York: Grosset and Dunlap, 1915); Charles H. Sherrill, *Modernizing the Monroe Doctrine* (New York: Houghton and Mifflin Co., 1916).

35. *PAUB*, 36 (June 1913), pp. 833—35; George H. Blakeslee, ed., *Latin America, Clark University Addresses, November 1913* (New York: G. E. Stechert and Co., 1924).

36. *The Atlantic Monthly*, 111 (June 1913), pp. 721—34; Thomas L. Karnes, "Hiram Bingham and His Obsolete Shibboleth," *Diplomatic History* 3 (Winter 1979), pp. 45—46; Bingham to Wilson, 20 June 1913, 710. 11/149, RDS; Bingham to Wilson, 3 Oct. 1913, #693, series 4, case files, WWP.

37. Diary, 2 May 1913, EMHP; Lorillard to Bryan, 28 March 1913, 710/3, Post Records, R. G. 84, RDS.

38. Barrett to Wilson, 26 Feb., 26 July, box 14, JBP; *PWW*, 28:139; Fletcher to Bryan, Garrett to Bryan, Morgan to Bryan, 16 Aug. 1913, series 2, WWP.

39. Lind to Bryan, 19 Sept. 1913, Bryan-Wilson Correspondence, RDS; Grieb, *U.S. and Huerta*, chap. 6; Hill, *Emissaries*, chap. 4; Peter Calvert, *The Mexican Revolution, 1910—1914, The Diplomacy of Anglo-American Conflict* (Cambridge: The Univ. Press, 1968), chap. 7; John Milton Cooper, Jr., *Walter Hines Page, The Southerner as American, 1855—1918* (Chapel Hill: Univ. of North Carolina Press, 1977), pp. 262—64, 276; Meyer, *Huerta*, chap. 6; Katz, *The Secret War*, chap. 5.

40. *PWW*, 28:448—52.

41. Diary, 30 Oct. 1913, EMHP; Bryan to Wilson, 20 Nov. 1913, Bryan-Wilson Correspondence, RDS; *PWW*, 29:121—22.

42. Diary, 30 Oct. 1913, EMHP; *PWW*, 28:483—84.

43. *PWW*, 28:485; *FR 1914*, pp. 443—44.

44. *PWW*, 28:528, 543—44, 29:121—22.

45. Page to Wilson, 8 Jan., 22 Feb., 19 March 1914, series 2, WWP; Calvert, *Mexican Revolution*, p. 267; Katz, *The Secret War*, chap. 5.

46. Fletcher to House, 31 March 1914, series 2, WWP; E. Bradford Burns, *The Unwritten Alliance, Rio-Branco and Brazilian American Relations* (New York: Columbia Univ. Press, 1966); Harold F. Peterson, *Argentina and the United States, 1810—1960* (New York: State Univ. of New York, 1964); Thomas F. McGann, *Argentina, the United States, and the Inter-American System, 1880—1914* (Cambridge: Harvard Univ. Press, 1957); Frederick B. Pike, *Chile and the United States, 1880—1962, The Emergence of Chile's Social Crisis and the Challenge to United States Diplomacy* (Notre Dame: Univ. of Notre Dame Press, 1963); Dawson Memorandum, 1 Feb. 1912, 725.3211/33, RDS.

47. *DCTR*, no. 61, 15 March 1913, p. 1307, no. 244, 18 Oct. 1913, pp. 321—26; *PAUB*, 38 (Jan. 1914), pp. 98—101.

48. *PAUB*, 39 (July, Aug. 1914), pp. 122—49, 258; *DCTR*, no. 211, 10 Sept. 1913, p. 1410, no. 223, 24 Sept. 1913, p. 1677.

49. David Rock, *Politics in Argentina, 1890—1930, The Rise and Fall of Radicalism* (Cambridge: The Univ. Press, 1975), p. 1—2.

50. Rock, *Politics in Argentina*, pp. 3, 5—7.

51. Rock, *Politics in Argentina*, p. 34 ff.

52. Peterson, *Argentina and the United States*, chap. 17; McGann, *Argentina, the United States, and the Inter-American System*.

53. Burns, *Unwritten Alliance*, pp. 1—4; *PAUB*, 38 (March 1914), p. 440; *DCTR*, no. 157, 8 July 1913, pp. 129—34.

54. Burns, *Unwritten Alliance*, chaps. 3, 4; Leon F. Sensabaugh, "The Coffee-Trust Question in United States-Brazilian Relations, 1912—1913," *Hispanic American Historical Review* 26 (Nov. 1946), pp. 480—96; Lawrence F. Hill, *Diplomatic Relations Between the United States and Brazil* (Durham: Duke Univ. Press, 1932), chap. 11; *PAUB*, 37 (July 1913), pp. 1—4.

55. Pike, *Chile and the U.S.*, p. 37 ff; *PAUB*, 37 (Nov. 1913), pp. 736—47.

56. *PAUB*, 36 (Feb. 1913), pp. 207—23; Report from C, no. 23, 13 May 1913, box 453, C-9-d, 2975, R. G. 38, Records of the Chief of Naval Operations, Naval Intelligence Reports, 1886—1939, National Archives, Washington, D.C.

57. Pike, *Chile and the U.S.*, chaps. 3—5.

58. Pike, *Chile and the U.S.*, p. 86; Fletcher to Bryan, 9 May 1913, 825.00/40, Morgan to Bryan, 17 Nov. 1913, 723.2515/293, RDS.
59. Harold Eugene Davis, John J. Finian, and F. Taylor Peck, *Latin American Diplomatic History* (Baton Rouge: Louisiana State Univ. Press, 1977), chaps. 6, 7; Robert N. Burr, *By Reason or Force, Chile and the Balance of Power in South America, 1830–1905* (Berkeley: Univ. of California Press, 1967).
60. Seward W. Livermore, "Battleship Diplomacy in South America, 1905–1925," *Journal of Modern History* 16 (March 1944), pp. 31–48; Peterson, *Argentina and the U.S.*, pp.291–97.
61. Chandler to Bryan, 10 Feb. 1914, 710.11/170, Lorillard to Bryan, 14 Apr. 1913, 735.00/1, RDS; *DCTR*, no. 18, 22 Jan. 1914, p. 286, no. 28, 3 Feb. 1914, p. 445; *PAUB*, 38 (March 1914), pp. 385–87.
62. *DCTR*, no. 4, 6 Jan. 1914, p. 53; Robert Mayer, "The Origins of the American Banking Empire in Latin America, Frank A. Vanderlip and the National City Bank," *Journal of InterAmerican Studies and World Affairs* 15 (Feb. 1973), pp. 60–72; U.S. Dept. of Commerce, Bureau of Foreign and Domestic Commerce, *Special Agents Series*, no. 90, *Banking and Credit in Argentina, Brazil, Chile, and Peru* by Edward N. Hurley (Washington: Govt. Printing Office, 1914), pp. 7–8 ff.
63. *Special Agents*, no. 90, p. 65; Arthur S. Link, *Wilson*, vol. 2: *The New Freedom* (Princeton: Princeton Univ. Press, 1956), chap. 7; *PAUB*, 38 (Jan. 1914), p. 76.
64. *PAUB*, 38 (Jan. 1914), pp. 27–36; *DCTR*, no. 4, 6 Jan. 1914, p. 57, no. 163, 14 July 1914, p. 268.
65. Jeffrey J. Safford, *Wilsonian Maritime Diplomacy, 1913–1921* (New Brunswick: Rutgers Univ. Press, 1978), chaps, 1, 2; *PAUB*, 36 (March 1913), p. 733.
66. *DCTR*, no. 11, 14 Jan. 1914, p. 161; *Special Agents*, no. 90, pp. 38–39.
67. Barrett Memorandum, 13 March 1914, box 15, JBP; *PAUB*, 38 (March 1914), pp. 378–80, 39 (June 1913), pp. 853–54; U.S. Congress, House, Ambassador to Argentine Republic, Report to Accompany H. R. 13667, 12 March 1914, Ambassador to Chile, Report to Accompany H. R. 15503, 27 April 1914, Ambassador to Argentina, Report to Accompany S. 4553, 12 May 1914, 63d Cong., 2d sess., 1914, H. Repts, 372, 583, 664; Senate, Appointment of an Ambassador to Argentina to Accompany S. 4553, 4 March 1914, Ambassador to Chile to Accompany S. 5203, 63rd Cong., 2nd sess., 1914, S. Repts. 313, 424; *El Mercurio* 2, 25 July 1914; Lorillard to Bryan, 5 Aug. 1914, 701, Post Records, R. G. 84, RDS.
68. *PWW*, 29:211.
69. Lorillard to Knox, 19 Feb. 1913, 710/3, Post Records, R. G. 84, RDS.
70. Lorillard to Bryan, 27 Feb. 1914, 835.00/118, RDS; *La Prensa*, 23 March, 27 Apr. 1914.
71. Robert E. Quirk, *An Affair of Honor, Woodrow Wilson and the Occupation of Veracruz* (n.p.: The Univ. of Kentucky Press, 1962), chaps. 1, 2; Grieb, *Huerta*, chap. 9.
72. Mark T. Gilderhus, *Diplomacy and Revolution, U.S.–Mexican Relations under Wilson and Carranza* (Tucson: Univ. of Arizona Press, 1977), pp. 9–14.
73. Naón, da Gama, and Suárez to Bryan, 25 Apr. 1914, 812.00/16525, Lorillard to Bryan, 29 April 1914, 710.3, Post Records, R. G. 84, RDS.
74. Meyer, *Huerta*, chap. 10.
75. Lorillard to Bryan, 29 April 1914, 710.3, Post Records, R. G. 84, RDS; *La Prensa*, 20, 24, 27, 28 April, 1 June, 13 July 1914; *El Mercurio*, 15, 19, 26, 27 June, 22 July 1914.
76. Barrett to his mother Caroline, 5 May 1914, box 14, JBP; *PAUB*, 39 (July 1914), p. 83; Eliot to Wilson, 7 May 1914, series 2, WWP.
77. Diary, 15 April 1914, 11 May 1914, EMHP.
78. *PWW*, 29:516–24.
79. *PWW*, 30:130–31, 143.
80. *PWW*, 30:77–78.

81. *FRLP*, 2:459—65.
82. *PWW*, 30:255—57, 271—72.

NOTES TO CHAPTER 2

1. *PAUB*, 45 (Sept. 1917), p. 393.
2. H. S. Ferns, *Britain and Argentina in the Nineteenth Century* (Oxford: The Clarendon Press, 1960); D.C.M. Platt, *Finance, Trade, and Politics in British Foreign Policy, 1815—1914* (Oxford: The Clarendon Press, 1968); and *Latin America and British Trade, 1806—1914* (London: Adam and Charles Black, 1972); Platt, ed., *Business Imperialism, 1840—1930, An Inquiry Based on British Experience in Latin America* (Oxford: The Clarendon Press, 1977); Tony Smith, *The Pattern of Imperialism, The United States, Great Britain and the Late-Industrializing World since 1815* (Cambridge: The Univ. Press, 1981).
3. *PAUB*, 46 (Jan. 1918), pp. 39—48, 47 (Oct., Dec. 1918), pp. 542—46, 782—810; *DCTR*, no. 189, 13 Aug. 1913, pp. 850—55, no. 275, 24 Nov. 1913, p. 993; David Rock, *Politics in Argentina, 1890—1930 The Rise and Fall of Radicalism* (Cambridge: The Univ. Press, 1975), p. 105; Lorillard to Bryan, 19 June 1914, 835.00/119, 14 Aug. 1914, 835.001/38, RDS; Lansing to Colville Barclay, 10 Aug. 1914, vol. 3, RLP.
4. L. J. Keena Report, 14 Sept. 1914, 835.51/112, RDS; *DCTR*, no. 272, 19 Nov. 1914, pp. 810—11; *La Prensa*, 8 Oct. 1914.
5. *DCTR*, no. 272, 19 Nov. 1914, p. 811, no. 244, 17 Oct. 1914, p. 317, no. 256, 31 Oct. 1914, no. 265, 11 Nov. 1914, p. 689, no. 270, 17 Nov. 1914, pp. 776—77; *CR*, no. 14, 18 Jan. 1915, p. 243; Lorillard to Bryan, 24 Nov. 1914, 835.51/114, RDS.
6. *PAUB*, 39 (Sept. 1914), pp. 453—55; L. J. Keena Report, 14 Sept. 1914, 835.51/112, RDS; *DCTR*, no. 265, 11 Nov. 1914, p. 689; *CR*, no. 40, 5 Dec. 1914, p. 667.
7. *Jornal do Commércio*, 6 May 1914; *DCTR*, no. 208, 6 Sept. 1913, p. 1329 ff., no. 214, 12 Sept. 1914, pp. 1377—95; *PAUB*, 40 (Jan. 1915), pp. 97—109; Consul General to Bryan, 12 Aug., 7 Oct. 1914, 832.51/61, 62, Morgan to Bryan, 1 April 1914, 832.00/122, 27, 30 June, 19 Aug. 1914, 832.51/66, 69, 79, RDS.
8. Morgan to Bryan, 10 March, 30 Apr. 1914, 832.00/120, 124, 3 Aug., 22 Oct. 1914, 832.51/71, 81, Griffith to Bryan, 15 Aug. 1914, 832.00/125, RDS; *DCTR*, no. 232, 3 Oct. 1914, pp. 46—48.
9. Morgan to Bryan, 3 Aug., 19 Oct. 1914, 832.51/71, 80, Unsigned Memorandum to Bryan, 2 Sept. 1914, 832.73/78, RDS; *DCTR*, no. 232, 3 Oct. 1914, pp. 46—48.
10. *DCTR*, nos. 168, 169, 20, 21 July 1914, pp. 375, 415.
11. Fletcher to Bryan, 11 Aug. 1914, 825.51/68, RDS; *DCTR*, no. 242, 15 Oct. 1914, p. 269, no. 288, 9 Dec. 1914, pp. 1078—79; *CR*, no. 18, 22 Jan. 1915, pp. 310—11.
12. Frederick B. Pike, *Chile and the United States, 1880—1962, The Emergence of Chile's Social Crisis and the Challenge to United States Diplomacy* (Notre Dame: Notre Dame Univ. Press, 1963), chaps. 3—5; William Jefferson Dennis, *Tacna and Arica, An Account of the Chilean-Peruvian Boundary Dispute and of the Arbitration by the United States* (Hamden, Conn.: Archon Books, 1967, fp. 1931); Huntington Wilson to Fletcher, 17 March 1913, 723.2515/289, RDS; *El Mercurio*, May—June 1914.
13. John Bassett Moore to Bryan, 8 May 1913, 710E/4, Roland B. Harvey to Bryan, 5 Dec. 1913, 710E/10, E. Suárez Mújica to Bryan, 31 July 1914, 710E/18, Fletcher to Bryan, 19 Sept. 1914, 710E/28, E. Suárez Mújica to Bryan, 10 Oct. 1914, 710E/33, Bryan to Wilson, 10 March 1914, Wilson to Bryan, 30 Aug. 1914, Wilson-Bryan Correspondence, RDS; James F. Vivian, "Wilson, Bryan and the American Delegation to the Abortive Fifth Pan American Conference, 1914," *Nebraska History* 59 (Spring 1978), pp. 56—69.
14. *El Mercurio*, 28 Nov. 1914; *CR*, no. 98, 27 Apr. 1915, p. 461.
15. *PAUB*, 38 (May 1914), p. 696, 39 (July 1914), p. 74; Development of South American Trade, Commerce Dept., 12 Aug. 1914, series 2, WWP; *DCTR*, no. 198, 24 Aug. 1914, p. 1041.

16. *PAUB*, 39 (Sept. 1914), p. 445; Memorandum, 7 Aug. 1914, 610.11/21, RDS,
17. *DCTR*, no. 211, 9 Sept. 1914, pp. 1339–40.
18. *PAUB*, 39 (Oct., Nov. 1914), pp. 617–18, 794–97; Redfield to McAdoo and James M. Baker, 17 Sept. 1914, E 305, box 947, R. G. 43, U.S. Participation in International Conferences, Commissions, and Expositions, U.S. Section of the International High Commission, 1916–1933, National Archives, Washington, D.C.; Straight to Fletcher, 18 Sept. 1914, Willard Straight Papers, Cornell University, Ithaca, N.Y.
19. *PAUB*, 39 (Oct., Nov. 1914), pp. 512–31, 618, 798; Straight to Morgan, 20 Oct. 1914, Straight Papers; *CR*, no. 30, 5 Feb. 1915, p. 512; McAdoo to Wilson, 28 Oct. 1914, McAdoo to Redfield, 20 Nov. 1914, E 305, box 947, R. G. 43, U.S. Section, International High Commission; U.S. Dept. of Commerce, Bureau of Foreign and Domestic Commerce, *Special Agents Series*, no. 106, *Banking Opportunities in South America* by William H. Lough (Washington: Govt. Printing Office, 1915), pp. 16–19.
20. *FR 1913*, pp. xi–xii.
21. Bryan to Wilson, 22 June 1914, box 66, William Jennings Bryan Papers, Library of Congress, Washington, D.C.
22. Straight to Fletcher, 6 Apr. 1914, 3 June 1914, Straight Papers; *PWW*:29:449; Oath of Allegiance and Office, 2 Oct. 1914, box 3, HPFP.
23. Bryan to Wilson, 22 June 1914, box 66, 19 Aug. 1914, box 43, Bryan Papers; Frederick J. Stimson, *My United States* (New York: Charles Scribner's, 1931), pp. 202, 265–69, 329; Mabel Stimson to her mother, to Harriet, 16, 21 Sept. 1914, Bryce to Stimson, 15 Sept. 1914, box 2, Frederick J. Stimson Papers, Massachusetts Historical Society, Boston, Mass.
24. Stimson, *My United States*, pp. 268–69, 294.
25. Bryan to Wilson, 17 Aug. 1914, Wilson-Bryan Correspondence, RDS.
26. Fletcher to House, 3 Oct. 1914, folio 1909, box 44, series 1, EMHP; Morgan to Bryan, 22 Sept. 1914, 710E/34, Division of Latin American Affairs Memorandum, 16 Oct. 1914, 710E/41, RDS; Wilson to Lansing, 19 Nov. 1914, series 3, WWP.
27. Memorandum for Bryan, 7 Oct. 1914, 763.72119, Bryan to Wilson, Wilson to Bryan, 7, 8 Oct. 1914, Bryan-Wilson Correspondence, RDS.
28. Diary, 25 Nov. 1914, EMHP.
29. Diary, 30 Nov. 1914; EMHP; *PAUB*, 39 (Dec. 1914), pp. 880–82; Minutes of the Governing Board, 8 Dec. 1914, 710.001/121, Bryan to Wilson, 9 Dec. 1914, Bryan-Wilson Correspondence, RDS.
30. Diary, 16 Dec. 1914, EMHP; Bryan to Wilson, Wilson to Bryan, 24 Jan. 1914, 710.11/167, RDS; the original version under the date of 29 Jan. 1915 is in series 2, WWP.
31. Diary, 17, 19 Dec. 1914, EMHP.
32. Diary, 29, 30 Dec. 1914, 13 Jan. 1915, EMHP; House to Wilson, 26 Dec. 1914, series 2 WWP.
33. E. Suárez Mújica to House, 19 Jan. 1915, House to Wilson, 21 Jan. 1915, series 2, WWP.
34. Diary, 24, 25 Jan. 1915, EMHP; Robert E. Quirk, *The Mexican Revolution, 1914–1915, The Convention of Aguascalientes* (New York: Citadel Press, 1963).
35. House to Wilson, 26 Jan. 1915, series 2, WWP; *FRLP*, 2:472–73.
36. *FRLP*, 2:473; The Negotiations of the Pan-American Treaty (1915), Notes, n.d., box 1, HPFP.
37. *PWW*, 32:191.
38. Eliot to Wilson, 19, 25 Feb. 1915, WWP.
39. *FRLP*, 2:529–32; Charles Seymour, ed., *The Intimate Papers of Colonel House* (New York: Houghton Mifflin, Co., 1926), vol. 1, p. 220.
40. *FRLP*, 2:473–75; *PWW*, 32:364.
41. Negotiations (1915), n.d., box 1, Morgan to Fletcher, 2 April 1915, box 3, HPFP; Fletcher to House, early April 1915, folio 1409, box 44, series 1, EMHP; *FRLP*, 2:475–83; Memorandum, 18 May 1915, 710.11/204 1/2, RDS.

42. Fletcher to Bryan, 2 Jan. 1915, Bryan to Fletcher, 6 Jan. 1915, 725.3211/39, Fletcher to Bryan, 12 Jan. 1915, 725.3211/41, Stimson to Bryan, 11 April 1915, 725.3211/50, Wilson to Bryan, 26 April 1915, 725.3211/46 1/2, Summerlin to Bryan, 26 May 1915, 725.3211/56, RDS; *El Mercurio*, 18–25 May 1915; Mario Barros, *Historia Diplomática de Chile (1541–1938)* (Barcelona; Ediciones Ariel, 1970), pp. 615–17.

43. U.S. Dept. of the Treasury, *Proceedings of the First Pan American Financial Conference, Washington, May 24 to 29, 1915* (Washington: Govt. Printing Office, 1915), p. 87.

44. Quoted in *PAUB*, 40 (Feb. 1915), pp. 221–22; Barrett, *Pan America* (New York: Harper and Brothers, 1915).

45. *PAUB*, 40 (March, April 1915), pp. 286–87, 492–94.

46. *PAUB*, 40 (Feb. 1915), pp. 190–93.

47. *PAUB*, 40 (March 1915), pp. 355–57; *CR*, no. 45, 24 Feb. 1915, p. 753, no. 105, 5 May 1915, pp. 580–82.

48. Morgan to Bryan, 27 Jan. 1915, 832.51/88, Gottschalk to Bryan, 16 March 1915, 832.51/90, RDS; *CR*, no. 117, 19 May 1915, p. 812, no. 133, 8 June 1915, p. 1107.

49. *El Mercurio*, 19 March 1915; *CR*, no. 112, 13 May 1915, p. 733.

50. *CR*, no. 112, 13 May 1915, p. 733, no. 121, 24 May 1915, pp. 874–75, no. 166, 17 July 1915, p. 277.

51. Otto Willson Memorandum, 8 May 1915, E 305, box 948, R. G. 43, U.S. Section, International High Commission.

52. *Proceedings, First Pan American Financial Conference*, pp. 7–20, 90, 201–2.

53. *Proceedings, First Pan American Financial Conference*, p 9; *PAUB*, 40 (June 1915), pp. 747–54.

54. *PAUB*, 40 (May 1915), p. 569; *El Mercurio*, 24 May 1915; *La Prensa*, 6, 26 May 1915; Dr. Equis, *La Invasión Yankee, Cartilla de Política Internacional Sur Americana* (Buenos Aires: Larrea 258, n.d.), in Stimson to Bryan, 29 March 1915, 710.11/194, RDS.

55. *FR 1915*, pp. 694–95; Bryan to Wilson, 2 June 1915, Bryan-Wilson Correspondence, RDS.

56. Paola E. Coletta, *William Jennings Bryan*, vol. 2: *Progressive Politician and Moral Statesman, 1909–1915* (Lincoln: Univ. of Nebraska Press, 1969), chap. 12; Kendrick A. Clements, *William Jennings Bryan, Missionary Isolationist* (Knoxville: Univ. of Tennessee Press, 1982), chap. 6; Daniel M. Smith, "Robert Lansing (1915–1920)," in *An Uncertain Tradition: American Secretaries of State in the Twentieth Century*, ed. Norman A. Graebner (New York: McGraw-Hill Book Co., Inc., 1961), pp. 101–27; House to Wilson, 16 June 1915, series 2, WWP.

57. Diary, 24 June 1915, EMHP.

58. Diary, 18 June 1915, Fletcher to House, 23 July 1915, folio 1409, box 44, series 1, EMHP; *PWW*, 33:533.

59. House to Wilson, 5 July 1915, series 2, WWP; Diary, 11 July 1915, vol. 1, RLP; Barrett to House, 15 July 1915, folder 319, box 10, series 1, Diary, 24 July 1915, EMHP.

60. *FRLP*, 2:543–45.

61. Isidro Fabela, ed., *Documentos Históricos de la Revolución Mexicana, Revolución y Régimen Constitucionalista*, vol. 3: *Carranza, Wilson y el ABC* (México: Fondo de Cultura Económica, 1962), pp. 253 ff.; vol. 20: *Las Relaciones Internacionales en la Revolución y Régimen Constitucionalista y la Cuestión Petrolera, 1913–1919*, tomo 1 (México: Editorial Jus, S. A., 1970), pp. 205 ff.; *FR 1915*, pp. 755–56; *FRLP*, 2:550–54, Diary, 10 Oct. 1915, vol. 1, RLP, Louis Kahle, "Robert Lansing and the Recognition of Venustiano Carranza," *Hispanic American Historical Review* 38 (Aug. 1958), pp. 353–72.

62. *FR 1915*, p. x.

63. *FRLP*, 2:486.

64. *FRLP*, 2:486–87; *PWW*, 35:66–68; Diary, 15 Oct. 1915, EMHP.

65. *PWW*, 35:111–14; *FRLP*, 2:488–90; Fletcher to Bryan, 20 Sept. 1915, 825.00/113, RDS; Fletcher to Lansing, early Nov. 1915, vol. 14, RLP.

66. *PWW*, 35:188 – 89; Wilson to Lansing, 17 Nov. 1915, vol. 15, RLP; Lansing to Wilson, 18 Nov. 1915, Lansing-Wilson Correspondence, Stimson to Bryan with enclosure, 26 Nov., 710.11/216, RDS; *La Prensa*, 24 Nov. 1915.

67. *FR 1915*, pp. ix – xi; Barrett to his mother Caroline, 11 Dec. 1915, box 14, JBP.

68. Pan American Union, *Proceedings of the Second Pan American Scientific Congress* (Washington: Govt. Printing Office, 1917), vol. 7, pp. xii, 6 – 11, 14 – 15, 122 – 28, vol. 9, pp. 7 – 9, vol. 11, pp. 254 – 62.

69. *PWW*, 35:441 – 46, 520; *FRLP*, 2:492; Fletcher to Lansing, 21 Jan. 1916, 711, Post Records, R. G. 84, RDS; E. Suárez Mújica to Lansing, 14 Jan. 1916, vol. 16, RLP; Lansing to Wilson, 19 Feb. 1916, Lansing-Wilson Correspondence, RDS.

70. Wilson to Lansing, 25 Jan. 710.11/463, Morgan to Lansing, 21 Feb. 1916, 710.11/252, RDS; *FR 1916*, p. 3: Diary, 20 – 22 Feb., 23 March 1916, EMHP.

71. *CR*, no. 201, 27 Aug. 1915, p. 1020, no. 209, 7 Sept. 1915, p. 1175, no. 223, 23 Sept. 1915, p. 1413; *PAUB*, 43 (Oct. 1916), p. 586.

72. *FR 1915*, p. 23; Minutes, Meeting of 23 Sept. 1915, box 45, vol. 1, R. G. 43, U.S. section, International High Commission.

73. *CR*, no. 154, 2 July 1915, p. 19, no. 168, 20 July 1915, pp. 326, 330, no. 182, 5 Aug. 1915, pp. 638 – 39, no. 195, 20 Aug. 1915, p. 907, no. 224, 24 Sept. 1915, p. 1425.

74. *CR*, no. 220, 20 Sept. 1915, p. 1361; Morgan to Latin American Affairs Division, 12 Sept. 1915, 832.51/129, RDS.

75. *PAUB*, 41 (Sept. 1915), pp. 459 – 63.

76. *CR*, no. 199, 25 Aug. 1915, p. 986, no. 202, 28 Aug. 1915, pp. 1028 – 29, no. 230, 1 Oct. 1915, p. 5, no. 84, 10 April 1916, pp. 123 – 25; *PWW*, 36:43 – 44; Jeffrey J. Safford, *Wilsonian Maritime Diplomacy, 1913 – 1921* (New Brunswick: Rutgers Univ. Press, 1978), chaps. 2 – 4.

77. *CR*, no. 15, 19 Jan. 1916, p. 257, no. 67, 21 March 1916, p. 1132, no. 40, 17 Feb. 1916, p. 664, no. 85, 11 April 1916, p. 132.

78. *FR 1916*, pp. 21 – 22; U.S. Congress, House, *Report of the United States Section of the International High Commission on the First General Meeting of the Commission held at Buenos Aires, April 3 – 12, 1916*, 64th Cong., 2d sess., 20 Dec. 1916, H. Doc. 1788, pp. 8 – 9; Mabel Stimson to her mother, 13 April 1916, box 3, Stimson Papers.

79. U.S. Congress, House, *Report, International High Commission, Buenos Aires*, pp. 6, 9 – 14, 26 – 28.

80. *PAUB*, 42 (March, April 1916), pp. 453 – 54, 460; *FR 1916*, p. 23.

81. *PWW*, 36:278; Clarence C. Clendenen, *The United States and Pancho Villa: A Study in Unconventional Diplomacy* (Ithaca: Cornell Univ. Press, 1961), chaps. 18, 19, 20; Friedrich Katz, *The Secret War in Mexico: Europe, the United States, and the Mexican Revolution* (Chicago: Univ. of Chicago Press, 1981), chap. 8.

82. Confidential Diary, 16 March 1916, drawer 88, Frank L. Polk Papers, Yale University, New Haven Conn.; Polk to Wilson, 17 March 1916, Lansing-Wilson Correspondence, RDS; *FR 1916*, p. 4; Diary, 29, 31 March 1916, EMHP; *PWW*, 36:398.

83. *FRLP*, 2:495; Diary, 6, 11 April, 3 May 1916, Fletcher to House, 20 April 1916, folio 1410, box 44, series 1, EMHP; Naón to Lansing, 13 April 1916, 710.11/225 1/2B, RDS; *PWW*, 36: 478 – 79, 412 – 13, 595 – 96.

84. Clendenen, *U.S. and Villa*, chaps. 21, 22; Mark T. Gilderhus, *Diplomacy and Revolution, U.S. – Mexican Relations under Wilson and Carranza* (Tucson: Univ. of Arizona Press, 1977), chap. 3.

85. Eliseo Arredondo to Carranza, 21 June 1916, Carranza to Arredondo, 24 June 1916, tomo 3, leg. 1, L-E-1443, III252 (72:73)/10, Expediente Personal de Venustiano Carranza, Archivo de la Secretaría de Relaciones Exteriores, México, D. F.; Arthur S. Link, *Wilson*, vol. 4: *Confusions and Crises, 1915 – 1916* (Princeton: Princeton Univ. Press, 1964), pp. 307 ff.; Mexico, *Labor Internacional de la Revolución Constitucionalista de México (Libro Rojo)* (México; n.p., 1960, fp. 1919), pp. 288 – 89; also see Isidro Fabela and Josefina E. de Fabela, *Documentos Históricos de la Revolución Mexicana*, vols. 12, 13: *Expedición Punitiva* (México: Editorial Jus, S. A., 1967 – 68).

86. *FRLP*, 2:558 – 59.

87. Gilderhus, *Diplomacy and Revolution*, chap. 3; Arredondo to Carranza, 28, 30 June, tomo III, leg. 1, Expediente Personal de Carranza, Archivo de la Secretaría de Relaciones Exteriores; *FRLP*, 2:559–62; *PWW*, 37: 306–7.

88. Gilderhus, *Diplomacy and Revolution*, chap. 3.

89 .*PWW*, 37:240–45, 398–400; Fletcher to Lansing, Lansing to Wilson, 16, 17 June 1916, vol. 19, RLP; House to Wilson, 16, 18 June 1916, series 2, WWP; Fletcher to House, 4 May, 15 June 1916, folios 1410, 1411, box 4, series 1, diary, 18 Sept. 1916, EMHP; *FRLP*, 2:496–97.

90. *CR*, no. 124, 26 May 1916, p. 756.

91. *CR*, no. 87, 13 Apr. 1916, pp. 164–65, no. 116, 17 May 1916, p. 630, no. 173, 25 July 1916, p. 307, no. 176, 28 July 1916, p. 362, no. 254, 28 Oct. 1916, p. 381, no. 268, 14 Nov. 1916, p. 594; Morgan to Lansing, 14 Sept. 1916, 832.51/122, RDS; *PAUB*, 43 (Oct. 1916), pp. 601–6.

92. Carl P. Parrini, *Heir to Empire, United States Economic Diplomacy, 1916–1923* (Pittsburgh: Univ. of Pittsburgh Press, 1969), chap. 2; Burton I. Kaufman, *Efficiency and Expansion, Foreign Trade Organization in the Wilson Administration, 1913–1921* (Westport, Conn.: Greenwood Press, 1974), pp. 165–75.

93. Lansing to Wilson, 23 June 1916, Lansing-Wilson Correspondence, RDS.

94. *CR*, no. 257, 1 Nov. 1916, pp. 481–91.

95. Diary, 1 Oct. 1916, Fletcher to House, folio 1411, box 44, series 1, EMHP.

NOTES TO CHAPTER 3

1. Ernest R. May, *The World War and American Isolation, 1914–1917* (Cambridge: Harvard Univ. Press, 1959), chaps. 18, 19.

2. Arthur S. Link, *Woodrow Wilson, Revolution, War, Peace* (Arlington Heights, Ill.: AHM Publishing Corp., 1979), chap. 3; Lansing's circular instruction, 3 Feb. 1917, 763.72/3438, RDS.

3. Percy Alvin Martin, *Latin America and the War* (Gloucester, Mass.: Peter Smith, 1967, first published, 1925); *FR 1917*, supp. 1, pp. 221–39.

4. G. Messersmith to Lansing, Lansing's circular instruction, 6 Feb. 1917, 763.72/3338, Lansing-Wilson, 6, 7 Feb. 1917, 763.72/3314 ½, W. J. Price to Lansing, enclosures, 8 Feb. 1917, 763.72/3359, RDS.

5. Brasil, Ministerio das Relacões Exteriores, *Guerra da Europa, Documentos Diplomaticos, Attitude do Brasil* (Rio de Janeiro: Imprensa Nacional, 1917), pp. 15–17; Benson to Lansing, 8 Feb. 1917, 763.72/3266, 5 April 1917, 763.72/4315, 832.635/1, Redfield to Lansing, 3 April 1917, 832.635/2, Lansing to Benson, 5 April 1917, 832.635/6, RDS.

6. *FR 1917*, supp. 1, p. 227; Shea to Lansing, 9, 10 Feb. 1917, 763.72/3286, 3448, RDS.

7. *La Prensa*, 5 Feb. 1917.

8. Stimson to Lansing, 15 July 1916, 711.35/24, 7 Feb. 1917, 763.72/3546, Frederick de Billier to Lansing, 14 Oct. 1916, 835.0011r4, RDS; Mabel Stimson to her mother, 9 Feb. 1917, box 4, Frederic J. Stimson Papers, Massachusetts Historical Society, Boston, Mass.

9. Stimson to Lansing, 3 Jan. 1917, 835.0011r4/2, 8, 10 Feb. 1917, 763.72/3274, 3547, 3548, Naón to Lansing, 9 Feb. 1917, 763.72/3328, RDS; Stimson to Hugh Wilson, 8 May 1916, letterbook, Stimson Papers; David Rock, *Politics in Argentina, 1890–1930, The Rise and Fall of Radicalism* (Cambridge Univ. Press, 1975), pp. 100–4.

10. Mark T. Gilderhus, *Diplomacy and Revolution, U.S.–Mexican Relations under Wilson and Carranza* (Tucson: Univ. of Arizona Press, 1977), chap. 4; Robert Freeman Smith, *The United States and Revolutionary Nationalism in Mexico, 1916–1932* (Chicago: Univ. of Chicago Press, 1972), chaps. 4, 5, 6, pp. 267–70.

11. *War Memoirs of Robert Lansing, Secretary of State* (New York: Bobbs-Merrill Co., 1935), p. 308.

12. *Labor Internacional de la Revolución Constitucionalista de México* (*Libro Rojo*) (México: n.p., 1960), pp. 372—75.

13. *Labor Internacional*, pp. 375—91; Stimson to Lansing, enclosure, 15 Feb. 1917, 763.72/3576, RDS; *FR 1917*, supp. 1, p. 233; Wilson to Lansing, 20 Feb. 1917, series 2, WWP.

14. *FR 1917*, supp. 1, p. 236; *FRLP*, 1:246.

15. Michael C. Meyer, *Huerta, A Political Biography* (Lincoln: Univ. of Nebraska Press, 1972), chap. 11; Friedrich Katz, *The Secret War in Mexico: Europe, the United States and the Mexican Revolution* (Chicago: The Univ. of Chicago Press, 1981), chaps. 9, 10.

16. Katz, *Secret War*, p. 354.

17. *FR 1917*, supp. 1, pp. 160—61; Katz, *Secret War*, pp. 355—67.

18. Gilderhus, *Diplomacy and Revolution*, chap. 4; Katz, *Secret War*, chap. 10.

19. Goodwin to Lansing, 24 March 1917, 763.72119/542, RDS; Page to Wilson, 28 March 1917, series 2, WWP.

20. Lansing to Wilson, 26 March 1917, Lansing-Wilson correspondence, RDS.

21. Lansing to Wilson, 26 March 1917, Lansing-Wilson correspondence, Wilson to Lansing, 27 March 1917, 763.72/3759 3/4, RDS; E. David Cronon, ed., *The Cabinet Diaries of Josephus Daniels, 1913 —1921* (Lincoln: Univ. of Nebraska Press, 1963), pp. 106—7; draft. 1917, memorandum re: W. R. Grace and Co., 4 Aug. 1917, drawer 77, file 187, Frank L. Polk Papers, Yale Univ., New Haven, Conn.

22. Lansing to Wilson, 29 Jan. 1917, Lansing-Wilson correspondence, RDS; Stimson to Lansing, 29 Jan. 1917, Wilson to Lansing, 22 March 1917, series 2, WWP; William Phillips to House, 4 Jan. 1917, series 1, box 89, folio 3096, EMHP; confidential diary, 12 March 1917, drawer 80, Polk papers; *FR 1917*, supp. 1, pp. 67—68, 242.

23. Martin, *Latin America and the War*; *FR 1917*, supp. 1, pp. 244—55; Lansing to all diplomatic missions, 22 May 1917, 763.72/4858b, RDS; press release, 10 April 1917, box 16, JBP.

24. Ministerio das Relacões Exteriores, *Guerra da Europa*, pp. 25—37; *FR 1917*, supp. 1, 252; consul general to Lansing, 10 April 1917, 732.62/4, Benson to Lansing, 11 April 1917, 763.72/4452, Samuel T. Lee to Lansing, 28 April 1917, 832.00/142, Lansing to Wilson, 8 April 1917, Lansing-Wilson correspondence, da Gama to Lansing, 10 April 1917, 832.635/4, RDS; Polk to Lansing, 7 April 1917, Lansing to Wilson, 8 April 1917, da Gama to Lansing, 9 April 1917, vol. 26, RLP.

25. Polk to da Gama, enclosure, 12 April 1917, da Gama to Polk, 14 April 1917, vol. 26, RLP.

26. Polk memorandum, 16 April 1917, Lansing to Wilson, 17 April 1917, Polk to Wilson, 19 April 1917, vol. 26, RLP.

27. *FRLP*, 2:499.

28. Lansing to Wilson, 19 Apr. 1917, Lansing-Wilson correspondence, RDS; Wilson to Lansing, 20 April 1917, vol. 27, RLP.

29 .Stimson-Lansing, 20, 22 April 1917, 763.72119/587, Fletcher to Lansing, 11 April 1917, 763.72/3909, RDS; *FR 1917*, supp.1, pp. 262, 264.

30. Shea to Lansing, 21, 23 April 1917, 763.72/4713, 4714, Stabler to Lansing, 18 April 1917, 711.25/25, RDS; *El Mercurio*, 21 April 1917.

31. *FR 1917*, supp. 1, pp. 264—65; Stimson to Lansing, enclosure, 27 April 1917, 763.62119/628, RDS; *La Prensa*, 1, 4 May 1917.

32. *FR 1917*, supp. 1, pp. 265—66.

33. Barrett to Baker, 11 March 1917, 763.72/5146, Benson to Lansing, 7 May 1917, 832.021/30, 11 May 1917, 763.72/5042, RDS.

34. Confidential diary, 15 May 1917, drawer 88, Polk papers; *FR 1917*, supp. 1, pp. 283—84.

35. Gottschalk to Lansing, 16 May 1917, 832.635/16, RDS; confidential diary, 18, 22 May 1917, drawer 88, Polk papers; *FRLP*, 2:500.

36. Ministerio das Relacões Exteriores, *Guerra da Europa*, pp. 54—56, 60—61; Morgan to Lansing, 20 May 1917, 763.72/4942, enclosures, 2 June 1917, 763.72/5703, RDS; *FR 1917*, supp. 1, p. 295; *Jornal do Commercio*, 9 June 1917.

37. Shea to Lansing, 19, 21 May 1917, 763.72/5322, 4816, RDS; confidential diary, 12 June 1917, Polk papers.
38. Statement, 4 June 1917, box 16, JBP; *FR 1917*, supp. 1, pp. 282–93, 297, 300.
39. *La Prensa*, 30 May, 8 June 1917; consul general to Lansing, 31 May 1917, 711.35/26, Stimson to Lansing, 8 June 1917, 763.72119/675, RDS.
40. From B, #9, 15 June 1917, box 512, C-10-f, 8755, U.S. Dept. of the Navy, Record Group 38, Records of the Chief of Naval Operations, Intelligence Divison, Naval Attaché Reports, National Archives, Washington, D.C.
41. Morgan to Lansing, 20 June 1917, 763.72/5871, Daniels to Lansing, 22 June 1917, 832.34/114, RDS.
42. Report No. 61, 22 June 1917, Buenos Aires (U.S. Naval Intelligence, WX-7), U.S. Dept. of the Navy, Record Group 45, Naval Records Collection of the Office of Naval Records and Library, Subject File, 1911–27, National Archives, Washington, D.C.
43. *FR 1917*, p. 26; *PAUB*, 45 (Oct. 1917), pp. 424, 433.
44. *FR 1917*, pp. 5–8, 26; *FR 1917*, supp. 1, pp. 313–15; Morgan to Lansing, 23 July 1917, 763.72/6393, RDS; Samuel Guy Inman to Daniels, 28 Dec. 1917, box 503, Josephus Daniels Papers, Library of Congress, Washington, D.C.
45. McAdoo to Sen. William J. Stone, 29 Dec. 1916, E 305, box 948, Dept. of State, Record Group 43, U.S. Participation in International Conferences, Commissions, and Expositions, U.S. Section of the International High Commission, 1916–1933, National Archives, Washington, D.C.
46. *CR*, no. 261, 6 Nov. 1916, p. 485, no. 99, 28 April 1917, p. 382; *PAUB*, 45 (July, Aug. 1917), pp. 1–23, 141–65; Stimson to Lansing, 9 Dec. 1916, 711.35/25, RDS.
47. Consul general to Lansing, 13 Dec. 1916, 610, Dept. of State, Record Group 84, Records of the Service Posts of the Dept. of State, Legations, Embassies, Consular Posts, National Archives, Washington, D.C.; Robbins memorandun, 29 Nov. 1916, 835.51/132, Stimson to Lansing, 835.51/153, RDS; *CR*, no. 4, 3 Jan. 1917, p. 26; *PAUB*, 44 (May 1917), pp. 626–27.
48. Polk to Morgan, 21 Oct. 1916, 832.51/125, Morgan to Lansing, 23 Oct. 1916, 832.51/131, J. Butler Wright to Morgan, 21 Nov. 1917, 832.51/143, Benson to Lansing, 22 Nov. 1916, 832.51/133, Hoover to Lansing, 25 Nov. 1916, 832.51/140, Redfield to Polk, 27 Jan. 1917, 832.51/141, Gottschalk to Lansing, 7 Feb., 19 March 1917, 832.51/145, 151, RDS; *CR*, no. 256, 31 Oct. 1916, p. 403.
49. *CR*, no. 65, 20 March 1917, p. 1041; *PAUB*, 44 (May 1917), pp. 553–59.
50. U.S. Dept. of Commerce, *Brazil, A Study of Economic Conditions since 1913*, by Arthur H. Redfield, No. 86, *Miscellaneous Series* (Washington: Government Printing Office, 1920), pp. 21–22, 27–29, 51–52, 56, 61–63; *CR*, no. 196, 22 Aug. 1917, p. 691.
51. Consul general to Lansing, 17 Aug. 1917, 832.20/12, RDS.
52. Morgan to Lansing, 13, 16 Aug. 1917, 832.73/111, 115, Gottschalk to Lansing, 25 Nov., 17 Dec. 1917, 832.73/111, 115, RDS.
53. Morgan to Lansing, 17 Aug. 1917, 832.635/23, Roger Welles to Leland Harrison, 6 Sept. 1917, 832.635/23, Gottschalk to Lansing, 24 Sept. 1917, 832.635/38, Lansing to Morgan, 27 Sept. 1917, 832.635/23, Morgan to Lansing, 2 Oct. 1917, 832.635/32, RDS.
54. Morgan to Lansing, 21 July 1917, 832.85/7, RDS.
55. Daniels to Lansing, 2, 22, 23 Aug. 1917, 832.85/8, 12, 13, Morgan to Lansing, 14 Aug., 4 Sept. 1917, 832.85/11, 19, memorandum from the British Embassy, 3 Sept. 1917, 832.85/21, RDS.
56. Daniels to Lansing, 6 Sept. 1917, 832.85/20, Morgan to Lansing, 27 Sept. 3, 12, 28 Oct. 1917, 832.85/34, 832.635/32, 832.85/40, 43, 49, RDS.
57. *FR 1917*, supp. 1, pp. 351–52; Morgan to Lansing, 5 Nov. 1917, 832.20/15, RDS.
58. Morgan to Lansing, 13 Nov. 1917, 832.20/16, RDS.
59. *FR 1917*, supp. 1, pp. 379–80; Morgan to Lansing, 6, 9 Nov., 1, 8 Dec. 1917, 832.24/28, 832.20/13, 832.30/22, 832.34/121, RDS.

60. *FR 1917*, supp. 1, pp. 309–10; Shea to Lansing, 3 July, 4, 10 Aug. 1917, 763.72/6094, 6180, 6799, RDS.

61. Shea to Lansing, 7 Aug. 1917, 825.6374/40, Walter Hines Page to Lansing, 7, 13 Sept. 1917, 825.6374/39, 41, RDS.

62. Cronon, ed., *Cabinet Diaries*, p. 209; Shea to Lansing, 9, 30 Oct. 1917, 763.72/7551, 7964, Johnson to Lansing, 763.72/7482, Lansing to Page, 5 Nov., 4 Dec. 1917, 825.6374/41, 61, Polk to Page, 16 Nov. 1917, 825.6374/549, Lansing to American consulates, London, 22 Nov. 1917, 825.6374/53, Bernard Baruch to Lansing, 2 March 1918, 825.6374/120, RDS; Fletcher to Daniels, 13 Nov. 1917, box 77, Daniels papers.

63. Caperton to Daniels, 29 July 1917, 835.00/144, RDS.

64. Harold F. Peterson, *Argentina and the United States, 1810–1960* (New York: State Univ. of New York, 1964), pp. 312–15.

65. Stimson to Lansing, 28 Sept. 1917, 763.72/8423, RDS; Mabel Stimson to her mother, 12 Sept. 1917, box 4, Stimson papers.

66. Stimson to Lansing, 13 Oct. 1917, 763.72/7270, Navy Dept., Argentine Political Situation, 6 Nov. 1917, 835.00/145, RDS; naval attaché, Rio de Janeiro, to director of naval intelligence, 14 Nov. 1917, box 511, C-10-f, 8724, from A, 19 Nov. 1917, box 514, C-10-f, 9219, R. G. 38, Records of the Chief of Naval Operations.

67. U.S. Dept. of Commerce, *The Economic Position of Argentina During the War*, by L. Brewster Smith, Harry T. Collings, and Elizabeth Murphey, No. 88, *Miscellaneous Series* (Washington: Govt. Printing Office, 1920), p. 7; *CR*, no. 158, 9 July 1917, p. 85, no. 274, 22 Nov. 1917, p. 721.

68. J. M. Lay to Polk, 2 Nov. 1917, 835.613/11, Crosby to McAdoo, 11 Nov. 1917, 835.6131/5, Stimson to Lansing, 7, 28 Dec. 1917, 835.6131/46, 39, Stimson to Lansing, 28 Dec. 1917, 763.72119/1048, RDS; *FR 1917*, supp. 1, 380, 389, 392, 395.

69. Lawrence E. Gelfand, *The Inquiry, American Preparations for Peace, 1917–1919* (New Haven: Yale Univ. Press, 1963), chap. 2.

70. A Program. . . ., by Henry Bruere, 13 Oct. 1917, entry 19, box 85, doc. #912, American Commission to Negotiate Peace, Record Group 256, Records of the Inquiry, Latin American Division, National Archives, Washington, D.C.

71. House to Wilson, 27 Oct. 1917, series 2, WWP.

72. U.S. Dept. of the Treasury, *Annual Report of the Secretary of the Treasury on the State of the Finances for the Fiscal Year Ended on 30 June 1918* (Washington: Govt. Printing Office, 1919), pp. 117–23.

73. *FRPPC, 1919*, 1:22–25.

74. Barrett memorandum, 17, 19 Nov. 1917, box 17, JBP.

75. Confidential diary, 1, 27, 28 Dec. 1917, drawer 88, Polk papers; Lansing to Barrett, 30 Nov. 1917, box 17, JBP.

76. Digest of Latin American Affairs, entry 4, box 79, doc. #787, pp. 2–3, R. G. 256, Records of the Inquiry; consul general to Lansing, 4 Jan. 1918, 711.2, R. G. 84, Post Records, RDS.

77. Morgan to Lansing, 4 Jan. 1918, 832.30/27, Stimson to Lansing, 3 Jan. 1918, 835.6131/43, Shea to Lansing, 11 Jan. 1918, 825.6374/88, RDS.

78. Lay to Polk, 22 Jan. 1918, drawer 77, file 182, Polk papers.

79. Lansing to Morgan, 9 Jan. 1918, Morgan to Lansing, 12, 21 Jan. 1918, 832.85/62a, 71, 47, RDS.

80. Lansing-Morgan, 10, 12 Jan. 1918, 832.34/121a, 122, Daniels to Lansing, 16, 18 Jan. 1918, 832.30/25, 832.34/124, RDS.

81. *FR 1918*, supp. 1, p. 66; Morgan to Lansing, 26 Jan., 6 Feb. 1918, 832.635/53, 763.72/9019, RDS.

82. Lansing-Morgan, 7 Feb. 1918, 832.30/27, 2, 8, 14 March 1918, 832.635/63, 832.00/147, 832.73/139, Albert Strauss to J. G. Lay, 18 Feb. 1918, 832.73/42, John L. Merrill to William Phillips, 832.73/144, RDS; from B, No. 122, O.N.I., 25 March 1918, WA-7, R. G. 45, Naval Records Collections, Subject File.

83. Stimson to Lansing, 15, 19 Jan., 22 March 1918, 835.6131/51, 54, 763.72119/1652, Price to Lansing, 763.72119/1347, RDS; from A (B.A.) to O.N.I., 11 June 1918, box 528, C-10-9, R.G. 38, Records of the Chief of Naval Operations; *FR 1917*, supp. 1, p. 380; *FR 1918*, supp. 1, 1:662, 665.

84. *FR 1918*, supp. 1, 1:671–72.

85. *FR 1918*, supp. 1, 1:673–80.

86. Shea to Lansing, 18, 20 Jan. 1918, 825.6374/99, 763.72/8998, Sharp to Lansing, 12 Jan. 1918, 825.6374/91, Lansing to Skinner, to Shea, 21, 29 March 1918, 825.6374/147a, 155b, RDS.

87. Unsigned memorandum, April 1918, entry 4, box 34, doc. #103, Latin America—Attitude Toward the War, 13 April, 1918, entry 4, box 73, doc. #645, R. G. 256, Records of the Inquiry; Morgan to Lansing, 12 April 1918, 832.00/181, RDS.

88. Phillips to Lansing, 15, 23 April 1918, Wilson to Lansing, 18 April 1918, series 2, WWP.

89. *FRPPC 1919*, 1:77; Lansing to Mezes, 17 April 1918, Lansing-Wilson correspondence, RDS.

90. Walter Hines Page to Stimson, summer 1918, 701/710, enclosures, R. G. 84, Post Records, RDS.

91. Memorandum, Division of Latin American Affairs, 31 May 1918, drawer 77, file 185, Polk papers.

92. Stabler memorandum, 22 April 1918, 832.51/176, L. Rowe to G. Auchincloss, 23 May 1918, 832.635, McAdoo to Lansing, 832.51/185, John L. Merrill to Lansing, 832.63/150, Morgan to Lansing, 31 May, 22 July 1918, 832.3421/38, 42, RDS.

93. Morgan to Lansing, 6 July 1918, 832.00/155, Polk to Lansing, 5 Oct. 1918, 832.00/197, RDS; Klein to Thomas B. McGovern, 10 Oct. 1918, box 2232, 432, U.S. Dept. of Commerce, Record Group 40, General Records, National Archives, Washington, D.C.

94. *FR 1918*, supp. 1, 1:691, 730–33; confidential diary, 16 July 1918, Polk papers.

95. Robbins to Lansing, 26 Aug. 1918, 835.00/155, RDS.

96. Chilean Finance, by Verne L. Havens, June 1918, entry 19, box 85, doc. #921, R. G. 256, Records of the Inquiry; editorials from *La Nación*, 12 Aug. 1918, *El Mercurio*, 25 Aug. 1918, C-10-f, 10697, box 521, R. G. 38, Records of the Chief of Naval Operations; Shea to Lansing, 4 Oct. 1918, 711.25/32, RDS.

97. Gilderhus, *Diplomacy and Revolution*, chap. 5.

98. *FR 1918*, pp. 577–79.

99. Fletcher to C. Aguilar, 2 April 1918, 711.12/104, RDS.

100. *El Pueblo*, 14, 29, 30 June 1918; *FR 1918*, pp. 584–600; Fletcher to Lansing, 3 July 1918, 711.12/116, RDS; *Labor Internacional*, p. 421.

101. *FR 1918*, p. 584; Fletcher to House, 17 July 1918, series 1, box 44, folio 1412, EMHP; Fletcher to Lansing, 3 July 1918, 711.12/116, RDS.

102. Boaz Long's Memorandum to Lansing, 10 Aug. 1918, 711.12/130, RDS.

NOTES TO CHAPTER 4

1. *PAUB*, 45 (Sept. 1917), p. 393, 47 (Dec. 1918), p. 792.

2. Latin American Trade—A Comparative View, by John Barrett and W. C. Wells, entry 18, box 117, American Commission to Negotiate Peace, Record Group 256, Records of the Inquiry, National Archives, Washington, D.C.

3. *PAUB*, 46 (Jan. 1918), p. 44; 47 (Oct. 1918), pp. 542–43.

4. *CR*, no. 232, 4 Oct. 1917, pp. 49–50, no. 275, 23 Nov. 1917, pp. 346–47, no. 275, 23 Nov. 1917, p. 747, no. 176, 29 July 1918, pp. 376–78; Shea to Lansing, 4 Nov. 1918, 825.6374/430, RDS; *PAUB*, 50 (Feb. 1920), pp. 160–61.

5. *PAUB*, 47 (Sept. 1918), pp. 385–86.

6. *PAUB*, 48 (Feb. 1919), pp. 158—60.

7. *CR*, no. 194, 19 Aug. 1918, p. 659, no. 305, 30 Dec. 1918, pp. 1204—10.

8. Max Winkler, *Investments of United States Capital in Latin America, World Peace Foundation Pamphlets*, vol. 11, no 6 (Boston: 1929), pp. 1031, 1034, 1036, 1039; U.S. Dept. of Commerce, *Investments in Latin America and the British West Indies*, by Frederick M. Halsey, no. 169, *Special Agents Series* (Washington: Govt. Printing Office, 1918), p. 17.

9. *Investments*, no. 169, *Special Agents Series*, pp. 19—21.

10. Sidney Mezes to Lansing, 2 Aug. 1918, Record Group 59, Records of the Dept. of State, Division of Latin American Affairs, 1904—1944, National Archives, Washington, D.C.; Report of Progress, 25 Sept. 1918, entry 19, box 86, doc. #948, Appendix to Vital Issues in Relation to the Peace Conference, n.d., entry 19, box 87, R. G. 256, Records of the Inquiry.

11. Willis to Stabler, 31 Oct. 1919, box 1, R. G. 59, Division of Latin American Affairs; *FRPPC*, 1:108—9, 116.

12. *PWW*, 40:538—39.

13. *PWW*, 45:534—39.

14. "The Monroe Doctrine and the American Policy of Isolation in Relation to a Just and Durable Peace," *The Annals of the American Academy of Political and Social Science*, 72 (July, 1917), pp. 100—3; quoted in William C. Widenor, *Henry Cabot Lodge and the Search for an American Foreign Policy* (Berkeley: Univ. of California Press, 1980), pp. 316—17.

15. John Barrett, "What the War Has Done to the Monroe Doctrine," *Current Opinion*, 65 (Nov. 1918), pp. 291—93; The Pan American Union—A Working Prototype of a World League of Nations, 2 Dec. 1918, entry 18, box 117, Barrett to Lansing, enclosures, entry 18, box 117, R. G. 256, Records of the Inquiry; Practical Pan Americanism—Past, Present and Future, in Barrett to Stimson, 11 March 1919, 711, Dept. of State, Record Group 84, Records of the Service Posts of the Dept. of State, Legations, Embassies, Consular Posts, National Archives, Washington, D.C.

16. *FRPPC*, 1:223—26; Morgan to Lansing, 11 Feb. 1919, 832.00/170, RDS; Vogelgesang to Daniels, 13 Dec. 1918, box 503, Josephus Daniels Papers, Library of Congress, Washington, D.C.

17. *FRPPC*, 1:224:—26; The Attitude of the Latin American Countries During the War, by John Barrett and Benite Javier Perez Verdia, 2 Dec. 1918, entry 18, box 117, Notes on the Status of Latin-American Nations before the Peace Conference, by Willis and Stabler, 19 Dec. 1918, entry 19, box 87, R. G. 256, Records of the Inquiry.

18. *FRPPC*, 1:228—30.

19. *FRPPC*, 1:234—35, 3:31—56, 172, 233, 533—34.

20. William Jefferson Dennis, *Tacna and Arica, An Account of the Chile-Peru Boundary Dispute and the Arbitration by the United States* (Archon Books, 1967, first pub. 1931), pp. 201—9; *FR 1919*, 1:124—25, 144.

21. *FR 1919*, 1:25—26.

22. *FR 1919*, 1:127—31.

23. *FR 1919*, 1:132—35, 137—38; *FRPPC*, 1:552—54.

24. *FRPPC*, 1:555—56.

25. *FRPPC*, 1:556—59.

26. *FRPPC*, 1:560—62; *FR 1919*, 1:148.

27. Thomas A. Bailey, *Woodrow Wilson and the Lost Peace* (New York: The Macmillan Co., 1944), chaps. 8, 9, 10.

28. Bailey, *Wilson and the Lost Peace*, chap. 12.

29. *FRPPC*, 11:67, 90, 553, 3:1—5, 190.

30. Stabler to Polk, 1 March 1919, drawer 78, file 48, Frank L. Polk Papers, Yale University, New Haven, Conn.; *FRPPC*, 11:531—32.

31. *FRPPC*, 11:532; Stabler to Polk, 25 March 1919, drawer 78, file 18, Polk Papers.

32. Memorandum from the Chilean Embassy, 19 Dec. 1918, 825.6374/469, Arnold A.

McKay to Lansing, 23 Jan. 1919, 825.6374/494, RDS; *FR 1919*, 1:143, 145–46, 150–51, 156–57.

33. *FR 1919*, 1:157, 159.

34. Alberto J. Pani, *Mi Contribución al Nuevo Régimen* (México, D. F. Editorial Cultura, 1936), pp. 250–54; Pani, *Cuestiones Diversas* (México: Imprenta Nacional, S. A., 1922), pp. 19–20, 250–57.

35. *FRPPC*, 13:92; Pani, *Cuestiones Diversas*, pp. 218–28.

36. *FR 1919*, 2:545–48.

37. Fletcher's confidential memorandum to Wilson, 1 March 1919, 711.12/187, RDS.

38. Mark T. Gilderhus, "Senator Albert B. Fall and 'The Plot against Mexico'," *New Mexico Historical Review*, 48 (Oct. 1973), 299–311; Clifford W. Trow, "Woodrow Wilson and the Mexican Interventionist Movement of 1919," *Journal of American History*, 58 (June 1971), pp. 46–72; William Gates to Root, 3 June 1919, General Correspondence, box 137, Elihu Root Papers, Library of Congress, Washington, D.C.

39. Aguilar to Eliseo Arredondo, 6 June 1919, reel 37, microfilm copy of the Albert B. Fall Papers, University of Nebraska, Lincoln, Neb.; Aguilar to Carranza, 2 July 1919, III/628 (010)/1, 1914–1918—Reglamentación de la Ley del Petróleo Mexicano, Controversia entre México y los Estados Unidos de A. con motivo de la Reglamentación de la Fracción I del Artículo 27 Constitucional, Archivo General de la Secretaría de Relaciones Exteriores de México, México, D. F.; Jara to Carranza, 3 June, Archivo de Venustiano Carranza, Centro de Estudios de Historia de México, Departamento Cultural de Condumex, S. A., México, D. F.; Lansing to Wilson, enclosures, 21 Aug. 1919, 812.00/2311c, RDS; Hermila Galindo, *La Doctrina Carranza y El Aceramiento Indo-Latino* (México: n.p., 1919), and *Labor Internacional de la Revolución Constitucionalista de México (Libro Rojo)* (México, D. F.; n.p., 1960, first pub. 1919).

40. Fletcher to Lansing, 30 July 1919, 711.12/216, Wilson to Lansing, 4 Aug. 1919, Fletcher to Wilson, 18 Aug. 1919, 711.12/187, Lansing to Wilson, enclosures, 21 Aug. 1919, 711.12/192 1/2, RDS; Mark T. Gilderhus, *Diplomacy and Revolution, U.S.–Mexican Relations under Wilson and Carranza* (Tucson: Univ. of Arizona Press, 1977), chap. 6; U.S. Congress, Senate, *Investigation of Mexican Affairs*, 66th cong., 2d sess., doc. #285, 2 vols. (Washington: Government Printing Office, 1920); Gonzales to Carranza, 18 Aug. 1919, Archivo de Carranza.

41. Stimson to Lansing, 20 Nov. 1918, series 2, WWP; Stimson to Lansing, 31 Dec. 1917, 835.02/3, 22 Jan. 1919, 835.6131/73, 25 Jan. 1919, 835.51/198, 2 May 1919, 710.11/399, Weekly Reports, 1 May, 31 July, 14 Aug. 1919, 810.00/2, RDS; From RC, 19 Nov. 1918, #1470, 10987-54, Dept. of the Army, Record Group 165, Records of the Military Intelligence Division, 1918–1941, National Archives, Washington, D.C.

42. Morgan to Lansing, 30 Nov. 1918, 611.32/5, 3 Dec. 1918, 832.00/22, 2 Jan. 1919, 832.20/23, 8 Jan. 1919, 832.3421/44, 5 Feb. 1919, 832.34/140, RDS.

43. Morgan to Lansing, 26 Feb. 1919, 832.00/171, Da Gama to Lansing, 18 April 1919, 711.32/23, RDS; From Maj. Fenton R. McCreery, 2 June 1919, box 772, 2052-68, R. G. 165, Records of the Military Intelligence Division.

44. *FR 1919*, 1:xi.

45. *PAUB*, 49 (July 1919), pp. 1–2.

46. Rowe to C. E. McGuire, 18 Nov. 1919, E 305, box 948, Minutes, 24 March 1919, 29 May 1919, box 45, vol. 1, Glass to Wilson, 25 Feb. 1919, E 305, box 948, Dept. of State, Record Group 43, U.S. Participation in International Conferences, Commissions, and Expositions, U.S. Section of the International High Commission, 1916–1933, National Archives, Washington, D.C.

47. U.S. Dept. of the Treasury, *Annual Report of the Secretary of the Treasury on the State of the Finances for the Fiscal Year Ended on 30 June 1920* (Washington: Govt. Printing Office, 1919), p. 179; Summary reports to Glass, Jan. 1920, E 305, box 949, R. G. 43, International High Commission; *FR 1919*, 1:37, 39, 40–41.

48. *PAUB*, 50 (Feb. 1920), pp.126, 137–39; 50 (Jan. 1920), pp. 46–57.

49. U.S. Dept. of the Treasury, *Annual Report of the Secretary of the Treasury on the State of the Finances for the Fiscal Year Ended on 30 June 1921* (Washington: Govt. Printing Office, 1920), pp. 232–34.

50. Edwin A. Weinstein, *Woodrow Wilson: A Medical and Psychological Biography* (Princeton: Princeton Univ. Press, 1981), chap. 21; Thomas A. Bailey, *Woodrow Wilson and the Great Betrayal* (New York: The Macmillan Co., 1945), chap. 17; Widenor, *Lodge*, chap. 7, 8.

51. Gilderhus, *Diplomacy and Revolution*, chap. 6; Robert Freeman Smith, *The United States and Revolutionary Nationalism in Mexico, 1916–1932* (Chicago: Univ. of Chicago Press, 1972), chap. 7.

52. Fall to Lansing, 13 Nov. 1919, 711.12/227, RDS; Fall to Fletcher, 4 Dec. 1919, box 7, HPFP; Charles C. Cumberland, "The Jenkins Case and Mexican-American Relations," *Hispanic-American Historical Review*, 31 (Nov. 1951), pp. 586–607; David H. Stratton, "President Wilson's Smelling Committee," *The Colorado Quarterly* 5 (Autumn 1956), pp. 164–84; Edith Bolling Wilson, *My Memoir* (New York : Bobbs-Merrill Co., 1938), pp. 298–99; Gilderhus, *Diplomacy and Revolution*, chaps. 6, 7.

53. Alexander L. and Juliette L. George, *Woodrow Wilson and Colonel House, A Personality Study* (New York: Dover Publications, Inc., 1964), chap. 13; Daniel M. Smith, "Robert Lansing and the Wilson Interregnum, 1919–1920," *The Historian*, 21 (Nov. 1959), pp. 135–52; Joyce G. Williams, "The Resignation of Secretary Robert Lansing," *Diplomatic History*, 3 (Summer 1979), pp. 337–44; Fletcher to Lansing, 20 Jan. 1920, box 8, HPFP; Polk to Wilson, 16 April 1920, series 2, WWP; Colby to Wilson, 28 April 1920, box 3A, Bainbridge Colby Papers, Library of Congress, Washington, D.C.

54. Daniel M. Smith, "Bainbridge Colby and the Good Neighbor Policy, 1920–1921," *Mississippi Valley Historical Review*, 50 (June 1963), pp. 56–78; Joseph S. Tulchin, *The Aftermath of War: World War I and U.S. Policy Toward Latin America* (New York: New York Univ. Press, 1971), pp. 56–57; Daniel M. Smith, *Aftermath of War: Bainbridge Colby and Wilsonian Diplomacy, 1920–1921* (Philadelphia, Pa.: American Philosophical Society, 1970).

55. Anti-American Activities in Latin America, WP, n.d. [1920], box 687, Dept. of Navy, Record Group 45, Naval Records Collection of the Office of Naval Records and Library, Subject File, 1911-27, National Archives, Washington, D.C.

56. Colby's statements, 16, 25 March 1920, box 70, Colby Papers.

57. Tulchin, *The Aftermath of War*, chap. 2; Polk to Morgan, 21 June 1919, 832.73/170a, Norman H. Davis to Polk, 2 April 1920, 835.51/235, Morgan to Colby, 6 May 1920, 832.3421/57, RDS; memorandum of a conversation with the Brazilian ambassador, 10 Aug. 1920, box 9, Norman H. Davis Papers, Library of Congress, Washington, D.C. Davis replaced Polk in the State Department. Colby to Wilson, 15 April 1920, series 2, WWP; Wilson to Colby, 16 April 1920, box 3A, Colby Papers; *FR 1920*, 1:373 ff.; Dennis, *Tacna and Arica*, chap. 13.

58. Smith, "Colby and the Good Neighbor Policy," pp. 73 ff.; Colby-Wilson, 2, 4 Oct. 1920, box 3B, 2 scrapbooks of the trip to South America, box 23, Colby Papers.

59. Extracts from a speech, 2 March 1921, box 70, Colby Papers.

Bibliographical Note

PRIMARY SOURCES AVAILABLE IN THE UNITED STATES form the basis of this study. The following bibliographical note provides a list of archival manuscripts and published documents and also a brief commentary on the most pertinent secondary works. Various guides and aids make additional information available. These include the revised edition of the *Harvard Guide To American History*, directed by Frank Freidel (Cambridge: Belknap Press of Harvard University Press, 1974); the *Handbook of Latin American Studies* (Cambridge: Harvard University Press; Gainesville: University of Florida Press, 1936 ff.); the *Guide to American Foreign Relations Since 1700*, edited by Richard Dean Burns (Santa Barbara: ABC-CLIO, Inc., 1983); *A Bibliography of United States – Latin American Relations Since 1810, A Selected List of Eleven Thousand Published References*, put together by David F. Trask, Michael C. Meyer, and Roger R. Trask (Lincoln: University of Nebraska Press, 1968); the *Supplement to A Bibliography of United States – Latin American Relations Since 1810*, compiled by Michael C. Meyer (Lincoln: University of Nebraska Press, 1979); the *Guide to Materials on Latin America in the National Archives of the United States*, assembled by George S. Ulibarri and John P. Harrison (Washington: National Archives and Records Service, 1974); and the *Catalog of National Archives Microfilm Publications* (Washington: National Archives and Records Service, 1974).

PRIMARY SOURCES: ARCHIVAL MANUSCRIPTS

Library of Congress, Washington, D.C.

Chandler P. Anderson Papers.
Newton D. Baker Papers.
Ray Stannard Baker Papers.
John Barrett Papers.
William Jennings Bryan Papers.
Albert Burleson Papers.
Wilbur J. Carr Papers.
Bainbridge Colby Papers.
George Creel Papers.
Josephus Daniels Papers.
Norman H. Davis Papers.
Henry P. Fletcher Papers.
Lindley M. Garrison Papers.
Leland Harrison Papers.
Charles Evans Hughes Papers.
Samuel Guy Inman Papers.
Robert Lansing Papers.
Breckinridge Long Papers.
William Gibbs McAdoo Papers.
John Bassett Moore Papers.
William Redfield Papers.
Elihu Root Papers.
Joseph P. Tumulty Papers.
Edith Bolling Galt Wilson Papers.
Woodrow Wilson Papers.

National Archives, Washington, D.C.

American Commission to Negotiate Peace. R.G. 256. Records of the Inquiry.
U.S. Dept. of the Army. R.G. 165. Records of the Military Intelligence Division, 1918–1941.
U.S. Dept. of Army. R.G. 165. Records of the War College Divison and Related General Staff Office, 1903–1919.
U.S. Dept. of Commerce, R.G. 40. General Records.
U.S. Dept. of Commerce, R.G. 151. Records of the Bureau of Foreign and Domestic Commerce.
U.S. Dept. of the Navy. R.G. 38. Records of the Chief of Naval Operations, Intelligence Division, Naval Attaché Reports, 1886–1939.
U.S. Dept. of the Navy. R.G. 45. Naval Records Collection of the Office of Naval Records and Library, Subject File 1911–1927.
U.S. Participation in International Conferences, Commissions, and Expositions. R.G. 43. Records of the U.S. Section of the International High Commission.

U.S. Dept. of State. R.G. 59. Correspondence of Secretary of State Bryan with President Wilson, 1913–1914. Microcopy 841, 1963.

U.S. Dept. of State. R.G. 59. Decimal File, 1910–1929.

U.S. Dept. of State. R.G. 59. Personal and Confidential Letters from Secretary of State Lansing to President Wilson, 1915–1918. Microcopy 743, 1968.

U.S. Dept. of State. R.G. 59. Records of Division of Latin American Affairs, 1904–1944.

U.S. Dept. of State. R.G. 84. Records of the Foreign Service Posts of the Dept. of State, Legations, Embassies, Consular Posts.

U.S. Dept. of State. R.G. 59. Records Relating to Internal Affairs of Argentina, 1910–1929. Microcopy 514, 1963.

U.S. Dept. of State. R.G. 59. Records Relating to Internal Affairs of Brazil, 1910–1929. Microcopy 519, 1963.

U.S. Dept. of State. R.G. 59. Records Relating to Internal Affairs of Chile, 1910–1929. Microcopy 487, 1963.

U.S. Dept. of State. R.G. 59. Records Relating to Political Relations Between Argentina and Other States, 1910–1929. Microcopy 516, 1963.

U.S. Dept. of State. R.G. 59. Records Relating to Political Relations Between Brazil and Other States, 1910–1929. Microcopy 526, 1963.

U.S. Dept. of State. R.G. 59. Records Relating to Political Relations Between Chile and Other States, 1910–1929. Microcopy 490, 1963.

U.S. Dept. of State. R.G. 59. Records Relating to Political Relations Between the United States and Argentina, 1910–1929. Microcopy 515, 1963.

U.S. Dept. of State. R.G. 59. Records Relating to Political Relations Between the United States and Brazil, 1910–1929. Microcopy 525, 1963.

U.S. Dept. of State. R.G. 59. Records Relating to Political Relations Between the United States and Chile, 1910–1929. Microcopy 489, 1963.

U.S. Dept. of State. R.G. 43. Records Relating to World War I and Its Termination, 1914–1929. Microcopy 367, 1962.

Pan American Union, Columbus Library, Washington, D.C.

Leo S. Rowe Papers.

Cornell University, Ithaca, N.Y.

Willard Straight Papers.

Yale University Library, New Haven, Conn.

Gordon Auchincloss Papers.
Edward M. House Papers.
Frank L. Polk Papers.

Massachusetts Historical Society, Boston, Mass.

Henry Cabot Lodge Papers.
Frederick J. Stimson Papers.

Minnesota State Historical Society, St. Paul, Minn.

John Lind Papers.

University of Nebraska, Lincoln, Neb.

Albert B. Fall Papers (microfilm copy).

University of Texas, Austin, Tex.

William F. Buckley Papers.

**Archivo de la Secretaría de Relaciones Exteriores,
México, D.F.**

Revolución Mexicana durante los Años 1910 a 1920. Informaciones Diversas de la República y de las Oficinas de México en el Exterior.
Reglamentación de la Ley de Petróleo Mexicano, 1914–1928. Controversia entre México y los Estados Unidos de A. con motivo de la Fracción I de Artículo 27 Constitucional.

**Centro de Estudios de Historia de México,
Departamento Cultural de Condumex, S.A., México, D.F.**

Archivo de Venustiano Carranza.

PRIMARY SOURCES: PUBLISHED DOCUMENTS

Brasil. Ministerio das Relacões Exteriores. *Guerra da Europa, Documentos Diplomaticos, Attitude do Brasil, 1914–1917*. Rio de Janeiro: Imprensa Nacional, 1917.
Fabela, Isidro, et al., eds. *Documentos Históricos de la Revolución Mexicana*. México, D.F.: Fondo de Cultural Económica, Editorial Jus, 1960 ff.
Gantenbein, James W., ed. *The Evolution of Our Latin-American Policy, A Documentary Record*. New York: Octagon Books, 1971.
Link, Arthur S., et al., eds. *The Papers of Woodrow Wilson*. Princeton, N.J: Princeton University Press, 1966 ff
México. *Labor Internacional de la Revolución Constitucionalista de México (Libro Rojo)*. México: 1960, first published, 1919.

Pan American Union. *Proceedings of the Second Pan American Scientific Congress*. Washington: Government Printing Office, 1917.

United States. Dept. of Commerce. Bureau of Foreign and Domestic Commerce. *Commerce Reports*. Washington: Government Printing Office, 1915–19.

United States. Dept. of Commerce. Bureau of Foreign and Domestic Commerce. *Daily Consular and Trade Reports*. Washington: Government Printing Office, 1913–14.

United States. Dept. of Commerce. Bureau of Foreign and Domestic Commerce. *Miscellaneous Series*. Washington: Government Printing Office, 1913–21.

United States. Dept. of Commerce. Bureau of Foreign and Domestic Commerce. *Special Agents Series*. Washington: Government Printing Office, 1913–21.

United States. Dept. of Commerce. Bureau of Foreign and Domestic Commerce. *Trade Information Bulletins*. Washington: Government Printing Office, 1920–21.

United States. Dept. of State. *Papers Relating to the Foreign Relations of the United States, 1913–21*. Washington: Government Printing Office, 1920–36.

United States. Dept. of State. *Papers Relating to the Foreign Relations of the United States, The Lansing Papers, 1914–20*. 2 vols. Washington: Government Printing Office, 1939.

United States. Dept. of State. *Papers Relating to the Foreign Relations of the United States, 1919, The Paris Peace Conference*. 13 vols. Washington: Government Printing Office, 1942–47.

United States. Dept. of the Treasury. *Annual Report of the Secretary of the Treasury on the State of the Finances of the Fiscal Year ended 30 June 1916–21*. Washington: Government Printing Office, 1917–22.

United States. Dept. of the Treasury. *Proceedings of the First Pan American Financial Conference, Washington, May 24 to 29, 1915*. Washington: Government Printing Office, 1915.

United States. Congress. Senate. *Investigation of Mexican Affairs*. 66th Cong. 2d Sess. Document 285. 2 vols. Washington: Government Printing Office, 1920.

SECONDARY SOURCES

The Pan American theme figures implicitly in much of the literature on United States–Latin American relations, particularly in broad surveys and institutional studies focusing on the conduct of inter-American conferences. Older accounts, classics of a sort generally favorable toward the United States, include Samuel Flagg Bemis, *The Latin American Policy of the United States, An Historical Interpretation* (New York: W.W. Norton, Inc., 1967, first published in 1943); Dexter Perkins, *A History of the Monroe Doctrine* (Boston: Little, Brown and Co., 1963, first published in 1941); and Arthur P. Whitaker, *The Western*

Hemisphere Idea: Its Rise and Decline (Ithaca, N.Y.: Cornell University Press, 1954). More modern interpretations are found in Thomas F. McGann, *Argentina, the United States and the Inter-American System, 1889–1914* (Cambridge, Mass.: Harvard University Press, 1957); J. Lloyd Mecham, *The United States and Inter-American Security, 1889–1960* (Austin: University of Texas Press, 1961); and the two volumes by Gordon Connell-Smith, *The Inter-American System* (New York: Oxford University Press, 1966), and *The United States and Latin America, An Historical Analysis of Inter-American Relations* (New York: John Wiley & Sons, 1975). Samuel Guy Inman's *Inter-American Conferences, 1826–1954*, edited by Harold Eugene Davis (Washington, D.C.: The University Press, 1965), provides a simplistic account of proceedings and resolutions.

Views from the other side are developed in *Latin American Diplomacy*, by Harold Eugene Davis, John J. Finian, and F. Taylor Peck (Baton Rouge: Louisiana State University, 1977); and John T. Reid, *Spanish American Images of the United States, 1790–1960* (Gainesville: University Presses of Florida, 1977). Latin American perspectives are also expressed by Enrique Gil, *Evolución del Panamericanismo, El Credo de Wilson y El Panamericanismo* (Buenos Aires: Libreria y Casa de Jesús Menéndez, 1933), an effusive tribute by an unabashed champion; Ricardo A. Martínez, *De Bolívar a Dulles: El Panamericanismo, Doctrina y Práctica Imperialista* (México, D.F.: n.p., 1959), a more critical examination, and Alonso Aguiles Monteverde, *Pan Americanism from Monroe to the Present: A View from the Other Side*, translated by Asa Zatz (New York: Monthly Review Press, 1968), a Marxist treatise.

Dependency theory, though not an explicit concern of this study, bears on the subject, particularly by setting forth a sense of victimization, the presumed result of an international economic system over which Latin Americans wielded little control. Introductions to and critiques of this complex body of theoretical literature are contained in *Latin America: The Struggle with Dependency and Beyond*, edited by Ronald H. Chilcote and Joel Edelstein (New York: John Wiley & Sons, 1974); *Latin America: Underdevelopment or Revolution, Essays on the Development of Underdevelopment and the Immediate Enemy*, by André Gunder Frank (New York: Monthly Review Press, 1969); *Dependency and Development in Latin America*, by Fernando Henrique Cardoso and Enzo Faletto and translated by Marjory Mattingly Urquidi (Berkeley: Univeristy of California Press, 1979); *Latin America, the United States, and the Inter-American System*, edited by John D. Martz and Lars Schoultz (Boulder, Colo.: Westview Press, 1980); "'Liberal,' 'Radical,' and 'Bureaucratic' Perspectives on U.S.–Latin American Policy: The Alliance for Progress in Retrospect," by Abraham F. Lowenthal in *Latin America and the United States: The Changing Political Realities*, edited by Julio Cotler and Richard R. Fagen (Stanford: Stanford University Press, 1974), pp. 212–35; "Consensus and Divergence: The State of the Literature on Inter-American Relations in the 1970s," by Jorge I. Domínguez in the

Latin American Research Review, 13 (No. 1, 1977), pp. 87–126; *Economic Development of Latin America, A Survey From Colonial Times to the Cuban Revolution*, by Celso Furtado and translated by Suzette Macedo (Cambridge: At the University Press, 1970); and *The Pattern of Imperialism, The United States, Great Britain, and the Late-Industrializing World since 1815*, by Tony Smith (Cambridge: The University Press, 1981).

Studies of the peace movement and the drive toward international organization, against which this book is set, include important works by Warren F. Kuehl, *Seeking World Order, The United States and International Organization to 1920* (Nashville: Vanderbilt University Press, 1969); Calvin DeArmond Davis, *The United States and the First Hague Conference* (Ithaca, N.Y.: Cornell University Press, 1962), and *The United States and the Second Hague Peace Conference, American Diplomacy and International Organization, 1899–1914* (Durham, N.C.: Duke University Press, 1975); Charles DeBenedetti, *The Peace Reform in American History* (Bloomington: University of Indiana Press, 1980); C. Roland Marchand, *The American Peace Movement and Social Reform, 1898–1918* (Princeton, N.J.: Princeton University Press, 1972); and David S. Patterson, *Toward a Warless World: The Travail of the American Peace Movement, 1887–1914* (Bloomington: University of Indiana Press, 1976). The article by Russell H. Bastert in the *Hispanic American Historical Review*, "A New Approach to the Origins of Blaine's Pan American Policy," 39 (May 1959), pp. 375–412, applies to the western hemisphere.

The Wilson presidency has produced a vast body of historical works. The beginning place is Arthur S. Link's *Wilson*, 5 vols. (Princeton, N.J.: Princeton University Press, 1947 ff.). Important biographical studies in recent times include Henry Wilkinson Bragdon, *Woodrow Wilson, The Academic Years* (Cambridge, Mass.: The Belknap Press of Harvard University Press, 1967); John M. Mulder, *Woodrow Wilson, The Years of Preparation* (Princeton, N.J.: Princeton University Press, 1978); and Edwin A. Weinstein, *Woodrow Wilson: A Medical and Psychological Biography* (Princeton, N.J.: Princeton University Press, 1981), a careful but controversial endeavor, among other reasons because it criticizes an earlier psycho-analytical study, George L. and Juliette L. George, *Woodrow Wilson and Colonel House, A Personality Study* (New York: Dover Publications, 1964, first published in 1956). John Milton Cooper, Jr., *The Warrior and the Priest, Woodrow Wilson and Theodore Roosevelt* (Cambridge, Mass.: The Belknap Press of Harvard University Press, 1983) presents an intriguing comparative perspective.

Other biographies, used in connection with published memoirs and diaries, provide understanding of the processes of policymaking. These include the second volume of Paolo E. Coletta's, *William Jennings Bryan, Progressive Politician and Moral Statesman, 1909–1915* (Lincoln: University of Nebraska Press, 1969); Kendrick A. Clements' persuasive interpretation, *William Jennings Bryan, Missionary Isolationist* (Knoxville: University of Tennessee Press, 1982); Salvador Prisco III's *John Bar-*

rett, *Progressive Era Diplomat: A Study of a Commerical Expansionist, 1887 –
1920* (University of Alabama Press, 1973); John Milton Cooper, Jr.'s
Walter Hines Page, The Southerner as American, 1855 –1918 (Chapel Hill:
University of North Carolina Press, 1977); and William C. Widenor's
Henry Cabot Lodge and the Search for an American Foreign Policy (Berkeley:
University of California Press, 1980). Further insights emerge from the
War Memoirs of Robert Lansing, Secretary of State (New York: Bobbs-
Merrill Co., 1935); *The Cabinet Diaries of Josephus Daniels, 1913 –1921*,
edited by E. David Cronon (Lincoln: University of Nebraska Press,
1963); *The Wilson Years*, Daniels' own account in two volumes (Chapel
Hill: University of North Carolina Press, 1946); *The Intimate Papers of
Colonel House*, edited in two volumes by Charles Seymour (New York:
Houghton Mifflin Co., 1926); and *My United States*, by Frederick Jesup
Stimson (New York: Charles Scribner's Sons, 1931). The machineries
of diplomacy come under discussion in Richard Hume Werking, *The
Master Architects, Building the United States Foreign Service, 1890 –1913*
(University Press of Kentucky, 1977); and Rachel West, O.S.F., *The
Department of State on the Eve of the First World War* (Athens: University of
Georgia Press, 1978).

The economic context of foreign affairs has inspired many studies.
William Appleman Williams' *The Tragedy of American Diplomacy*, 2d ed.
rev. (New York: Dell Publishing Co., 1972) is a seminal work. William
Diamond's *The Economic Thought of Woodrow Wilson*, vol. 61, no. 4, in *The
Johns Hopkins University Studies in Historical and Political Science* (Baltimore, Md., 1943), and Sidney Bell's *Righteous Conquest, Woodrow Wilson
and the Evolution of the New Diplomacy* (Port Washington, N.Y.: Kennikat
Press, 1972) center attention on the period under consideration in this
book. Other prominent works, some of them quite specialized, encom-
pass the two volumes by Mira Wilkins, *The Emergence of Multinational
Enterprise: American Business Abroad from the Colonial Era to 1914* (Cambridge, Mass.: Harvard University Press, 1970), and *The Maturing of
Multinational Enterprise: American Business Abroad from 1914 to 1970*
(Cambridge, Mass.: Harvard University Press, 1974); Burton I. Kauf-
man, *Efficiency and Expansion: Foreign Trade Organization in the Wilson
Administration, 1913 –1921* (Westport, Conn.: Greenwood Press, 1974);
Carl P. Parrini, *Heir to Empire, United States Economic Diplomacy,
1916 –1923* (University of Pittsburgh Press, 1969); William H. Becker,
*The Dynamics of Business-Government Relations, Industry and Exports,
1893 –1921* (Chicago: University of Chicago Press, 1982); and Jeffrey
J. Safford, *Wilsonian Maritime Diplomacy, 1913 –1921* (New Brunswick,
N.J.: Rutgers University Press, 1978). Statistical information is con-
tained in Max Winkler, *Investments of United States Capital in Latin
America, World Peace Foundation Pamphlets*, vol. 11, no. 6 (Boston: 1929);
and Cleona Lewis and Karl T. Schlotterbeck, *America's Stake in International Investments* (Washington, D.C.: The Brookings Institution, 1938).

The conduct of Woodrow Wilson's policies in Latin America has
also engendered a great deal of scholarly writing. Stephen Goodell's

essay, "Woodrow Wilson in Latin America: Interpretations," *The Historian*, 28 (November 1965), pp. 96–127, presents a now dated introduction. Standard references include Dana G. Munro, *Intervention and Dollar Diplomacy in the Caribbean, 1900–1921* (Princeton, N.J.: Princeton University Press, 1964); and a string of articles by George W. Baker, Jr., including "The Wilson Administration and Cuba, 1913–1921," *Mid-America*, 46 (January 1964), pp. 48–63; "Ideals and Realities in the Wilson Administration's Relations with Honduras," *The Americas*, 21 (January 1964), pp. 3–19; "The Woodrow Wilson Administration and Guatemalan Relations," *The Historian*, 27 (June 1965), pp. 155–69; "Woodrow Wilson's Use of Non-Recognition Policy in Costa Rica," *The Americas*, 22 (January 1965), pp. 3–21; and "The Woodrow Wilson Administration and El Salvadoran Relations, 1913–1921," *Social Studies*, 56 (March 1965), pp. 97–103.

In recent times, monographic studies have illuminated understanding particularly of bilateral relations with Mexico and Caribbean countries and have focused attention on questions of intervention. Among the many pertaining to Mexico, three have special utility: Robert Freeman Smith's *The United States and Revolutionary Nationalism in Mexico, 1916–1932* (Chicago: University of Chicago Press, 1972), my *Diplomacy and Revolution, U.S.–Mexican Relations under Wilson and Carranza* (Tucson: University of Arizona Press, 1977), and Friedrich Katz's *The Secret War in Mexico, Europe, the United States and the Mexican Revolution* (Chicago: University of Chicago Press, 1981). Depictions of the Constitutionalist regime are found in *Mexican Revolution, The Constitutionalist Years*, by Charles C. Cumberland (Austin: University of Texas Press, 1972), and *Venustiano Carranza's Nationalist Struggle, 1893–1920*, by Douglas W. Richmond (Lincoln: Univeristy of Nebraska Press, 1983). For the Caribbean region, Lester D. Langley's survey, *The United States and the Caribbean in the Twentieth Century* (Athens: University of Georgia Press, 1980) provides an introduction. More specialized studies include Whitney T. Perkins, *Constraint of Empire: The United States and Caribbean Interventions* (Westport, Conn.: Greenwood Press, 1981); Louis A. Pérez, Jr., *Intervention, Revolution, and Politics in Cuba, 1913–1921* (Pittsburgh: University of Pittsburgh Press, 1978); Jules Robert Benjamin, *The United States and Cuba: Hegemony and Dependent Development, 1880–1934* (Pittsburgh: University of Pittsburgh Press, 1977); Hans Schmidt, *The United States Occupation of Haiti, 1915–1934* (New Brunswick, N.J.: Rutgers University Press, 1971); David Healy, *Gunboat Diplomacy in the Wilson Era, The U.S. Navy in Haiti, 1915–1916* (Madison: University of Wisconsin Press, 1976); Bruce Calder, *The Impact of Intervention, The Dominican Republic during the U.S. Occupation of 1916–1924* (Austin: University of Texas Press, 1984); and Lester D. Langley, *The Banana Wars, An Inner History of American Empire, 1900–1934* (University Press of Kentucky, 1983). Louis A. Pérez, Jr.'s essay, "Intervention, Hegemony, and Dependency: The United States in the Circum-Caribbean, 1898–1980," in the *Pacific Historical Review*, 51 (May 1982), pp. 165–94, serves up a historiographical appraisal.

More general accounts characterize the sparser literature on relations with South America. Harold F. Peterson's *Argentina and the United States, 1810–1960* (Albany: State University of New York Press, 1964) is basic. From an Argentine point of view, Roberto Etchepareborda, *La Política Externa Argentina: 1870–1920* (Córdoba, Argentina: Universidad Nacional de Córdoba, 1964–65) presents good material on dealings among the A.B.C. countries. Miguel A. Scenna, *Como Fueron las Relaciones Argentino-Norteamericanas* (Buenos Aires: Editorial Plus Ultra, 1970) is rudimentary. David Rock, *Politics in Argentina, 1890–1930, The Rise and Fall of Radicalism* (Cambridge: The University Press,1975) is indispensable for the Yrigoyen regime. No general survey exists for Brazil. For this reason, the works of E. Bradford Burns have special importance, notably, *The Unwritten Alliance, Rio-Branco and Brazilian-American Relations* (New York: Columbia University Press, 1966), and *Nationalism in Brazil, A Historical Survey* (New York: Frederick A. Praeger, Publishers, 1968). Interested readers also may wish to peruse Robert M. Levine, *Pernambuco in the Brazilian Federation, 1889–1937* (Stanford: Stanford University Press, 1978); the two works of Joseph L. Love, *Rio Grande do Sul and Brazilian Regionalism, 1882–1937* (Stanford: Stanford University Press, 1971), and *São Paulo in the Brazilian Federation, 1889–1937* (Stanford: Stanford University Press, 1977); and John D. Wirth, *Minas Gerais in the Brazilian Federation, 1889–1937* (Stanford: Stanford University Press, 1977). For Chile, Robert N. Burr's *By Reason or Force, Chile and the Balancing of Power in South America, 1830–1905* (Berkeley: University of California Press, 1967) establishes the background. Frederick B. Pike's *Chile and the United States, 1880–1962* (Notre Dame, Ind.: Notre Dame University Press, 1963) is standard. *Historia Diplomática de Chile (1541–1938)*, by Mario Barros, a professional diplomat (Barcelona: Ediciones Ariel, 1970), is encyclopedic; *Historia del Imperialismo en Chile*, by Hernán Ramírez Necochea, a history professor (Santiago: Empresa Editora Austral Ltda., 1960) employs Marxian models of analysis. The long controversy over Tacna and Arica comes under consideration in William Jefferson Dennis' *Tacna and Arica, An Account of the Chilean-Peruvian Boundary Dispute and of the Arbitration by the United States* (Hamden, Conn.: Archon Books, 1967, first published in 1931); and Michael Monteón's *Chile in the Nitrate Era, The Evolution of Economic Dependence, 1880–1930* (Madison: University of Wisconsin Press, 1982) argues that the Chilean elite accepted dependency as the price for retaining political power.

The British presence in South America has attracted a great deal of interest. Notable studies by D.C.M. Platt all reject the Marxian hypothesis. They include *Finance, Trade, and Politics in British Foreign Policy, 1815–1914* (Oxford: The Clarendon Press, 1968); *Latin America and British Trade, 1806–1914* (London: Adam & Charles Black, 1972); and *Business Imperialism, 1840–1930, An Inquiry Based on British Experi-*

ence in Latin America (Oxford: The Clarendon Press, 1977), an edited collection of essays. Relationships with the A.B.C. countries are addressed in H.S. Ferns' *Britain and Argentina in the Nineteenth Century* (Oxford: The Clarendon Press, 1960); Richard Graham's *Britain and the Onset of Modernization in Brazil, 1850–1914* (Cambridge: The University Press, 1968); and Harold Blakemore's *British Nitrates and Chilean Politics, 1886–1896: Balmaceda and North* (University of London: The Athlone Press, 1974).

The Pan American politics of the United States comes under scrutiny in two unpublished doctoral dissertations, "The Pan-American Policy of Woodrow Wilson, 1913–1921" (University of Colorado, 1968) by Alexander Waller Knott, and "Progressive Pan Americanism: Development and U.S. Policy Toward South America, 1906–1931" (Cornell University, 1973) by Robert Neal Seidel. My own essays in *Diplomatic History*, "Pan American Initiatives: The Wilson Presidency and Regional Integration, 1914–1917," 4 (Fall 1980), pp. 409–24, and "Wilson, Carranza, and the Monroe Doctrine: A Question in Regional Organization," 7 (Spring 1983), pp. 103–16, set forth some preliminary notions.

The literature pertinent to the Pan American theme is surprisingly scant. In "The Creation and Development of the Pan American Union," *Hispanic American Historical Review*, 13 (November 1933), pp. 437–56, Clifford B. Casey provides a brief sketch. The activities of influential persons show up in Thomas L. Karnes' "Hiram Bingham and his Obsolete Shibboleth," *Diplomatic History*, 3 (Winter 1979), pp. 39–57; Robert Waller's "John Barrett: Pan American Promoter," *Mid-America*, 53 (July 1971), pp. 170–89; Selig Adler's "Bryan and Wilsonian Caribbean Penetration," *Hispanic American Historical Review*, 20 (May 1940), pp. 198–226; and Paolo E. Coletta's two articles, "Secretary of State William Jennings Bryan and 'Deserving Democrats'," *Mid-America*, 48 (April 1966), pp. 75–98; and "William Jennings Bryan's Plans for World Peace," *Nebraska History*, 58 (Summer 1977), pp. 193–217. Other items of interest are "The Coffee-Trust Question in United States-Brazilian Relations, 1912–1913," *Hispanic American Historical Review*, 26 (November 1946), pp. 480–96, by Leon F. Sensabaugh; "Wilson, Bryan and the American Delegation to the Abortive Fifth Pan American Conference, 1914," *Nebraska History*, 59 (Spring 1978), pp. 56–69, by James F. Vivian; "The Origins of the American Banking Empire in Latin America: Frank A. Vanderlip and the National City Bank," *Journal of Inter-American Studies and World Affairs*, 15 (February 1973), pp. 60–72, by Robert Mayer; "Battleship Diplomacy in South America, 1905–1925," *Journal of Modern History*, 16 (March 1944), pp. 31–48, by Seward W. Livermore; and "United States Trade and Latin America: The Wilson Years," *The Journal of American History*, 58 (September 1971), by Burton I. Kaufman.

Basic works for the war period consist of books by Percy Alvin Martin, *Latin America and the War* (Baltimore: The Johns Hopkins Press, 1925), now out of date; Joseph S. Tulchin, *The Aftermath of War*,

World War I and U.S. Policy Toward Latin America (New York: New York University Press, 1971), a successful modern treatment; and an important doctoral dissertation by Emily S. Rosenberg, "World War I and the Growth of the United States Preponderance in Latin America" (S.U.N.Y., Stony Brook, 1973). Happily, she has made her findings readily available in a series of articles, among them, "Dollar Diplomacy Under Wilson: An Ecuadorean Case," in *Inter-American Economic Affairs*, 25 (No. 2, 1971), pp. 47–53; "Economic Pressures in Anglo-American Diplomacy in Mexico, 1917–1918," in the *Journal of Inter-American Studies*, 17 (May 1975), pp. 123–52; "World War I and 'Continental Solidarity'," in *The Americas*, 31 (January 1975), pp. 313–34; "The Exercise of Emergency Controls over Foreign Commerce: Economic Pressure on Latin America," in *Inter-American Economic Affairs*, 31 (Spring 1978), pp. 81–96, and "Anglo-American Economic Rivalry in Brazil During World War I," in *Diplomatic History*, 2 (Spring 1978), pp. 131–52. Rosenberg draws on this material in *Spreading the American Dream, American Economic and Cultural Expansion, 1890–1945* (New York: Hill and Wang, 1982). In "World War I as an Entrepreneurial Opportunity: Willard Straight and the American International Corporation," *Political Science Quarterly*, 84 (Summer 1969), pp. 484–511, Harry Schreiber explores a similar theme. The German connection comes under consideration in Warren Schiff. "The Influence of the German Armed Forces and Industry on Argentina, 1880–1914," *Hispanic American Historical Review*, 52 (August 1972), pp. 436–55; Loretta S. Baum, "German Political Designs with Reference to Brazil," *Hispanic American Historical Review*, 2 (November 1919), pp. 586–99; and Melvin Small, "The United States and the German 'Threat' to the Hemisphere, 1905–1914," *The Americas*, 28 (January 1972), pp. 252–70.

For the immediate postwar period, the works of Daniel M. Smith have special importance, notably "Bainbridge Colby and the Good Neighbor Policy, 1920–21," in the *Mississippi Valley Historical Review*, 50 (June 1963), pp. 56–78; and *Aftermath of War: Bainbridge Colby and Wilsonian Diplomacy, 1920–1921* (Philadelphia, Pa.: American Philosophical Society, 1970). No scholarly secondary accounts consider Latin America's role at the peace conference in any detail. Basic studies, otherwise, include Lawrence E. Gelfand's *The Inquiry, American Preparations for Peace, 1917–1919* (New Haven: Yale University Press, 1963); Thomas A. Bailey's *Woodrow Wilson and the Lost Peace* (New York: The Macmillan Co., 1944); Paul Birdsall's *Versailles Twenty Years After* (New York: Harcourt, Brace & World, Inc., 1941); N. Gordon Levin, Jr's *Woodrow Wilson and World Politics, America's Response to War and Revolution* (New York: Oxford University Press, 1968); Arno J. Mayer's *Politics and Diplomacy of Peacemaking, Containment and Counterrevolution at Versailles, 1918–1919* (New York: Alfred A. Knopf, 1967); Inga Floto's *Colonel House in Paris, A Study of American Policy at the Paris Peace Conference, 1919* (Universitetsforlaget I Aarhus, 1972); Seth P. Tillman's *Anglo-American Relations at the Paris Peace Conference of 1919* (Princeton, N.J.: Princeton University Press, 1961); Howard Elcock's *Portrait of a Decision, The Council of Four and the Treaty of Versailles* (Eyre Methuen, 1972); and Michael L. Dockrill and J. Douglas Goold's *Peace without Promise, Britain and the Peace Conferences, 1919–23* (Hamden, Conn.: Archon Books, 1982).

The debate over the Treaty of Versailles and the League of Nations comes under consideration in Thomas A. Bailey's *Woodrow Wilson and the Great Betrayal* (New York: The Macmillan Co., 1945). In "Woodrow Wilson's Neurological Illness," *Journal of American History*, 57 (September 1970), pp. 324–51, Edwin A. Weinstein scrutinizes the reasons for the president's collapse. The article by Clifford B. Trow, "Woodrow Wilson and the Mexican Interventionist Movement of 1919," *Journal of American History*, 58 (June 1971), pp. 46–72, and my own, "Senator Albert B. Fall and 'The Plot against Mexico'," *New Mexico Historical Review*, 48 (October 1973), pp. 299–311, examine the Mexican crisis. The Lansing problem is addressed by Daniel M. Smith in "Robert Lansing and the Wilson Interregnum, 1919–1920," *The Historian*, 21 (November 1959), pp. 135–42, and Joyce G. Williams in "The Resignation of Secretary Robert Lansing," *Diplomatic History*, 3 (Summer 1979), pp. 337–44.

Many publications contemporaneous with the Wilson presidency provide understanding of public perceptions. The *Bulletin* of the Pan American Union, vols, 36 ff. (Washington: Government Printing Office, 1913 ff.) contains a wealth of significant material and also synopses of periodical literature. The newspapers, *La Prensa* in Buenos Aires, *Jornal do Commercio* in Rio de Janeiro, and *El Mercurio* in Santiago, all available on microfilm from the Library of Congress, show South American preoccupations with European affairs and the immensity of the distance, both geographic and political, from Washington, D.C. Commentaries on the Pan American theme are found in *Latin America, Clark University Addresses, November, 1913*, edited by George H. Blakeslee (New York: G.E. Stechert and Co., reprinted in 1924); *Pan America and Pan Americanism, The Great American Opportunity, War Time and After*, by John Barrett (New York: Harper and Brothers, 1915); *Pan-Americanism: A Forecast of the Inevitable Clash Between the United States and Europe's Victor*, by Roland G. Usher (New York: Grosset and Dunlop, 1915); *Modernizing the Monroe Doctrine*, by Charles H. Sherrill (New York: Houghton Mifflin Co., 1916); and *Problems in Pan-Americanism*, by Samuel Guy Inman (New York: George R. Doran, 1921). Finally, David M. Kennedy's *Over Here, The First World War and American Society* (New York: Oxford University Press, 1980) presents a splendid portrait of the home front during the Wilson years.

Index

Aguilar, Cándido, 147
Alves, Rodrígues, 122, 138
American Commission to Negotiate Peace, 112
Argentina
  conference of neutrals, 118
  economic conditions, 21, 71, 101–2, 109–12
  economic consequences, First World War, 38–39, 58, 77–80
  foreign policy traditions, 22, 25–26
  neutrality, 92, 111
  Pan American treaty, 49–56, 74–77, 93–96
  Pan Hispanic alternatives, x, 81, 92
  Paris Peace Conference, 139
  U.S. break with Germany, 84–86, 87–88
  U.S. declaration of war, 93–96, 99
  visit of south Atlantic squadron, 100–1
  wartime relations with U.S., 118–19, 123
  Wheat Convention, 112, 148

Bailey, Thomas A., 152
Banking facilities in Latin America, U.S. branches, 28, 29, 71–72, 133
Barbosa, Ruy, 138, 148
Barrett, John, 3, 6, 16–17, 30, 33, 44, 56, 60–61, 68, 92, 96, 98, 114, 130, 137, 153
Bingham, Hiram, 15, 16, 20
Bolivia, 140, 145

Brazil
  economic conditions, 23, 71, 103–8
  economic consequences, First World War, 39–41, 58–59, 77–80
  foreign policy traditions, 23, 25–26
  naval cooperation with U.S., 107–8
  Pan American treaty, 49–56, 74–77, 93–96
  Paris Peace Conference, 137, 143–44
  revocation of neutrality, 97
  U.S. break with Germany, 83–84
  U.S. declaration of war, 93, 96–97
  visit of south Atlantic squadron, 100–1
  wartime relations with U.S., 96–101, 116–18, 122–23
Braz Pereira Gomes, Wenceslau, 40, 97, 106
Bryan, William Jennings, 10, 14–15, 19, 44, 47, 48, 51, 53, 60, 63
Bureau of Foreign and Domestic Commerce, 5, 20, 43, 101
Burns, E. Bradford, 23

Cabrera, Luis, 118
Calogeras, Pandía, 143
Calvo, Carlos, 22
Caperton, Admiral William B., 100, 108, 109, 123
Carranza, Venustiano
  Constitution of 1917, Article 27, 86, 124, 145–48, 152–53
  Constitutionalist revolt, 12, 32, 52
  de facto recognition, 62–65

Carranza, Venustiano (*continued*)
  neutrality, 92, 94
  Pershing punitive expedition, 74–77
  Zimmermann telegram, 88–92
Carranza Doctrine, 126–27, 145–48
Chilcote, Ronald H., xi
Chile
  economic conditions, 24–25, 71, 103,
    108–9
  economic consequences, First World
    War, 41–42, 59, 77–80
  foreign policy traditions, 24–26
  Nitrate of Soda Executive, 109, 120
  Pan American treaty, 49, 56, 66–67, 69,
    74–76, 93–96
  Paris Peace Conference, 139, 144–45
  Tacna and Arica dispute. *See* Tacna and
    Arica dispute
  U.S. break with Germany, 84–85
  U.S. declaration of war, 98
  wartime relations with U.S., 119–20,
    124
Colby, Bainbridge, 153–56
Coletta, Paolo, 15

da Gama, Domicio, 32, 51, 93, 97, 137, 148
Daniels, Josephus, 14, 106, 117
da Silva Pessôa, Epitacio, 148
de Bunsen, Maurice, 121–22, 131
de la Plaza, Victorino, 31, 38, 74
dependency model, xi, 157, 159–60
Díaz, Porfirio, 12
diffusion model, xi, 157, 159–60
Drago, Luis M., 22

Edelstein, Joel C., xi
Edwards, Augustín, 109, 145
Edwards, Carlos, 109, 145
Eliot, Charles W., 33, 54

Fall, Albert B., 147, 152–53
First World War
  economic consequences in Latin
    America, 37–41, 45, 77–80
  effects on trade in Latin America,
    101–12
  neutrality, U.S. and Latin America, 42,
    45
  political consequences in Latin America,
    42, 45–46, 47–52
  U.S. break with Germany, 82–88
  U.S. declaration of war, 92–96
Fletcher, Henry P.
  ambassador to Chile, 46, 48
  ambassador to Mexico, 75, 79–80,
    125–27, 146–48, 153
  minister to Chile, 13, 20, 25, 41–42, 46
  Pan American treaty, 53, 63–64, 69
Fourteen Points, 113, 129, 136, 143

Galt, Edith Bolling, 153
Garrett, John W., 13, 46
Germany, 11, 50, 64, 66, 69, 74–75, 78, 82,
  83, 88–92, 94, 98, 99, 105,
  110–11, 113, 131
Glass, Carter, 150, 151, 152
Gottschalk, Alfred L. M., 72, 105
Great Britain, 11, 13, 17, 19–20, 26, 79,
  82, 102, 104, 112, 131
Grey, Lord Edward, 19, 69–70, 75

Hitchcock, Gilbert M., 153
House, Edward M.
  deus ex machina, 10, 16, 18, 33, 49, 52
  Inquiry, the, 112–13
  Pan American treaty, 49–56, 63–64, 66,
    69–70, 74–76
  Paris Peace Conference, 138, 144, 153
Huerta, Victoriano, 12, 13, 30–31, 32, 88
Hurley, Edward N., 132

Inman, Samuel Guy, 100
Inquiry, the (on peace terms), 112, 121,
  124, 130, 134, 135
Inter-American High Commission, 151
International High Commission, 61–62,
  73–74, 114, 149, 150–51
Investment patterns in Latin America,
  133–34, 149–50

Karnes, Thomas L., x
Katz, Friedrich, 19, 89–92

Lansing, Robert
  counselor, 34–35, 54
  interpretation of Monroe Doctrine,
    34–35
  secretary of state, 63–64, 66, 74, 76, 79,
    84, 87, 88, 91–94, 96, 110, 114–15,
    120–21, 135, 138–39, 140–44, 148,
    153
Latané, John H., 136
Latin American Trade Conference, 44
League of Nations, 137, 152
Lind, John, 13, 17–18
Lodge, Henry Cabot, 137, 152
Long, Boaz, 127
Luxburg, Karl Von, 110

McAdoo, William G., 10, 56, 60–61, 68,
  70, 73, 101, 114
Madero, Francisco I., 12
Mexico
  A.B.C. mediation, 32
  Carranza Doctrine, 126–27, 145–48
  Constitution of 1917, Article 27, 86,
    124, 139, 145–48, 152–53
  Constitutionalist triumph, 52–54
  neutrality, 92–96, 118

Mexico (*continued*)
 Pan Hispanic alternatives, x, 81, 92
 Paris Peace Conference, 139, 145
 Pershing punitive expedition, 74–77
 recognition of Carranza, 63
 revolution in, 12, 16, 30–31
 seizure of Veracruz, 31
 Zimmermann telegram, 87–92
Mezes, Sidney E., 112, 114, 121
Mobile Address, 17–18, 49, 113, 156
Monroe Doctrine
 effects of First World War, 92–96,126
 multilateral definitions, 8, 15–16, 18,
  33–35, 49, 51, 135–36, 137
 Richard Olney corollary, 7
 Theodore Roosevelt corollary, 7,
  15–16, 22
Moreira, Delfim, 138
Morgan, Edwin V., 13, 40–41, 55, 71, 99,
  101, 102, 105, 116, 117, 122, 148
Müller, Lauro, 23, 56, 93, 96

Naón, Rómulo S., 32, 39, 50, 51, 58, 102,
  118–19, 123, 147, 158
National Foreign Trade Convention, 43
Naval arms race, 26

O'Shaughnessy, Nelson, 104, 118

Page, Walter Hines, 17, 18–19, 47
Panama Canal, 1, 24, 42
Pan American Commercial Conference
  (second), 149–50
Pan American Financial Conference, 56,
  59–62
Pan American Financial Conference
  (second), 101
Pan American International Conference
  (fifth), 42, 48
Pan Americanism
 definitions, ix, x
 Wilson's visions, xi, 1, 2–3, 8, 9, 11–12,
  17–18, 27, 34, 45, 52, 56, 67–68, 81,
  149, 156–58
Pan American Scientific Conference
  (second), 68–70
Pan American treaty
 attempted negotiation, 49–52, 63–64,
  66–68
 failure of negotiation, 74–77, 93–96,
  125, 158
Pan American Union, 48, 50, 61, 115, 137,
  149
Pan Hispanic alternatives, x, 81, 92,
  126–27, 145–48
Pani, Alberto J., 139, 145
Pardo, José, 140
Paris Economic Conference, 78–79

Paris Peace Conference, Latin American
  role, 129, 134, 138–39, 142–48
Patronage, 13
Pecanha, Nilo, 96
Pershing punitive expedition, 74–77, 86
Peru, 140–42
Polk, Frank L., 70, 93, 97–98, 123,
  140–42, 153
Pratt, E. E., 77, 79
Pueyrredón, Honorio, 85, 95, 110

Ramírez Necochea, Hernán, x
Redfield, William C., 10, 44, 102
Regional integration, ix, x, xi, 1, 2, 6, 37,
  148, 156
Rio-Branco, Baron of, 20, 23
Rock, David, 21, 22
Rowe, Leo S., 57, 62, 71, 150, 155

Sáenz Peña, Roque, 22, 31
Sanfuentes, Juan Luis, 67, 84–85
Shea, Joseph, 84–85, 95, 98, 108, 116,
  119, 121, 124, 131, 145
Smith, Daniel M., 154–55
Spring-Rice, Sir Cecil, 34
Stabler, Jordan H., 43, 95, 134, 143–44
Stimson, Frederick Jesup, 46–47, 67,
  85–86, 88, 92, 93, 95, 100, 101,
  110, 116, 118–19
Stimson, Mabel, 46, 73, 86, 110
Straight, Willard, 10, 13, 44
Súarez Mújica, Eduardo, 32, 50, 51, 66, 75

Tacna and Arica dispute, 25, 42, 48, 51,
  67, 69, 74, 134, 139–42, 145, 155,
  157
Tocornal, Ismael, 108
Trade in Latin America
 consequences of First World War,
  37–45, 58–60, 77–80, 101–12
 effects of tariffs, 57–58, 73
 expansion of U.S. share, 70, 130–32
 U.S. interest, 2–6, 20–24, 43–45, 57,
  62, 149–50
Transportation in Latin America,
  inadequacies, 29, 72
Treaty of Versailles, 152, 158
Tyrell, Sir William, 19

Union Cívica Radical, 22

Villa, Francisco, 74
Villard, Oswald Garrison, 9

Whitaker, Arthur P., ix
Widenor, William C., 137
Willis, Bailey, 134–35

Wilson, Woodrow
  cerebral thrombosis, 152–53
  effects of First World War, 45, 48–49
  embassies in Argentina and Chile, 30, 47
  Fourteen points, 113, 129, 136, 143
  interview with Samuel G. Blythe, 34
  Mexico, 9, 11, 12–13, 17–20, 30–32,
    52, 62–65, 74–77, 86–91, 94,
    124–27, 139, 145–47, 152–53
  Mobile Address, 17–18, 49
  Pan American treaty, 49–56, 66–68,
    74–77
  Pan American visions, xi, 1–3, 8–9,
    11–12, 17–18, 27, 34, 45, 52, 56,
    67–68, 81, 149, 156–58
  Paris Peace Conference, 138–39,
    143–48
  "peace without victory," 135
  speech before the Mexican editors,
    124–27
  Tacna and Arica dispute, 141–42, 145,
    155, 157
  U.S. break with Germany, 82–88
  U.S. declaration of war, 92–96
  Zimmermann telegram, 90–92

Yrigoyen, Hipólito, 22, 77, 85, 86, 92,
    109–12, 118–19, 123

Zeballos, Estanislao S., 12, 13, 67, 85, 99
Zimmermann, Arthur, 88–92
Zimmermann telegram, the test, 89